How to Start a Business in Texas

Traci Truly
Mark Warda
Attorneys at Law

Fourth Edition

SPHINX® PUBLISHING
AN IMPRINT OF SOURCEBOOKS, INC.®
NAPERVILLE, ILLINOIS
www.SphinxLegal.com

Copyright © 2002, 2004 by Traci Truly and Mark Warda
Cover design © 2004 by Sourcebooks, Inc™

All rights reserved. No part of this book may be reproduced in any form or by any electronic or mechanical means including information storage and retrieval systems—except in the case of brief quotations embodied in critical articles or reviews—without permission in writing from its publisher, Sourcebooks, Inc. Purchasers of the book are granted a license to use the forms contained herein for their own personal use. No claim of copyright is made to any official government forms reproduced herein.

Fourth Edition: 2004

Published by: Sphinx® Publishing, A Division of Sourcebooks, Inc.®

Naperville Office
P.O. Box 4410
Naperville, Illinois 60567-4410
630-961-3900
Fax: 630-961-2168
www.sourcebooks.com
www.SphinxLegal.com

This publication is designed to provide accurate and authoritative information in regard to the subject matter covered. It is sold with the understanding that the publisher is not engaged in rendering legal, accounting, or other professional service. If legal advice or other expert assistance is required, the services of a competent professional person should be sought.

*From a Declaration of Principles Jointly Adopted by a Committee of the
American Bar Association and a Committee of Publishers and Associations*

This product is not a substitute for legal advice.

Disclaimer required by Texas statutes.

Library of Congress Cataloging-in-Publication Data
Truly, Traci.
  How to start a business in Texas / by Traci Truly and Mark Warda.-- 4th ed.
       p. cm.
  Rev. ed. of: How to start a business in Texas / Michael T. Norman, Mark Warda. 3rd ed. 2002.
  Includes index.
  ISBN 1-57248-471-3 (alk. paper)
  1. Business enterprises--Law and legislation--Texas--Popular works. 2. Incorporation--Texas--Popular works. 3. Business law--Texas. I. Warda, Mark. II. Norman, Michael T., 1973- How to start a business in Texas. III. Title.
KFT1405.Z9B76 2004
346.764'065--dc22
                                                 2004004756

Printed and Bound in the United States of America
VH — 10 9 8 7 6 5 4 3 2 1

Contents

USING SELF-HELP LAW BOOKS IX

INTRODUCTION XIII

CHAPTER 1: DECIDING TO START A BUSINESS 1
Know Your Strengths
Know Your Business
Do the Math
Sources for Further Guidance

CHAPTER 2: CHOOSING THE FORM OF YOUR BUSINESS 15
Basic Forms of Doing Business
Start-Up Procedures
Foreign Nationals
Business Comparison Chart

CHAPTER 3: NAMING YOUR BUSINESS 23
Preliminary Considerations
Fictitious Names
Corporate, LLC, LLP, and Limited Partnership Names
Professional Associations, Professional Corporations, and Professional LLCs
Domain Names
Trademarks

CHAPTER 4: FINANCING YOUR BUSINESS **31**
  Growing with Profits
  Using Your Savings
  Borrowing Money
  Getting a Rich Partner
  Selling Shares of Your Business
  Understanding Securities Laws
  Using the Internet to Find Capital

CHAPTER 5: LOCATING YOUR BUSINESS **37**
  Working Out of Your Home
  Choosing a Retail Site
  Choosing Office, Manufacturing, or Warehouse Space
  Leasing a Site
  Buying a Site
  Checking Government Regulations

CHAPTER 6: LICENSING YOUR BUSINESS **43**
  Occupational Licenses and Zoning
  State-Regulated Professions
  Federal Licenses

CHAPTER 7: CONTRACT LAWS **49**
  Traditional Contract Law
  Statutory Contract Law
  Preparing Your Contracts

CHAPTER 8: INSURANCE **55**
  Workers' Compensation
  Liability Insurance
  Hazard Insurance
  Home Business Insurance
  Automobile Insurance
  Health Insurance
  Employee Theft

CHAPTER 9: YOUR BUSINESS AND THE INTERNET **59**
  Domain Names
  Web Pages
  Legal Issues
  Financial Transactions
  FTC Rules
  Fraud

CHAPTER 10: HEALTH AND SAFETY LAWS........................73
  Federal Laws
  Texas Laws

CHAPTER 11: EMPLOYMENT AND LABOR LAWS 79
  Hiring and Firing Laws
  Firing
  New Hire Reporting
  Employment Agreements
  Independent Contractors
  Temporary Workers
  Discrimination Laws
  Sexual Harassment
  Wage and Hour Laws
  Pension and Benefit Laws
  Family and Medical Leave Law
  Child Labor Laws
  Immigration Laws
  Hiring *Off the Books*
  Federal Contracts
  Miscellaneous Laws

CHAPTER 12: ADVERTISING AND PROMOTION LAWS 103
  Advertising Laws and Rules
  Internet Sales Laws
  Home Solicitation Laws
  Telephone Solicitation Laws
  Pricing, Weights, and Labeling
  Email Advertising
  Deceptive Practices

CHAPTER 13: PAYMENT AND COLLECTION 117
  Cash
  Checks
  Credit Cards
  Financing Laws
  Usury
  Collections

Chapter 14: Business Relations Laws 125
The Uniform Commercial Code
Commercial Discrimination
Restraining Trade
Commercial Bribery
Intellectual Property Protection

Chapter 15: Endless Laws 131
Federal Laws
Texas Laws

Chapter 16: Bookkeeping and Accounting. 139
Initial Bookkeeping
Accountants
Computer Programs
Tax Tips

Chapter 17: Paying Federal Taxes 143
Federal Income Tax
Federal Withholding, Social Security, and Medicare Taxes
Excise Taxes
Unemployment Compensation Tax

Chapter 18: Paying Texas Taxes 149
Sales and Use Tax
Franchise Tax
Unemployment Taxes
Local Property Taxes
Other Texas Taxes

Chapter 19: Out-of-State Taxes 155
State Sales Taxes
Business Taxes
Internet Taxes
Canadian Taxes

Chapter 20: The End...and the Beginning **159**

Glossary **161**

Appendix A: Business Start-Up Checklist **169**

Appendix B: Sample Filled-in Forms **171**

Appendix C: Blank Forms **185**

Index **241**

Using Self-Help Law Books

Before using a self-help law book, you should realize the advantages and disadvantages of doing your own legal work and understand the challenges and diligence that this requires.

The Growing Trend

Rest assured that you won't be the first or only person handling your own legal matter. For example, in some states, more than seventy-five percent of the people in divorces and other cases represent themselves. Because of the high cost of legal services, this is a major trend and many courts are struggling to make it easier for people to represent themselves. However, some courts are not happy with people who do not use attorneys and refuse to help them in any way. For some, the attitude is, "Go to the law library and figure it out for yourself."

We write and publish self-help law books to give people an alternative to the often complicated and confusing legal books found in most law libraries. We have made the explanations of the law as simple and easy to understand as possible. Of course, unlike an attorney advising an individual client, we cannot cover every conceivable possibility.

Cost/Value Analysis

Whenever you shop for a product or service, you are faced with various levels of quality and price. In deciding what product or service to buy, you make a cost/value analysis on the basis of your willingness to pay and the quality you desire.

When buying a car, you decide whether you want transportation, comfort, status, or sex appeal. Accordingly, you decide among such choices as a Neon, a Lincoln, a Rolls Royce, or a Porsche. Before making a decision, you usually weigh the merits of each option against the cost.

When you get a headache, you can take a pain reliever (such as aspirin) or visit a medical specialist for a neurological examination. Given this choice, most people, of course, take a pain reliever, since it costs only pennies; whereas a medical examination costs hundreds of dollars and takes a lot of time. This is usually a logical choice because it is rare to need anything more than a pain reliever for a headache. But in some cases, a headache may indicate a brain tumor and failing to see a specialist right away can result in complications. Should everyone with a headache go to a specialist? Of course not, but people treating their own illnesses must realize that they are betting on the basis of their cost/value analysis of the situation. They are taking the most logical option.

The same cost/value analysis must be made when deciding to do one's own legal work. Many legal situations are very straight forward, requiring a simple form and no complicated analysis. Anyone with a little intelligence and a book of instructions can handle the matter without outside help.

But there is always the chance that complications are involved that only an attorney would notice. To simplify the law into a book like this, several legal cases often must be condensed into a single sentence or paragraph. Otherwise, the book would be several hundred pages long and too complicated for most people. However, this simplification necessarily leaves out many details and nuances that would apply to special or unusual situations. Also, there are many ways to interpret most legal questions. Your case may come before a judge who disagrees with the analysis of our authors.

Therefore, in deciding to use a self-help law book and to do your own legal work, you must realize that you are making a cost/value analysis. You have decided that the money you will save in doing it yourself outweighs the chance that your case will not turn out to your satisfaction. Most people handling their own simple legal matters never have a problem, but occasionally people find that it ended up costing them more to have an attorney straighten out the situation than it would have if they had hired an attorney in the beginning. Keep this in mind while handling your case, and be sure to consult an attorney if you feel you might need further guidance.

Local Rules

The next thing to remember is that a book which covers the law for the entire nation, or even for an entire state, cannot possibly include every procedural difference of every jurisdiction. Whenever possible, we provide the exact form needed; however, in some areas, each county, or even each judge, may require unique forms and procedures. In our state books, our forms usually cover the majority of counties in the state, or provide examples of the type of form which will be required. In our national books, our forms are sometimes even more general in nature but are designed to give a good idea of the type of form that will be needed in most locations. Nonetheless, keep in mind that your state, county, or judge may have a requirement, or use a form, that is not included in this book.

You should not necessarily expect to be able to get all of the information and resources you need solely from within the pages of this book. This book will serve as your guide, giving you specific information whenever possible and helping you to find out what else you will need to know. This is just like if you decided to build your own backyard deck. You might purchase a book on how to build decks. However, such a book would not include the building codes and permit requirements of every city, town, county, and township in the nation; nor would it include the lumber, nails, saws, hammers, and other materials and tools you would need to actually build the deck. You would use the book as your guide, and then do some work and research involving such matters as whether you need a permit of some kind, what type and grade of wood are available in your area, whether to use hand tools or power tools, and how to use those tools.

Before using the forms in a book like this, you should check with your court clerk to see if there are any local rules of which you should be aware, or local forms you will need to use. Often, such forms will require the same information as the forms in the book but are merely laid out differently or use slightly different language. They will sometimes require additional information.

Changes in the Law

Besides being subject to local rules and practices, the law is subject to change at any time. The courts and the legislatures of all fifty states are constantly revising the laws. It is possible that while you are reading this book, some aspect of the law is being changed.

In most cases, the change will be of minimal significance. A form will be redesigned, additional information will be required, or a waiting period will be extended. As a result, you might need to revise a form, file an extra form, or wait out a longer time period; these types of changes will not usually affect the outcome of your case. On the other hand, sometimes a major part of the law is changed, the entire law in a particular area is rewritten, or a case that was the basis of a central legal point is overruled. In such instances, your entire ability to pursue your case may be impaired.

Introduction

Texas has been, and will continue to be, a great place to start a business. The rugged individualism that gave rise to the legendary maverick cattle barons of the nineteenth century today finds its expression in the thousands of Texans each year who set out to start their own business and to be their own boss. In this age of instantaneous information transfer, rapid transportation, and worldwide business interaction, no business goal is too large. The sky is the limit!

As the Texas economy has moved from dependence on the oil industry to being a leader in technology, telecommunications, and international trade (particularly with Mexico), the opportunities for enterprising people to fill needs that were not even conceivable twenty years ago is incredible. It is not uncommon for entrepreneurs to take a start-up venture and grow it into a business worth millions of dollars in as little as a few years.

This book is intended to give you an overview of the legal environment in which you will establish your new Texas business. It includes information on where to find special rules for different types of businesses, as well as sample and blank forms for you to use.

If you have not yet started your business, you should read this entire book first, as most of the issues presented in the book are things you should think about as a new business owner. If you have problems that are not covered in this book or do not fully understand the issues discussed, seek out a qualified attorney who can help you. If you are already in business, this book will serve as a resource for you to consult as issues and problems arise.

For your benefit, this book has been conveniently grouped as follows. Chapters 1 through 6 deal primarily with the actual steps necessary to properly begin your business. Chapters 7 through 20 deal with individual substantive legal issues that face an ongoing business, such as employment laws, tax payment and collection, insurance, and the like. Consult these chapters often as your business grows.

Sample forms have also been provided at the end of this book, which will prove helpful as you navigate the myriad of requirements that the federal and state governments put on business owners. Forms are changed from time to time, so check the various websites provided in this book to ensure that you are using the most up-to-date forms available.

This book provides an abundance of information to actualize your dream of owning your own business. Do not be overwhelmed! As you read, note the incredible resources available to you to help you succeed. Take advantage of them and do not be afraid to go for it!

I DECIDING TO START A BUSINESS

If you are reading this book, then you have probably made a serious decision to take the plunge and start your own business. Hundreds of thousands of people make the same decision each year and many of them become very successful. Some barely make a living, others become billionaires. A lot of them also fail. Knowledge can only help your chances of success. You need to know why some succeed while others fail. Some of what follows may seem obvious, but for a person wrapped up in a new business idea, some of this information is occasionally overlooked.

Know Your Strengths

The last thing a budding entrepreneur wants to hear is that he or she is not cut out for running his or her own business. Those *do you have what it takes* quizzes are ignored with the fear that the answer might be one the entrepreneur does not want to hear. But even if you lack some skills, you can be successful if you know where to get them.

You should consider all of the skills and knowledge that running a successful business entails and decide whether you have what it takes. If you do not, it does not necessarily mean you are doomed to be an employee all your life. Perhaps you just need a partner who has the skills you lack. Perhaps you can hire someone with the skills you need or you can structure your business to avoid areas where you are weak. If those do not work, maybe you can learn the skills.

For example, if you are not good at dealing with employees (either you are too passive and get taken advantage of or too tough and scare them off), you can:

- handle product development yourself and have a partner or manager deal with employees;

- take seminars in employee management; or,

- structure your business so that you do not need employees—either use independent contractors or set yourself up as an independent contractor.

The following are some of the factors to consider when planning your business.

- If it takes months or years before your business turns a profit, do you have the resources to hold out? Businesses have gone under or have been sold just before they were about to take off. Staying power is an important ingredient to success.

- Are you willing to put in a lot of overtime to make your business a success? Owners of businesses do not set their own hours—the business sets the hours for the owner. Many business owners work long hours seven days a week, but they enjoy running their business more than family picnics or fishing.

- Are you willing to do the dirtiest or most unpleasant work of the business? Emergencies come up and employees are not always dependable. You might need to mop up a flooded room, spend a weekend stuffing 10,000 envelopes, or work Christmas day if someone calls in sick.

- Do you know enough about the product or service? Are you aware of the trends in the industry and what changes new technology might bring? Think of the people who started typesetting or printing businesses just before type was replaced by laser printers.

- Do you know enough about accounting and inventory to manage the business? Do you have a good *head for business*? Some people naturally know how to save money and do things profitably. Others are in the habit of buying the best and the most expensive of everything. The latter can be fatal to a struggling new business.

- Are you good at managing employees?

- Do you know how to sell your product or service? You can have the best product on the market but people do not know about it. If you are a wholesaler, shelf space in major stores is hard to get, especially for a new company without a record, a large line of products, or a large advertising budget.

- Do you know enough about getting publicity? The media receive thousands of press releases and announcements each day. Most are thrown away. Do not count on free publicity to put your name in front of the public.

Know Your Business

Not only do you need to know the concept of a business, but you need the experience of working in a business. Maybe you always dreamed of running a bed and breakfast or having your own pizza place. Have you ever worked in such a business? If not, you may have no idea of the day-to-day headaches and problems of the business. For example, do you really know how much to allow for theft, spoilage, and unhappy customers?

You might feel silly taking an entry level job at a pizza place when you would rather start your own, but it might be the most valuable preparation you could have. A few weeks of seeing how a business operates could mean the difference between success and failure.

Working in a business as an employee is one of the best ways to be a success at running such a business. New people with new ideas who work in old stodgy industries have been known to revolutionize the industires with obvious improvements that no one before dared to try.

Do the Math

Conventional wisdom says you need a business plan before committing yourself to a new venture. However, lots of businesses are started successfully without the owner even knowing what a business plan is. They have a great concept, put it on the market, and it takes off. But you need to at least do some basic calculations to see if the business can make a profit. Here are some examples.

- If you want to start a retail shop, figure out how many people are close enough to become customers and how many other stores will be competing for those customers. Visit some of those other shops and see how busy they are. Without giving away your plans to compete, ask some general questions like *how is business?*, and maybe they will share their frustrations or successes.

- Whether you sell a good or a service, do the math to find out how much profit is in it. For example, if you plan to start a house painting company, find out what you will have to pay to hire painters; what it will cost you for all of the insurance; what bonding and licensing you will need; and, what the advertising will cost you. Figure out how many jobs you can do per month and what other painters are charging. In some industries in different areas of the country, there may be a large margin of profit or there may be almost no profit.

- Find out if there is a demand for your product or service. Suppose you have designed a beautiful new kind of candle and your friends all say you should open a shop because *everyone will want them*. Before making a hundred of them and renting a store, bring a few to craft shows or flea markets and see what happens.

- Figure out what the income and expenses would be for a typical month of your new business. List monthly expenses such as rent, salaries, utilities, insurance, taxes, supplies, advertising, services, and other overhead. Then figure out how much profit you will average from each sale. Next, figure out how many sales you will need to cover your overhead and divide by the number of business days in the month. Can you reasonably expect that many sales? How will you get those sales?

Most types of businesses have trade associations, which often have figures on how profitable their members are. Some even have start-up kits for people who want to start businesses. One good source of information on such organizations is the Encyclopedia of Associations published by Gale Research Co., available in many library reference sections. Producers of products to the trade often give assistance to small companies getting started to win their loyalty. Contact the largest suppliers of the products your business will be using and see if they can be of help.

Sources for Further Guidance

The following offices offer free or low-cost guidance for new businesses.

SCORE The *Service Corps of Retired Executives* (SCORE) is a nonprofit association dedicated to entrepreneur education and the formation, growth, and success of small business nationwide. SCORE is a resource partner with the *Small Business Administration* (SBA). SCORE volunteers serve as *Counselors to America's Small Business*. Working and retired executives and business owners donate their time and expertise as volunteer business counselors free of charge.

Contact SCORE toll free at 800-634-0245 or visit their website at **www.score.org**. Below is a list of SCORE counseling locations.

Austin SCORE
4100 Ed Bluestein Boulevard
Austin, TX 78721
512-928-2425
email: info@scoreaustin.com

Golden Triangle SCORE
John Gray Building
855 Florida Avenue, Buidling B-104
Beaumont, TX 77705
email: score512@pnx.com

Corpus Christi SCORE
3649 Leopard Street, Suite 411
Corpus Christi, TX 78408
phone: 361 879-0017
fax: 361-879- 0764
email: score221@interconnect.com

Dallas SCORE
5646 Milton Street, Suite 303
Dallas, TX 75206
phone: 214-987-9491
fax: 214-987-9491
email: score220@flash.net

El Paso SCORE
10 Civic Center Plaza
El Paso, TX 79901
phone: 915-534-0541
fax: 915-534-0513
email: score@elpasoscore.org

Ft. Worth SCORE
1150 Freeway, Suite 108
phone: 817-871-6002
fax: 817-871-6031
email: ftwscorechapt120@juno.com

Lower Rio Grande Valley
222 E. Van Buren, Suite 500
Harlingen, TX 78550
phone: 956-427-8533
fax: 956-427-8537
email: chs1956@aol.com

Houston SCORE
8701 S. Gessner, Suite 1200
Houston, TX 77074
phone: 713-773-6565
fax: 713-773-6550
email: score37@scorehouston.org

Lubbock SCORE
1205 Texas Avenue, Room 411D
phone: 806-472-7462
fax: 806-472-7487
sharondale.bruni@sba.gov

San Antonio SCORE
17319 San Pedro
Building 2, Suite 200
San Antonio, TX 78232
phone: 210-403-5931
fax: 210-403-5935
email: sanantonio.score@sba.gov

Texarkana SCORE
819 State Line Avenue
Texarkana, TX 75501
phone: 903-792-7191
fax: 903-793-4304
email: score@texarkana.org

East Texas SCORE
RTDC
1530 SSW Loop 323, Suite 100
phone: 903-510-2975
fax: 903-510-2978
email: easttexasscore@yahoo.com

Waco SCORE
401 Franklin Avenue
phone: 254-754-8898
fax: 254-756-0776
email: score@brc-waco.com

Small Business Development Centers

The *Association of Small Business Development Centers* (ASBDC) is a partnership program uniting private enterprise, government, higher education, and local non-profit economic development organizations. It is dedicated to the sound development of small business throughout America. Founded in 1979, the ASBDC provides a vehicle for continuous improvement of the Small Business Development Center program.

To find the Small Business Development Center location nearest you and to learn about the many programs available through ASBDC, visit their website at **www.asbdc-us.org**.

The following is a list of Small Business Development Center locations.

Abilene SBDC
500 Chestnut, Suite 601
Abilene, TX 79602
phone: 325-670-0300
fax: 325-670-0311

West Texas A&M University SBDC
2300 Western Street
Amarillo, TX 79124
phone: 806-373-5151
fax: 806-372-5261
email: sbdc@mail.wtamu.edu

Trinity Valley Community College
100 Cardinal Dr.
Athens, TX 75751
phone: 903-675-7403
       800-335-7232
fax: 903-675-5199
email: jloden@tvcc.edu

Texas State University SBDC
314 Highland Mall Boulevard
Suite 110
Austin, TX 78752-3735
phone: 512-225-9888
email: sbdc@business.txstate.edu
http://sbdc.utsa.edu

University of Houston Coastal Plains SBDC
2200 Seventh St., Suite 300
Bay City, TX 77414
phone: 979-244-8466

Lee College SBDC
200 Lee Drive
Rundell Hall
Baytown, TX 77522-0818
Mailing Address:
P.O. Box 818
Baytown, TX 775
phone: 281-425-6309
fax: 281-425-6307
www.lee.edu

Lamar University SBDC
855 E. Florida Avenue
Suite 101
Beaumont, TX 77705
phone: 409-880-2367
fax: 409-880-2201
email: hal@lamar.edu/~sbdc

Bonham Satellite SBDC
Sam Rayburn Library
1201 E. 9th Street, Building 2
phone: 903-583-7565
fax: 903-583-6706

Blinn College SBDC
902 College Avenue
Brenham, TX 7783
phone: 979-830-4137
fax: 979-830-4135
www.blinncol.edu/sbdc

Brazos Valley
Small Business Development Center
4001 East 29th Street
Suite 175
Bryan, TX 77805
Mailing Address:
P.O. Box 3695
Bryan, TX 77805-3695
phone: 979-260-5222
fax: 979-260-5229
www.bvsbdc.org

Best Southwest SBDC
207 Cannady Drive
Cedar Hill, TX 75104
phone: 972-860-7894
fax: 972-291-1320
email: bswcvcc@airmail.net

Del Mar College SBDC
101 Baldwin VB-351
Corpus Christi, TX 78404
phone: 361-698-1021
fax: 361-698-1024
www.delmar.edu/sbdc

Navarro SBDC
120 North 12th Street
Corsicana, TX 75110
phone: 903-874-0658
         800-320-7232
fax: 903-874-4187
email: torte@nav.cc.tx.us

Bill J. Priest Inst. for Econ Dev.
1402 Cornith, Suite 2111
Dallas, Texas 75215
phone: 214-860-5835
fax: 214-860-5813
email: dsbdc@dcccd.edu
www.ntsbdc.org

Grayson County College SBDC
6101 Grayson Drive
Denison, TX 75020
phone: 903-463-8787
         800-316-7232
fax: 903-463-5437
www.ntsbdc.org/grayson.html

Sul Ross State University SBDC
500 W. Avenue H, Suite 102
Box C-47
Alpine, TX 79832
phone: 432-837-8694
fax: 432-837-8104
www.sulross.edu/pages/730.asp

U. of Texas-Pan American SBDC
2412 S. Closner
Edinburg, TX 78539-2999
phone: 956-292-7535
fax: 956-292-7561
http://coservel.panam.edu/sbdc

Tarrant SBDC
1150 South Freeway, Suite 229
Ft. Worth, TX 76104
phone: 817-871-6028
fax: 817-871-6417
email: tcc_sbdc@fnbgc.com
www.tccd.net/cc_sbdc.asp

Small Business Development
Center for Enterprise Excellence
7300 Jack Newell Boulevard, South
Fort Worth, TX 76118
phone: 817-272-5930
fax: 817-272-5952

North Central Texas College SBDC
1525 West California
Gainesville, TX 76240
Phone: 940-668-4220
Fax: 940-668-6049
email: nctc_sbdc@lists.nctc.edu
www.nctc.edu/continuing_
   education/sbdc.html

Galveston College SBDC
1130 Del Mar
LaMarque, TX 77550
phone: 409-938-1221 x450
email: GCSBDC@yahoo.com

Texas Gulf Coast SBDC
University of Houston
2302 Fannin, Suite 200
Houston, TX 77002
phone: 713-752-8444
fax: 713-756-1500
www.smbizsolutions.uh.edu

North Harris Montgomery
5000 Research Forest
The Woodlands, TX 77381
phone: 832-813-6674
www.cbed.org/sbdc

Sam Houston State University SBDC
2424 Sam Houston Avenue, Building A
Huntsville, TX 77340
Mailing Address:
P.O. Box 2058
Huntsville, TX 77341-2058
phone: 936-294-3737
fax: 936-294-3738
www.shsu.edu/~sbdc

Laredo Development Foundation SBDC
616 Leal Street
Laredo, TX 78041
phone: 956-722-0563
fax: 956-722-6247
www.laredo-ldf.com/ldfsbdc.htm

Kilgore College SBDC
911 Loop 281, Suite 209
Longview, TX 75604
phone: 903-757-5857
          838-338-7232
fax: 903-753-7920
email: bradbunt@aol.com
www.kilgore.edu/sbdc

Northwestern Texas
Texas Tech University
SBDC at Lubbock
2579 South Loop, 289
Suite 114
Lubbock, TX 79423
phone: 806-745-3973
fax: 806-745-6207
email: cbean@nwtsbdc.org
www.nwtsbdc.org

Angelina County SBDC
3500 S. First Street
Lufkin, TX 75901-1768
phone: 936-633-5400
www.angelina.cc.tx.us/SBDC/SATOP.htm

University of Houston Fort Bend County SBDC
2440 Texas Parkway, Suite 220
Missouri City, TX 77489
phone: 281-499-9787
www.sbdc.uh.edu/offices.html

Kingsville Chamber of Commerce SBDC
635 East King
Kingsville, TX 78363
phone: 361-595-5088
fax: 361-592-0866

Brazosport College SBDC
500 College Drive
Lake Jackson, TX 77566
phone: 979-230-3380
fax: 979-230-3482
www.brazosport.cc.tx.us/~sbdc
UT/Permian Basin SBDC
1400 N. FM 1788, Highway 191
Midland, TX 79707
phone: 432-552-2455

Paris Community College SBDC
2400 Clarksville Street
Paris, TX 75460
phone: 903-782-0224
fax: 903-782-0219
email: pbell@paris.cc.tx.us
www.paris.cc.tx.us

San Jacito College SBDC
2006 E. Broadway, Suite 1101
Pearland, TX 77581
phone: 281-485-5214
www.sjcd.cc.tx.us/sbdc

Courtyard Center for Professional
and Economic Development
4800 Preston Park Boulevard
Suite A 126, Box 15
Plano, TX 75093
phone: 972-985-3770
fax: 972-985-3775
email: sbdc@ccccd.edu
www.ccccd.edu/sbdc

Northeast/Texarkana SBDC
P.O. Box 1307
Mt. Pleasant, TX 75455
phone: 903-897-2956
fax: 903-897-1106
email: sbdcnetcc@aol.com
www.bizcoach.org

South-West Texas Border Region SBDC
501 Durango Boulevard
San Antonio, TX 78207
phone: 210-458-2450
fax: 210-458-2444
email: rmckinley@utsa.edu
www.iedtexas.org

Tarleton State University SBDC
College of Business Administration
Box T-0650
Stephenville, TX 76402
phone: 254-968-9330
fax: 254-968-9329
www.tarleton.edu/~sbdc

Tyler SBDC
1530 South SW Loop 323
Suite 100
Tyler, TX 75701
phone: 903-510-2975
fax: 903-510-2972
email: dpro@tjc.tyler.cc.tx.us
www.tjc.edu/sbdc

McLennan Community College SBDC
1400 College Drive
Waco, TX 76708
phone: 254-299-8141
fax: 254-299-8054
email: sbdc@sbdc-waco.com
www.mcweb.mcc.cc.tx.us/sbdc

Lamar State College SBDC-Port Arthur
1401 Procter
Port Arthur, TX 77641
phone: 409-984-6531
www.portarthur.com/sbdc

Angelo State University-SBDC
Rasmussen Building
2222 Dena Drive, Room 201
San Angelo, TX 76909
phone: 325-942-2098
fax: 325-942-2096
www.angelo.edu/services/sbdc

Midwestern State University SBDC
3410 Taft Boulevard
Wichita Falls, TX 76308
phone: 940-397-4373
fax: 940-397-4374
http://sbdc.mwsu.edu

College of the Mainland SBDC
Texas City, Texas
SBDC has temporary offices at the school-operated through University of Houston. Contact 713-752-8444 for current information.

The *Small Business Economic Development Centers* also have a number of specialty centers. These centers address specific business concerns. For example, if you have a specific issue related to risk management, contact 214-860-5821. For an issue regarding government contracting, contact 214-860-5889. Other specialty centers are:

International Assistance Center
Small Business Development Center
World Trade Center, Suite #156A
2050 Stemmons Freeway
P.O. Box 58299
Dallas, TX 75258
phone: 214-747-1300
       800-320-7232
fax: 214-748-7939

Center for Government Contracting/
Technology Assistance Center
Small Business Development Center
1402 Cornith Street
Dallas, TX 75215
phone: 214-860-5850
fax: 214-860-5881

Texas Mfg. Assistance Center-Gulf Coast
1100 Lousisana, Suite 500
Houston, TX 77002
phone: 713-752-8440
fax: 713-756-1500

UH Texas Information
Procurement Services
University of Houston SBDC
1100 Louisiana, Suite 500
Houston, TX 77002
phone: 713-752-8477
       800-252-7232
fax: 713-756-1515

The *Texas Economic Development Office of International Business* has five centers around the state to assist businesses with international concerns.

Austin Community College SBDC
5930 Middle Fiskville Road
Austin, TX 78752
Phone: 512-473-3510

North Texas International Business Center
World Trade Center
2050 Stemmons Freeway
Suite 156
Dallas, TX 75258
phone: 214-747-1300
　　　　800-337-7232
fax: 214-748-5774

UTSA International Trade Center
501 W. Durango Boulevard
San Antonio, TX 78207
phone: 210-458-2470
fax: 210-458-2464

U of Houston International
　Trade Center
302 Fannin
Houston, TX 77002
phone: 713-752-8404
fax: 713-756-1500

Northwest Texas SDBC Lubbock
2579 S. Loop 289
Lubbock, TX 79423
phone: 806-745-1673
fax: 806-745-6207

County and Municipal Economic Development Organizations

While not all counties or municipalities will have SCORE offices or Small Business Development Centers, almost every county or municipality has organizations dedicated to furthering the economic development of its area. These organizations will often go by the names *Chamber of Commerce, Economic Development Council,* or the like. Some of these organizations will be more helpful than others, but you should at least see what your local office has to offer.

In counties with smaller populations, Texas law has authorized the creation of local Economic Development Corporations. These corporations are created by qualifying cities in local elections and have the authority to make grants and loans as well as to assist businesses with tax abatements. Some areas also have been designated by the legislature as enterprise zones. If you locate your new business in one of these zones, you may be able to obtain tax breaks and other economic incentives.

Small Business Administration

The *United States Small Business Administration* (SBA), established in 1953, provides financial, technical, and management assistance to help Americans start, run, and grow their businesses. With a portfolio of business loans, loan guarantees, and disaster loans worth more than $45 billion, in addition to a venture capital portfolio of $13 billion, the SBA is the nation's largest single financial backer of small businesses. In addition to its lending activities, the SBA provides management and technical advice to small businesses and plays a major role in the government's disaster relief efforts by making low-interest recovery loans to both homeowners and businesses.

Texas has SBA offices in Houston, Dallas, Ft. Worth, San Antonio, El Paso, Harlingen, and Lubbock. To find the contact information for the Small Business Administration location nearest you and to learn about the many programs and resources available through SBA, visit their website at:

www.sba.gov

2: Choosing the Form of Your Business

One of the most important decisions you must make as you begin a new business venture is the selection of the form of business in which you will operate. Over time, various types of entities have been created by the state legislature. Each type of entity offers distinct advantages and disadvantages from a liability, flexibility, and tax standpoint. However, as you will see below, for some people the best answer may be not to choose a new entity at all. Instead, they may prefer to do business either under their own names or under an assumed name. As this choice is very important, if you do not know what to do, consult an attorney.

Basic Forms of Doing Business

The four most common forms for a business in Texas are sole proprietorships, general partnerships, corporations, and limited partnerships. Laws have been passed in recent years that allow the creation of two new types of enterprise—limited liability companies and limited liability partnerships. These offer new benefits for certain kinds of businesses. The characteristics, advantages, and disadvantages of each follow.

Sole Proprietorship

Characteristics. A sole proprietorship is one person doing business in his or her own name or under a *fictitious* name.

Advantages. The main advantage is simplicity. There is no organizational expense and no extra tax forms or reports to fill out.

Disadvantages. The sole proprietor is personally liable for all debts and obligations of the business. This means that personal assets are possibly at risk. There is also no continuation of the business after death and it may be difficult to keep business and personal records separate.

General Partnership

Characteristics. This involves two or more people carrying on a business together and sharing the profits and losses.

Advantages. Partners can combine expertise and assets. A general partnership allows liability to be spread among more than one person. Also, the business can be continued after the death of a partner if bought out by a surviving partner. General partnerships are formed by the actions of two or more persons. No written agreement or state filings are necessary (although a written agreement between the partners is advisable).

Disadvantages. Each partner is liable for the acts of other partners within the scope of the business. This means, for example, that if your partner harms a customer or signs a million-dollar credit line in the partnership name, you can be personally liable. Even if left in the business, all profits are taxable. Control is shared by all parties and the death of a partner may result in liquidation. In a general partnership, it is often hard to get rid of a bad partner.

Corporation

Characteristics. A corporation is a legally made *person* that carries on business through its board of directors and officers for the benefit of its shareholders. (In Texas, one person may form a corporation and be the sole shareholder and officer.) Laws covering the formation and operation of business corporations are contained in the *Texas Business Corporation Act* and the *Texas Miscellaneous Corporation Laws*. This legal person carries on business in its own name and shareholders are not usually liable for its acts.

An *S corporation* is a corporation that has filed Internal Revenue Service (IRS) Form 2553. By filing IRS Form 2553, the corporation has elected to have all of its profits taxed directly to its shareholders rather than the corporation. An S corporation files a tax return but pays no federal corporate income tax. The annual profit (or loss) of the S corporation is reported directly on the shareholder's personal income tax return. However, limitations apply as to which corporations may elect to be S corporations. (S corporations may only have one class of stock and a limited number of shareholders who, in most circumstances, must be individual persons who are residents of the United States.)

A *C corporation* is any corporation that has not elected to be taxed as an S corporation. A C corporation pays income tax on its profits. The effect of this is that when dividends are paid to shareholders, they are taxed twice, once for the corporation and once when they are paid to the shareholders.

A *professional service corporation* is a corporation formed by a professional such as a doctor or accountant. Texas has special rules for professional service corporations that differ slightly from those of other corporations. These rules are included in *Vernon's Texas Civil Statutes Article 1528e*. There are also special tax rules for professional service corporations.

A *nonprofit corporation* is usually used for organizations such as churches and condominium associations. With careful planning, some types of businesses can also be set up as nonprofit corporations and save a lot in taxes. While a non-profit corporation cannot pay dividends, it can pay its officers and employees fair salaries. Some of the major American nonprofit organizations pay their officers well over $100,000 a year. Texas' special rules for nonprofit corporations are included in the *Texas Non-Profit Corporation Act*.

Advantages. If properly organized, shareholders have no liability for corporate debts and lawsuits. Officers usually have no personal liability for their corporate acts. The existence of a corporation may be perpetual. There are tax advantages allowed only to corporations. There is prestige in owning a corporation. Capital may be raised by issuing stock and it is easy to transfer ownership upon death. A small corporation can be set up as an S corporation to avoid corporate taxes but still retain corporate advantages. Some types of businesses can be set up as nonprofit corporations that provide significant tax savings.

Disadvantages. The start-up costs for forming a corporation are higher than for a sole proprietorship or general partnership. There are certain formalities such as annual meetings, separate bank accounts, and tax forms that should be maintained. Unless a corporation registers as an S corporation, it must pay federal income tax separate from the tax paid by the owners. There have occasionally been proposals to tax S corporations with an exemption for small operations, but none of these have passed the legislature. Texas S corporations and C corporations are subject to the *Texas franchise tax*, which is essentially a corporate income tax of about 4.25% of income.

Limited Partnership

Characteristics. A limited partnership has characteristics similar to both a corporation and a partnership. There are *general partners* who have the control and personal liability, and there are *limited partners* who only put up money, whose liability is limited to what they paid for their share of the partnership (like corporate stock). A new type of limited partnership, a limited liability limited partnership, allows all partners to avoid liability.

Advantages. Capital can be contributed by limited partners who have no control of the business or liability for its debts.

Disadvantages. The disadvantage for limited partnership is high start-up costs. Also, an extensive partnership agreement is required because general partners are personally liable for partnership debts and for the acts of each other. (One solution to this problem is to use a corporation or limited liability company as the general partner.)

Limited Liabilitiy Company

Characteristics. The limited liability company (LLC) allows flexible management like a general partnership but without personal liability for its members like a corporation.

Advantages. The LLC may elect to be taxed like a partnership or a corporation, depending on the goals and needs of the business. Further, in contrast to an S corporation, an LLC may have different classes of ownership and an unlimited number of members (who do not have to be individuals or residents of the United States).

Disadvantages. If an LLC elects to be taxed as a partnership, it must pay Social Security tax on its profits (up to a limit), whereas S corporation profits are exempt from Social Security tax. Because LLCs are relatively new creations, there are not a lot of answers to legal questions that may arise. However, the courts will probably rely on corporation and limited partnership law for answers. Start-up fees are higher for LLCs than for general partnerships or sole proprietorships, and unlike general partnerships, LLCs are subject to *Texas Franchise Tax*.

Limited Liability Partnership

Characteristics. The limited liability partnership (LLP) is a relatively new entity created by the legislature to offer a combination of the benefits provided by general partnerships and corporations.

Advantages. This entity allows all of the partners in the partnership to participate in the management of the business while still maintaining limited liability. A partner is not liable individually for the errors or omissions of another partner. Additionally, partners are only liable for the errors and omissions of representatives of the partnership (such as employees) who are working under their supervision. The partners are not personally liable for the debts of the partnership. There are tax advantages as well. The limited liability partnership does not pay the franchise tax and other taxes pass through as they do in a general partnership.

Disadvantages. Like the LLC, the LLP is a new creation and there is not much case law available to provide guidance as situations arise. The LLP also has costs associated with it that a general partnership does not. The LLP must be registered with the state and there is an initial registration fee of $200 per partner. This registration must be renewed annually at the same $200 per partner fee. There is less liability protection for a partner in a limited liability partnership than for a limited partner in a traditional limited partnership.

Start-Up Procedures

Each form of business has its own unique start-up procedures.

Proprietorship

In a proprietorship, all accounts, property, and licenses are taken in the name of the owner. (See Chapter 3 for using a fictitious name.)

Partnership

To form a partnership, a written agreement should be prepared to spell out rights and obligations of the parties. Most accounts, property, and licenses can be in either the partnership name or in the names of the partners. General partnerships that carry on business under a name other than the names of the partners of the partnership or under a name with the suffix *and company* or *company*, must register such name with the county clerk of the counties where the general partnership has offices. If the general partnership does not have offices, then it must register in each of the offices of the county clerk in the counties in which the general partnership carries on business. (See Chapter 5 for more information.)

Corporation To form a corporation, *articles of incorporation* must be filed with the Secretary of State in Austin along with $300 in filing fees and taxes. An organizational meeting is then held. At the meeting, officers are elected, stock issued, and other formalities are complied with in order to avoid the corporate entity being set aside later and treated as though it never was formed. Licenses and accounts are titled in the name of the corporation. One person or more may form a corporation.

Limited Partnership A *certificate of limited partnership* must be filed with the Secretary of State in Austin, and a written *agreement of limited partnership* must be signed by the general partner and the limited partners. Because of the complex relationships embodied in the *agreement of limited partnership*, it is advisable to have an attorney assist you in organizing a limited partnership.

Limited Liability Company One or more persons may form a limited liability company by filing *articles of organization* with the Secretary of State in Austin. Licenses and accounts are in the name of the company.

Limited Liability Partnership The limited liability partnership is begun in the same way as a general partnership—with a partnership agreement between the partners. The next step is to file the application to register the partnership as a limited liability partnership with the Secretary of State. You should use the Form 701 provided by the Secretary of State. It is available by fax, mail, and from the Secretary of State website at **www.sos.tx.us**.

Foreign Nationals

Two legal issues that foreign persons should be concerned with when starting a business in Texas are their immigration status and the proper reporting of the business's foreign owners.

Immigration Status The ownership of a U.S. business does not automatically confer rights to enter or remain in the United States. Different types of visas are available to investors and business owners, but each of these has strict requirements.

A visa to enter the United States may be permanent or temporary. Permanent visas for business owners usually require investments from $500,000 to $1,000,000 that result in the creation of new jobs. However, there are ways to obtain visas for smaller investments, if structured correctly. For more information on this area, consult an immigration specialist or a book on immigration.

Temporary visas may be used by business owners to enter the U.S. However, these are hard to get because in most cases, the foreign person must prove that there are no U.S. residents qualified to take the job.

Reporting U.S. businesses that own real property and are controlled by foreign persons are required to file certain federal reports under the *International Investment Survey Act*, the *Agricultural Foreign Investment Disclosure Act*, and the *Foreign Investment in Real Property Tax Act* (FIRPTA). If these laws apply to your business, consult an attorney who specializes in foreign ownership of U.S. businesses.

Business Comparison Chart

	Sole Proprietorship	General Partnership	Limited Partnership	Limited Liability Co.	Corporation C or S	Nonprofit Corporation	Limited Liability Partnership
Liability Protection	No	No	For limited partners	For all members	For all shareholders	For all members	Yes
Taxes	Pass through	Pass through	Pass through	Pass through	S corps. pass through; C corps. pay tax	None on 501(c)(3) charities; Employees pay on wages	Pass through
Minimum # of Members	1	2	2 (1 general partner and 1 limited partner)	1	1	0 (may be a non-member, nonprofit corporation)	2
Start-Up filing fee	None	None	$750	$200	$300	$300	$200 per partner
Diff. Classes of Ownership	No	Yes	Yes	Yes	S corps. No; C corps. Yes	No ownership; Diff. classes of membership	No
Survives after Death	No	No	Yes	Yes	Yes	Yes	Yes, if renewed annually

3 Naming Your Business

The name of a business can be very important. For some businesses, the single greatest asset that the business has may be its name. Companies spend billions of dollars each year on advertising in an effort to enhance the public's awareness of their names. Often, as a business matures, the name will attract business because it is associated with quality and good practices.

Preliminary Considerations

Before deciding on a name for your business, make sure that it is not already being used by someone else. Many business owners have spent thousands of dollars on publicity and printing, only to throw it all away because another company owned the name. A company that owns a name can take you to court and force you to stop using that name. It can also sue you for damages if it thinks your use of the name cost it a financial loss.

Even if you will be running a small local shop with no plans for expansion, you should check out whether the name has been trademarked. If someone else is using the same name anywhere in the country and has registered it as a federal trademark, they can sue you if you use it. If you plan to expand or to deal nationally, then you should do a thorough search of the name.

The first places to look are the local phone books and official records of your county. Next, check with the Secretary of State's office in Austin to see if someone has registered a fictitious or corporate name that is the same as, or confusingly similar to, the one you have chosen. This can be done by calling 512-463-5555. Also, information is available at their website:

www.sos.state.tx.us

To do a national search, you should check trade directories and phone books of major cities. These can be found at many libraries and are usually reference books that cannot be checked out. The *Trade Names Directory* is a two volume set of names compiled from many sources published by Gale Research Co.

Using the Internet, you can search all of the yellow page listings in the U.S. at a number of sites at no charge. One website, **www.superpages.com**, offers free searches of the Yellow Pages for all states at once.

To be sure that your use of the name does not violate someone else's trademark rights, you should have a trademark search done of the mark in the *United States Patent and Trademark Office* (USPTO). In the past, this required a visit to their offices or the hiring of a search form for over a hundred dollars. Now USPTO trademark records can be searched online at:

www.uspto.gov

If you do not have access to the Internet, you might be able to search at a public library or have one of their employees order an online search for you for a small fee. If this is not available to you, you can have the search done through a firm. One such firm you can contact is:

Government Liaison Services, Inc.
200 N. Glebe Road, Suite 321
Arlington, VA 22203
703-524-8200
www.trademarkinfo.com

They also offer searches of 100 trade directories and 4800 phone books.

Make sure your search is thorough. There is no guaranty that there is not a local user somewhere with rights to the mark. If, for example, you register a name for a new chain of restaurants and later find out that someone in Tucumcari, New Mexico, has been using the name longer than you, that person will still have the right to use the name, but just in his or her local area. If you do not want his or her restaurant to cause confusion with your chain, you can try to buy it out. Similarly, if you are operating a small business under a unique name and a law firm in New York writes and offers to buy the right to your name, you can assume that some large corporation wants to start a major expansion under that name.

The best way to make sure a name you are using is not likely owned by someone else is to make up a name. Names such as *Xerox*, *Kodak*, and *Exxon* were made up and did not have any meaning prior to their use. Remember that there are millions of businesses and even something you make up may already be in use. Do a search regardless.

Fictitious Names

In Texas, as in most states, unless you do business in your own legal name you must register the name you are using—called a *fictitious name*. When you use a fictitious name you are *doing business as* (d/b/a) whatever name you are using.

A fictitious name registration is good for ten years. It can be renewed for additional ten year periods.

It is a misdemeanor to fail to register a fictitious name, and you may not sue anyone unless you are registered. If someone sues you and you are not registered, you may have to pay his or her attorney's fees and court costs.

If your name is *John Doe* and you are operating a masonry business, you may operate your business as *John Doe, Mason* without registering it. But any other use of a name should be registered, such as:

    Doe Masonry   Doe Masonry Company
    Doe Company   Texas Panhandle Masonry

NOTE: *Legally, you would use the full name John Doe d/b/a Doe Masonry.*

You cannot use the words *corporation*, *incorporated*, *corp.*, or *inc.* unless you are a corporation. However, corporations do not have to register the name they are using unless it is different from their registered corporate name.

For sole proprietorships, general partnerships, joint ventures, and any other entity other than a corporation, limited partnership, registered limited liability partnership, or limited liability company, you must file:

- in the office of the county clerk in each county you have a business location or

- in the office of the county in which you do business, if you do not have a business location.

Research to see if the name you intend to use is already being used by anyone else. Even persons who have not registered a name can acquire some legal rights to the name through mere use.

The assumed name form is available through your county clerk.

For corporations, limited partnerships, registered limited liability partnerships, or limited liability companies, you must file an **ASSUMED NAME CERTIFICATE FOR FILING WITH THE SECRETARY OF STATE** to register a fictitious name. (see form 2, p.189.) You must file the registration form:

- with the Secretary of State's office;

- in the office of the county clerk of the county in which you maintain your registered office; and,

- in the office of the county clerk of the county in which you maintain your principal business office (if your principal business office is in a different county than your registered office).

Corporate, LLC, LLP, and Limited Partnership Names

Corporations, limited liability companies, limited partnerships, and limited liability partnerships do not have to register a fictitious name because they already have a legal name. The name of a corporation must contain one of the following: *Incorporated*, *Company*, or *Corporation*, or the abbreviations *Inc.*, *Co.*, or *Corp.*

The name of a limited liability company must contain one of the following: *Limited Liability Company*, *Limited Company*, or the abbreviations *L.L.C.*, *LLC, L.C.,* or *LC.*

The name of a limited partnership must contain one of the following: *Limited Partnership*, *Limited*, or the abbreviations *Ltd., L.P.* or *LP.* Also, it may not contain the name of a limited partner unless that name is also the name of a general partner.

The name of a limited liability partnership must contain one of the following: *Limited Liability Partnership, Registered Limited Liability Partnership,* or one of the abbreviations *L.L.P.* or *LLP.*

If the name of a corporation, limited liability company, limited partnership, or limited liability partnership does not contain one of the above words, it will be rejected by the Secretary of State. It will also be rejected if the name used by it is already taken, is similar to the name of another corporation, or if it uses a forbidden word such as *Bank* or *Trust*. To check on a name, you may call the corporate name information number in Austin at 512-463-5555. You can also check their website at:

www.sos.state.tx.us

If a name you pick is taken by another company, you may be able to change it slightly and have it accepted. For example, if there is already a Tri-City Upholstery, Inc. and it is in a different county, you may be allowed to use Tri-City Upholstery of Liberty County, Inc. However, even if this is approved by the Secretary of State, you might get sued by the other company if your business is close to theirs or there is a likelihood of confusion.

Also, do not have anything printed until your corporate papers are returned to you. Sometimes a name is approved over the phone and rejected when submitted. Once you have chosen a corporate name and know it is available, you should immediately register your corporation.

If a corporation, limited liability company, limited partnership, or limited liability partnership wants to do business under a name other than its corporate name, it can register a fictitious name such as *Doe Corporation d/b/a Doe Industries*. See p.191 for instructions for filing form 2, **ASSUMED NAME CERTIFICATE FOR FILING WITH THE SECRETARY OF STATE**.

If the name used leads people to believe that the business is not one that shields its owners from liability, the right to limited liability may be lost. If you use such a name, it should always be accompanied by the corporate name.

Professional Associations, Professional Corporations, and Professional LLCs

Any one or more licensed professionals may form a professional association for the purpose of providing professional services. This includes doctors of medicine, podiatry, and dentistry. Any one or more licensed professionals—except physicians, surgeons, or other doctors of medicine—may form a professional corporation. Any licensed professionals, including doctors of medicine, may form a professional limited liability company for the purpose of rendering their particular professional service.

Historically, professionals were not allowed to form anything other than general partnerships. This subjected a professional to personal liability for the actions taken by another partner in the partnership. Therefore, the professional association, professional corporation, and professional limited liability company evolved. These types of entities are preferred because the personal liability for the actions of other professionals in the group is removed.

Professional associations must adopt a name followed by the word or words *Associated, Association, Professional Association, and Associates, Assoc.,* or *P.A.* Professional corporations may use the normal corporation designations, or *P.C.* Professional limited liability companies must adopt a name that contains the words *Professional Limited Liability Company* or the abbreviation *P.L.L.C.* or *PLLC.*

Domain Names

With the Internet being so new and changing so rapidly, all of the rules for Internet names have not yet been worked out. Originally, the first person to reserve a name owned it, and enterprising souls bought up the names of most of the *Fortune 500* corporations and held them for ransom. Then a few of the corporations went to court and the rule was developed that if a company had a trademark for a name, that company could stop someone else from using it as a domain name.

You cannot yet get a trademark merely for using a domain name. Trademarks are granted for the use of a name in commerce. Once you have a valid trademark, you will be safe in using it for your domain name.

In the next few years there will probably be several changes to the domain name system to make it more flexible and useful throughout the world. One proposed change is the addition of more *top level domains* (*TLDs*), which are the last parts of the names, like *com* and *gov*.

The following TLDs are either available now or will be soon:

aero	coop	llc	school
agent	family	llp	scifi
arts	free	love	shop
auction	game	ltd	soc
biz	golf	med	sport
bz	inc	mp3	tech
cc	info	museum	travel
chat	kids	names	tv
church	kids.us	nu	us
club	law	pro	video
			xxx

If you wish to protect your domain name the best thing to do at this point is to get a trademark for it. To do this you would have to use it on your goods or services. (See Chapter 9 for more information on domain names and the Internet.)

Trademarks

As your business builds goodwill, its name will become more valuable and you will want to protect it from others who may wish to copy it. To protect a name used to describe your goods or services, you can register it as a trademark (for goods) or a service mark (for services) with either the Secretary of State of the state of Texas or with the United States Patent and Trademark Office.

You cannot obtain a trademark for the name of your business, but you can trademark the name you use on your goods and services. In most cases, you use your company name on your goods as your trademark. In effect, it protects your company name. Another way to protect your company name is to incorporate. A particular corporate name can only be registered by one company in Texas.

State Registration

State registration would be useful if you only expect to use your trademark within the state of Texas. Federal registration would protect your mark anywhere in the country. The registration of a mark gives you exclusive use of the mark for the types of goods for which you register it. The only exception is people who have already been using the mark. You cannot stop people who have been using the mark prior to your registration.

Before a mark can be registered, it must be used in Texas. For goods, this means it must be used on the goods themselves, or on containers, tags, labels, or displays of the goods. For services, it must be used in the sale or advertising of the services. The use must be with regard to services rendered in Texas. A sample mailed to a friend is not an acceptable use.

You may only register the mark for one *class of goods*. If the mark is used on more than one class of goods, a separate registration must be filed. The registration is good for ten years and costs $50. Six months prior to its expiration, it must be renewed.

In Appendix B there is a sample filled-in **APPLICATION FOR THE REGISTRATION OF A TRADEMARK OR SERVICE MARK**. A blank form and instructions are in Appendix C. (see form 3, p.193.)

Federal Registration

For federal registration, the procedure is a little more complicated. There are two types of applications, depending upon whether you have already made *actual use* of the mark or whether you merely have an *intention to use* the mark in the future. For a trademark that has been in use, you must file an application form along with specimens showing actual use and a drawing of the mark that complies with all of the rules of the United States Patent and Trademark Office.

For an *intent to use* application, you must file two separate forms—one when you make the initial application and the other after you have made actual use of the mark—as well as the specimens and drawing. Before a mark can be entitled to federal registration, the mark must be used in *interstate commerce* (in commerce with another state). The fee for registration is $335, but if you file an *intent to use* application, there is a second fee of $100 for the filing after actual use.

4 | Financing Your Business

The way to finance your business is determined by how quickly you would like your business to grow and how much risk of failure you are willing to handle. Letting the business grow with its own income is the slowest but safest way to grow. Taking out a personal loan against your house to expand quickly is the fastest but riskiest way to grow.

Growing with Profits

Many successful businesses have started out with little money and used the profits to grow larger. If you have another source of income to live on (such as a job or a spouse) you can plow all the income of your fledgling business into growth.

Some businesses start as hobbies or part-time ventures on the weekend while the entrepreneur holds down a full-time job. Many types of goods or service businesses start this way. Even some multi-million dollar corporations, such as *Apple Computer*, started out this way.

This allows you to test your idea with little risk. If you find you are not good at running that type of business, or the time or location was not right for your idea, all you are out is the time you spent and your start-up capital.

However, a business can only grow so big from its own income. In many cases, as a business grows, it gets to a point in which the orders are so big that money must be borrowed to produce the product to fill them. With this kind of order, there is the risk that if the customer cannot pay or goes bankrupt, the business will also go under. At such a point, a business owner should investigate the credit worthiness of the customer and weigh the risks. Some businesses have grown rapidly, some have gone under, and others have decided not to take the risk and stayed small. You can worry about that down the road.

Using Your Savings

One of the best sources of money to fund the start of your business is often your personal savings. You will not have to pay high interest rates and you will not have to worry about paying someone back.

Home Equity If you have owned your home for several years, it is possible that the equity has grown substantially and you can get a second mortgage to finance your business. If you have been in the home for many years and have a good record of paying your bills, some lenders will make second mortgages that exceed the equity. Just remember—if your business fails, you may lose your house.

Retirement Accounts Be careful about borrowing from your retirement savings. There are tax penalties for borrowing from or against certain types of retirement accounts. Also, your future financial security may be lost if your business does not succeed.

Having Too Much Money It probably does not seem possible to have too much money with which to start a business, but many businesses have failed for that reason. With plenty of start-up capital available, a business owner does not need to watch expenses and can become wasteful. Employees get used to lavish spending. Once the money runs out and the business must run on its own earnings, it fails. Many *dot.com* start-ups recently faced this problem and failed.

Starting with the bare minimum forces a business to watch its expenses and be frugal. It necessitates finding the least expensive solutions to problems that arise and creative ways to be productive.

Borrowing Money

It is extremely tempting to look to others to get the money to start a business. The risk of failure is less worrisome and the pressure is lower, but that is a problem with borrowing. If it is others' money, you may not have the same incentive to succeed as you would if everything you own is on the line.

You should be even more concerned when using the money of others. Your reputation should be more valuable than the money, which can always be replaced. Yet that is not always the case. Many people borrow again and again from their parents for failed business ventures.

Family Depending on how much money your family can spare, it may be the most comfortable or most uncomfortable source of funds. If you have been assured a large inheritance and your parents have more funds than they need to live on, you may be able to borrow against your inheritance without worry. It will be your money anyway, and you need it much more now than you will ten or twenty or more years from now. If you lose it all, it is your own loss.

However, if you are borrowing your widowed mother's only source of income or asking her to cash in a CD she lives on to finance your get-rich-quick scheme, you should have second thoughts about it. Stop and consider all the real reasons your business might not take off and what your mother would do without the income.

Friends Borrowing from friends is like borrowing from family members. If you know they have the funds available and could survive a loss, you may want to risk it. If they would be loaning you their only resources, do not chance it.

Financial problems can be the worst thing for a relationship, whether it is a casual friendship or a long-term romantic involvement. Before you borrow from a friend, try to imagine what would happen if you could not pay it back and how you would feel if it caused the end of your relationship.

The ideal situation is if your friend were a co-venturer in your business and the burden would not be totally on you to see how the funds were spent. Still, realize that such a venture will put extra strain on the relationship.

Banks

A bank may be a more comfortable party from which to borrow money, because you do not have a personal relationship with it like you do with a friend or family member. If you fail, the bank will write your loan off rather than disown you. But a bank can also be the least comfortable party to borrow from because it will demand realistic projections and be on top of you to perform. If you do not meet the bank's expectations, it may call your loan just when you need it most.

The best thing about a bank loan is that it will require you to do your homework. You must have plans that make sense to a banker. If your loan is approved, you know that your plans are at least reasonable.

Bank loans are not cheap or easy. You will be paying interest and you will have to put up collateral. If your business does not have equipment or receivables, the bank may require you to put up your house and other personal property to guarantee the loan.

Banks are a little easier to deal with when you get a *Small Business Administration* (SBA) loan. That is because the SBA guarantees that it will pay the bank if you default on the loan. SBA loans are obtained through local bank branches.

Credit Cards

Borrowing against a credit card is one of the fastest growing ways of financing a business, but it can be one of the most expensive ways. The rates can go higher than twenty percent. However, some cards offer lower rates and many people are able to get numerous cards. Some successful businesses have used the partners' credit cards to get off the ground or to weather through a cash crunch, but if the business does not begin to generate the cash to make the payments, you could soon end up in bankruptcy. A good strategy is to use credit cards only for a long-term asset, like a computer, or for something that will quickly generate cash, like buying inventory to fill an order. Do not use credit cards to pay expenses that are not generating revenue.

Getting a Rich Partner

One of the best business combinations is a young entrepreneur with ideas and ambition and a retired investor with business experience and money. Together they can supply everything the business needs.

How can you find such a partner? Be creative. You should have investigated the business you are starting and know others who have been in such businesses. Have any of them had partners retire over the last few years? Are any of them planning to phase out of the business?

Selling Shares of Your Business

Silent investors are one of the the best sources of capital for your business. You retain full control of the business, and if it happens to fail, you have no obligation to them. Unfortunately, few silent investors are interested in a new business. It is only after you have proven your concept to be successful and built up a rather large enterprise that you will be able to attract such investors.

The most common way to obtain money from investors is to issue stock to them. For this, the best type of business entity is the corporation. It gives you almost unlimited flexibility in the number and kinds of shares of stock you can issue.

An alternative to forming a corporation is the limited partnership. In a limited partnership, you will be the general partner and the investor will be the limited partner. A limited partnership allows the general partner to maintain control of the day-to-day operations of the partnership while still allowing the investor the protection of limited liability. There may also be some tax advantages to using a limited partnership. Offering a share of a limited partnership to an investor is considered offering to sell a security.

Understanding Securities Laws

There is one major problem with selling stock, partnership, or membership interests in your business—there are many federal and state regulations with which you must comply. Both the state and federal governments have long and complicated laws dealing with the sales of *securities*. There are also hundreds of court cases attempting to explain what these laws mean. A thorough explanation of this area of law is obviously beyond the scope of this book.

Basically, securities have been held to exist in any case in which a person provides money to someone with the expectation that he or she will get a profit through the efforts of that person. This can apply to any situation where someone buys stock in or makes a loan to your business. What the laws require is disclosure of the risks involved and in some cases, registration of the securities with the government. There are some exemptions, such as for small amounts of money and for limited numbers of investors.

Penalties for violation of securities laws are severe, including triple damages and prison terms. Consult a specialist in securities laws before issuing any security. You can often get an introductory consultation at a reasonable rate to learn your options.

Using the Internet to Find Capital

The Internet does have some sources of capital listed. The following sites may be helpful.

America's Business Funding Directory
www.businessfinance.com

U.S. Small Business Administration (SBA)
www.sba.gov/financing

NVST
www.nvst.com

The Capital Network
www.thecapitalnetwork.com

Before attempting to market your company's shares on the Internet, be sure to get an opinion from a securities lawyer.

5 LOCATING YOUR BUSINESS

The right location for your business will be determined by what type of business it is and how fast you expect to grow. For some types of businesses, the location will not be important to your success or failure. In others it will be crucial.

Working Out of Your Home

Many small businesses get started out of the home. Chapter 6 discusses the legalities of home businesses. This section discusses the practicalities.

Starting a business out of your home can save you the rent, electricity, insurance, and other costs of setting up at another location. For some people this is ideal. They can combine their home and work duties easily and efficiently. For other people it is a disaster. Spouses, children, neighbors, television, and household chores can be so distracting that no other work gets done.

Since residential telephone rates are usually lower than business lines, many people use their residential telephone line to conduct business or add a second residential line. However, if you wish to be listed in the Yellow Pages, you will need to have a business line in your home. If you are running two or more types of businesses, you can probably add their names as additional listings on the original number and avoid paying for another business line.

You also should consider whether the type of business you are starting is compatible with a home office. For example, if your business mostly consists of making phone calls or calling clients, then the home may be an ideal place to run it. If your clients need to visit you or you will need daily pickups and deliveries by truck, then the home may not be a good location. This is discussed in more detail in Chapter 6.

Choosing a Retail Site

For most types of retail stores, the location is of prime importance. Such things to consider are how close it is to your potential customers, how visible it is to the public, and how easily accessible it is to both autos and pedestrians. The attractiveness and safety should also be considered.

Location would be less important for a business that was the only one of its kind in the area. For example, if there was only one moped parts dealer or Armenian restaurant in a metropolitan area, people would have to come to wherever you are if they want your products or services. However, even with such businesses, keep in mind that there is competition. People who want moped parts can order them by mail and restaurant customers can choose another type of cuisine.

Look up all the businesses similar to the one you plan to run in the phone book and mark them on a map. For some businesses, such as a cleaners, you would want to be far from the others. For other businesses, such as antique stores, you would want to be near the others that are similar. (Antique stores usually do not carry the same things, therefore they do not compete, and people like to go to an *antique district* and visit all the shops.)

Choosing Office, Manufacturing, or Warehouse Space

If your business will be the type in which customers will not come to you, then locating it near customers is not as much of a concern. You can probably save money by locating away from the high traffic central business districts. However, you should consider the convenience for employees and not locate in an area that would be unattractive to them or too far from where they would likely live.

For manufacturing or warehouse operations, consider your proximity to a post office, trucking company, or rail line. Where several sites are available, you might consider which one has the earliest or most convenient pick-up schedule for the carriers you plan to use.

Leasing a Site

A lease of space can be one of the biggest expenses of a small business, so do a lot of homework before signing one. There are a lot of terms in a commercial lease that can make or break your business. These are the most critical.

Zoning Before signing a lease, be sure that everything your business will need to do is allowed by the zoning of the property. Your county zoning board can explain what is and is not allowed for how your property is zoned.

Restrictions In some shopping centers, existing tenants have guarantees that other tenants do not compete with them. For example, if you plan to open a restaurant and bakery, you may be forbidden to sell carry out baked goods if the supermarket next door has a bakery and a noncompete clause.

Signs Business signs are regulated by zoning laws, sign laws, and property restrictions. If you rent a hidden location with no possibility for adequate signage, your business will have a lot smaller chance of success than with a more visible site or much larger sign.

ADA Compliance The *Americans with Disabilities Act* (ADA) requires that reasonable accommodations be made to make businesses accessible to the handicapped. When a business is remodeled, many more changes are required than if no remodeling is done. When renting space you should be sure that it complies with the law or that the landlord will be responsible for compliance. Be aware of the full costs you will bear.

Expansion As your business grows, you may need to expand your space. The time to find out about your options is before you sign the lease. Perhaps you can take over adjoining units when those leases expire.

Renewal Location is a key to success for some businesses. If you spend five years building up a clientele, you do not want someone to take over your locale at the end of your lease. Therefore, you should have a renewal clause on your lease. This usually allows an increase in rent based on inflation.

Guaranty Most landlords of commercial space will not rent to a small corporation without a personal guaranty of the lease. This is a very risky thing for a new business owner to do. The lifetime rent on a long-term commercial lease can be hundreds of thousands of dollars. If your business fails, the last thing you want to do is be personally responsible for five years of rent.

Where space is scarce or a location is hot, a landlord can get the guaranties he or she demands and there is nothing you can do about it (except perhaps set up an asset protection plan ahead of time). But where several units are vacant or the commercial rental market is soft, you can often negotiate out of the personal guaranty. If the lease is five years, maybe you can get away with a guaranty of just the first year.

Duty to Open Some shopping centers have rules requiring all shops to be open certain hours. If you cannot afford to staff it the whole time required or if you have religious or other reasons that make this a problem, negotiate it out of the lease or find another location.

Sublease At some point you may decide to sell your business, and in many cases the location is the most valuable aspect of it. For this reason you should be sure that you have the right to either assign your lease or to sublease the property. If this is impossible, one way around a prohibition is to incorporate your business before signing the lease, and then when you sell the business, sell the stock. Some lease clauses prohibit transfer of *any interest* in the business, so read the lease carefully.

Buying a Site

If you are experienced with owning rental property, you will probably be more inclined to buy a site for your business. If you have no experience with real estate, you should probably rent and not take on the extra cost and responsibility of property ownership.

One reason to buy your site is that you can build up equity. Rather than pay rent to a landlord, you can pay off a mortgage and eventually own the property.

Separating the Ownership One risk in buying a business site is that if the business gets into financial trouble, the creditors may go after the building as well. For this reason most people who buy a site for their business keep the ownership out of the business.

> **Example:** The business will be a corporation and the real estate will be owned personally by the owner or by a trust unrelated to the business.

Expansion Before buying a site, consider the growth potential of your business. If it grows quickly, will you be able to expand at that site or will you have to move? Might the property next door be available for sale in the future if you need it? Can you get an option on it?

If the site is a good investment whether or not you have your business, then by all means, buy it. But if its main use is for your business, think twice.

Zoning Some of the concerns when buying a site are the same as when renting. You will want to make sure that the zoning permits the type of business you wish to start or that you can get a variance without a large expense or delay. Be aware that just because a business is now using the site does not mean that you can expand or remodel the business at that site. Check with the zoning department and find out exactly what is allowed.

Signs Signs are another concern. Some cities have regulated signs and do not allow new or larger ones. Some businesses have used these laws to get publicity. A car dealer who was told to take down a large number of American flags on his lot filed a federal lawsuit and the community rallied behind him.

ADA Compliance   ADA compliance is another concern when buying a commercial building. Find out from the building department if the building is in compliance or what needs to be done to put it in compliance. If you remodel, the requirements may be more strict.

NOTE: *When dealing with public officials, keep in mind that they do not always know what the law is or do not accurately explain it. They occasionally try to intimidate people into doing things that are not required by law. Read the requirements yourself and question the officials if they seem to be interpreting it wrong. Seek legal advice if officials refuse to reexamine the law or move away from an erroneous position.*

Also consider that keeping them happy may be worth the price. If you are already doing something they have overlooked, do not make a big deal over a little thing they want changed or they may subject you to a full inspection or audit.

Checking Government Regulations

When looking for a site for your business, investigate the different government regulations in your area. For example, a location just outside the city or county limits might have a lower licensing fee, a lower sales tax rate, and less strict sign requirements.

6 Licensing Your Business

The federal and state legislatures and local governments have an interest in protecting consumers from bad business practices. Therefore, in order to ensure that consumers are protected from unscrupulous business people and to require a minimum level of service to the public, the federal, state, and local governments have developed hundreds of licensing requirements that cover occupations and services ranging from attorneys to barbers to day care providers and hundreds of others.

Occupational Licenses and Zoning

Some Texas counties and cities require you to obtain an occupational license. If you are in a city, you may need both a city and a county license. Businesses that do work in several cities, such as builders, must obtain a license from each city where they do work. This does not have to be done until you actually begin a job in a particular city.

County occupational licenses can be obtained from the tax collector in the county courthouse. City licenses are usually available at city hall. Be sure to find out if zoning allows your type of business before buying or leasing property. The licensing departments will check the zoning before issuing your license.

If you will be preparing or serving food, you will need to check with the local health department to be sure that the premises complies with their regulations. In some areas, if food has been served on the premises in the past, there is no problem getting a license. If food has never been served on the premises, then the property must comply with all the newest regulations. This can be very costly.

Home Business

Problems occasionally arise when persons attempt to start a business in their home. Small new businesses cannot afford to pay rent for commercial space and cities often try to forbid business in residential areas. Getting a county occupational license or advertising a fictitious name often gives notice to the city that a business is being conducted in a residential area.

Some people avoid the problem by starting their businesses without occupational licenses, figuring that the penalties for not having a license (if they are caught) are less expensive than the cost of office space. Others get the county license and ignore the city rules. If a person regularly parks commercial trucks and equipment on his or her property, has delivery trucks coming and going, or has employee cars parked along the street, there will probably be complaints from neighbors and the city will probably take legal action. But if a person's business consists merely of making phone calls out of the home and keeping supplies there, the problem may never become an issue.

If a problem does arise regarding a home business that does not disturb the neighbors, a good argument can be made that the zoning law that prohibits the business is unconstitutional. But court battles with a city are expensive and probably not worth the effort for a small business. The best course of action is to keep a low profile. Using a post office box for the business is sometimes helpful in diverting attention away from the residence.

State-Regulated Professions

The state of Texas requires many different businesses and occupations to obtain licenses prior to carrying on a regulated business or occupation. Often, the state will also require continuing education or recertification to ensure that licensed professionals maintain a proper level of expertise. If you are in a regulated profession or conducting a regulated business, you should be aware of the laws that apply to you. The following is a list of some of the most common regulated professions.

- Accountants
- Adult day care operators
- Air conditioning contractors
- Alcoholic beverage distributors
- Appraisers
- Architects
- Attorneys
- Auctioneers
- Barbers
- Career counselors
- Child care facility operators
- Cigarette and tobacco retailers
- Commercial vehicle drivers
- Dentists
- Dieticians
- Doctors
- Emergency medical services providers
- Engineers

- Firefighters
- Fireworks dealers
- Food wholesalers
- Funeral directors
- Insurance adjustors
- Land surveyors
- Manufactured housing retailers
- Massage therapists
- Nurses
- Nursing facility administrators
- Optometrists
- Pawnshop operators
- Pharmacists
- Physical therapists
- Plumbers
- Podiatrists
- Police officers
- Private investigators
- Psychologists
- Real estate agents/brokers

- Security officers

- Tanning facility operators

- Teachers

- Veterinarians

This list is not exhaustive. To find out information regarding the occupations listed and the many licenses and permits necessary to operate your business or provide certain services, see the following websites. They can provide a wealth of information to get your business started properly.

Texas Department of Economic Development
www.tded.state.tx.us

Texas Department of Licensing and Regulation
www.license.state.tx.us

Federal Licenses

There are few businesses that require federal registration. If you are in any of the types of businesses listed below, you should check with the federal agency below it.

Radio or television stations or manufacturers of equipment emitting radio waves:
Federal Communications Commission
445 12th Street, SW
Washington, DC 20554
www.fcc.gov

Manufacturers of alcohol, tobacco, firearms, or explosives:
Bureau of Alcohol, Tobacco, Firearms and Explosives
Office of Liaison and Public Information
650 Massachusetts Avenue, NW Room 8290
Washington, DC 20226
www.atf.treas.gov

Securities brokers and providers of investment advice:

Securities and Exchange Commission
Fort Worth District Office
801 Cherry Street, 19th Floor
Fort Worth, TX 76102
www.sec.gov

Manufacturers of drugs and processors of meat:

Food and Drug Administration
5600 Fishers Lane
Rockville, MD 20857
www.fda.gov

Interstate carriers:

Surface Transportation Board
1925 K Street, NW
Washington, DC 20423
www.stb.dot.gov

Exporting:

Bureau of Industry and Security
Department of Commerce
14th Street and Constitution Avenue, NW
Washington, DC 20230
www.bxa.doc.gov

7 Contract Laws

As a business owner, you will need to know the basics of forming a simple contract for your transactions with both customers and vendors. There is a lot of misunderstanding about what the law is and people may give you erroneous information. Relying on it can cost you money. This chapter gives you a quick overview of the principles that apply to your transactions and the pitfalls to avoid. If you face more complicated contract questions, consult a law library or an attorney familiar with small business law.

Traditional Contract Law

One of the first things taught in law school is that a contract is not legal unless three elements are present: *offer*, *acceptance*, and *consideration*. The rest of the semester dissects exactly what may be a valid offer, acceptance, and consideration. For your purposes, the important things to remember are as follows.

- ✪ If you make an offer to someone, it may result in a binding contract, even if you change your mind or find out it was a bad deal for you.

- ✪ Unless an offer is accepted and both parties agree to the same terms, there is no contract.

- A contract does not always have to be in writing. Some laws require certain contracts to be in writing, but as a general rule an oral contract is legal. The problem is in proving that the contract existed.

- Without consideration (the exchange of something of value or mutual promises), there is not a valid contract.

The most important rules for the business owner are as follows.

- An advertisement is not an offer. Suppose you put an ad in the newspaper offering *New IBM computers only $1995!* but there is a typo in the ad and it says $19.95? Can people come in and say, *I accept, here's my $19.95*, creating a legal contract? Fortunately, no. Courts have ruled that the ad is not an offer that a person can accept. It is an invitation to come in and make offers, which the business can accept or reject.

- The same rule applies to the price tag on an item. If someone switches price tags on your merchandise or if you accidentally put the wrong price on it, you are not required by law to sell it at that price. If you intentionally put the wrong price, you may be liable under the *bait and switch* law. Many merchants honor a mistaken price just because refusing to would constitute bad will and a lost customer.

- When a person makes an offer, several things may happen. It may be accepted, creating a legal contract. It may be rejected. It may expire before it has been accepted. Or, it may be withdrawn before acceptance. A contract may expire either by a date made in the offer (*This offer remains open until noon on January 29, 2005*) or after a reasonable amount of time. What is *reasonable* is a legal question that a court must decide. If someone makes you an offer to sell goods, clearly you cannot come back five years later and accept. Can you accept a week later or a month later and create a legal contract? That depends on the type of goods and the circumstances.

- A person accepting an offer cannot add any terms to it. If you offer to sell a car for $1,000 and the other party says they accept as long as you put new tires on it, there is no contract. An acceptance with changed terms is considered a rejection and a counteroffer.

- When someone rejects your offer and makes a counteroffer, a contract can be created by your acceptance of the counteroffer.

These rules can affect your business on a daily basis. Suppose you offer to sell something to one customer over the phone and five minutes later another customer walks in and offers you more for it. To protect yourself, you should call the first customer and withdraw your offer before accepting the offer of the second customer. If the first customer accepts before you have withdrawn your offer, you may be sued if you sell the item to the second customer.

There are a few exceptions to the basic rules of contracts. They are as follows.

- *Consent* to a contract must be voluntary. If it is made under a threat, the contract is not valid. If a business refuses to give a person's car back unless they pay $200 for changing the oil, the customer could probably sue and get the $200 back.

- Contracts to do *illegal acts* or acts *against public policy* are not enforceable. If an electrician signs a contract to put some wiring in a house that is not legal, the customer could probably not force him or her to do it because the court would refuse to require an illegal act.

- If either party to an offer *dies*, then the offer expires and cannot be accepted by the heirs. If a painter is hired to paint a portrait and dies before completing it, his wife cannot finish it and require payment. However, a corporation does not die, even if its owners die. If a corporation is hired to build a house and the owner dies, his or her heirs may take over the corporation and finish the job and require payment.

- Contracts made under *misrepresentation* are not enforceable. For example, if someone tells you a car has 35,000 miles on it and you later discover it has 135,000 miles, you may be able to rescind the contract for fraud and misrepresentation.

- If there was a *mutual mistake*, a contract may be rescinded. For example, if both you and the seller thought the car had 35,000 miles on it and both relied on that assumption, the contract could be rescinded. However, if the seller knew the car had 135,000 miles on it, but you assumed it had 35,000 and did not ask, you probably could not rescind the contract.

Statutory Contract Law

The previous section discussed the basics of contract law. These are not usually stated in the statutes but are the legal principles decided by judges over the past hundreds of years. In recent times, the legislatures have made numerous exceptions to these principles. In most cases, these laws have been passed when the legislature felt that traditional law was not fair. The important laws that affect contracts follow.

Statutes of Frauds

The *statutes of frauds* state when a contract must be *in writing* to be valid. Some people believe a contract is not valid unless it is in writing, but that is not so. Only those types of contracts mentioned in the statutes of frauds must be in writing. Of course, an oral contract is much harder to prove in court than one that is in writing.

In Texas, the statute of frauds is contained in Section 26.01 of the Texas Business and Commerce Code. The statute of frauds requires that the following types of contracts must be in writing:

- a promise by one person to answer for the debt, default, or miscarriage of another person;

- an agreement made on consideration of marriage or on consideration of nonmarital conjugal cohabitation;

- a contract for the sale of real estate;

- a lease of real estate for a term longer than one year;

- an agreement that is not to be performed within one year from the date of making the agreement; and,

- a promise or agreement to pay a commission for the sale or purchase of an oil and gas mining lease, an oil or gas royalty, minerals, or a mineral interest.

Consumer Protection Laws

Due to the alleged unfair practices by some types of businesses, laws have been passed controlling the types of contracts they may use. Most notable among these are health clubs and door-to-door solicitations. The laws covering these businesses usually give the consumer a certain time to cancel the contract. These laws are described in Chapter 12.

Preparing Your Contracts

Before you open your business, you should obtain or prepare the contracts or policies you will use in your business. In some businesses, such as a restaurant, you will not need much. Perhaps you will want a sign near the entrance stating *shirt and shoes required* or *diners must be seated by 10:30 p.m.*

However, if you are a building contractor or a similar business, you will need detailed contracts to use with your customers. If you do not clearly spell out your rights and obligations, you may end up in court and lose thousands of dollars in profits.

The best way to have an effective contract is to have one prepared by an attorney who is experienced in the subject. However, since this may be too expensive for your new operation, you may want to go elsewhere. Three sources for the contracts you will need are other businesses like yours, trade associations, and legal form books. Obtain as many different contracts as possible, compare them, and decide which terms are most comfortable for you.

8 Insurance

There are few laws requiring you to have insurance. However, if you do not have insurance, you could face liability that could ruin your business. You should be aware of the types of insurance available and weigh the risks of a loss against the cost of a policy.

Be mindful that there can be a wide range of prices and coverage in insurance policies. Get at least three quotes from different insurance agents and ask each one to explain the benefits of his or her policy.

Workers' Compensation

Chapter 406 of the *Texas Labor Code* governs the use of workers' compensation insurance by Texas employers. Unlike many states, Texas does not require an employer to carry workers' compensation insurance. However, to protect yourself from litigation, you may wish to carry it even though it is not required. This insurance can be obtained from most insurance companies and, at least for low-risk occupations, is not expensive.

If an employer purchases workers' compensation insurance, then the insurance company, by law, must compensate an injured employee. The insurance company pays if the injury *arises out of* or *occurs within* the scope of the employee's employment, without regard to the fault or negligence of the employer. Most importantly, in most situations, the employee may not then bring a claim against you as the employer for damages. This protects you against potentially ruinous claims by employees (or their heirs in case of accident or death).

If you do not carry workers' compensation insurance, you may be found liable for an employee's injuries, as well as his or her pain and suffering (and even *punitive* damages, which are designed to punish you).

Also, under Section 406.033 of the Texas Labor Code, employers who do not carry workers' compensation insurance may not defend themselves with the same arguments as employers who do carry the insurance. This can severely limit your ability to adequately defend against a claim.

If you choose not to carry workers' compensation insurance, you must notify the Texas Workers' Compensation Commission in writing using their form and provide certain information to them about your business. To obtain this form and get further information on the many requirements imposed by Chapter 406 of the Texas Labor Code, consult the Texas Workers' Compensation Commission website at www.twcc.state.tx.us. You may also contact them at:

Texas Workers' Compensation Commission
Public Information Office
7551 Metro Center Drive
Austin, Texas 78744
512-804-4000

Liability Insurance

Like workers' compensation insurance, Texas businesses are not required to carry liability insurance. However, you may wish to carry liability insurance in order to protect yourself from lawsuits.

Liability insurance can be divided into two main areas:

1. coverage for injuries on your premises and by your employees and

2. coverage for injuries caused by your products or services.

Coverage for the first type of injury is usually very reasonably priced. Injuries in your business or by your employees (such as in an auto accident) are covered by standard premises or auto policies. But coverage for injuries by products may be harder to find and more expensive. For now, if insurance is unavailable or unaffordable, you can go without and use a corporation and other asset protection devices to protect yourself from liability.

The best way to find out if insurance is available for your type of business is to check with other businesses. If there is a trade group for your industry, its newsletter or magazine may contain ads for insurers.

Umbrella Policy

As a business owner you will be a more visible target for lawsuits even if there is little merit to them. Lawyers know that a *nuisance suit* is often settled for thousands of dollars. Because of your greater exposure, you should consider getting a personal umbrella policy. This is a policy that covers you for claims of up to a million, or even two or five million, dollars and is very reasonably priced.

Hazard Insurance

One of the worst things that can happen to your business is a fire, flood, or other disaster. With lost customer lists, inventory, and equipment, many businesses have been forced to close after such a disaster.

The premium for such insurance is usually reasonable and could protect you from the loss of your business. You can even get business interruption insurance, which will cover your losses while your business is getting back on its feet.

Home Business Insurance

There is a special insurance problem for home businesses. Most homeowner and tenant insurance policies do not cover business activities. In fact, under some policies, you may be denied coverage if you used your home for a business.

If you merely use your home to make business phone calls and send letters, you probably will not have a problem and will not need extra coverage. But if you own equipment or have dedicated a portion of your home exclusively to the business, you could have a problem. Check with your insurance agent for the options that are available to you.

If your business is a sole proprietorship and you have a computer that you use both personally and for your business, it would probably be covered under your homeowner's policy. However, if you incorporate your business and bought the computer in the name of the corporation, coverage might be denied. If a computer is your main business asset, you could get a special insurance policy in the company name covering just the computer.

Automobile Insurance

If you or any of your employees will be using an automobile for business purposes, be sure that such use is covered. Sometimes a policy may include an exclusion for business use. Check to be sure your liability policy covers you if one of your employees causes an accident while running a business errand.

Health Insurance

While new businesses can rarely afford health insurance for their employees, the sooner they can obtain it, the better chance they will have to find and keep good employees. Those starting a business usually need insurance for themselves (unless they have a working spouse who can cover the family) and they can sometimes get a better rate if they get a small business package.

Employee Theft

If you fear employees may be able to steal from your business, you may want to have them *bonded*. This means that you pay an insurance company a premium to guaranty employees' honesty, and if they cheat you the insurance company pays you damages. This can cover all existing and new employees.

9 Your Business and the Internet

The Internet has opened up a world of opportunities for businesses. A few years ago getting national visibility cost a fortune. Today a business can set up a Web page for a few hundred dollars, and with some clever publicity and a little luck, millions of people around the world will see it.

But this new world has new legal issues and new liabilities. Not all of them have been addressed by laws or by the courts. Before you begin doing business on the Internet, you should know the existing rules and the areas where legal issues exist.

Domain Names

A *domain name* is the address of your website. For example, **www.apple.com** is the domain name of Apple Computer Company. The last part of the domain name, the *.com* (or *dot com*) is the *top level domain*, or TLD. *Dot com* is the most popular, but others are currently available in the United States, including *.net* and *.org*. (Originally, *.net* was only available to network service providers and *.org* only to nonprofit organizations, but regulations have eliminated those requirements.) (See p.29 for a complete list of existing or soon-to-exist TLDs.)

It may seem like most words have been taken as a dot com name, but if you combine two or three short words or abbreviations, a nearly unlimited number of possibilities are available. For example, if you have a business dealing with automobiles, most likely someone has already registered automobile.com and auto.com. But you can come up with all kinds of variations, using adjectives or your name, depending on your type of business. Some examples include:

autos4u.com	joesauto.com	autobob.com
myauto.com	yourauto.com	onlyautos.com
greatauto.com	autosfirst.com	usautos.com
greatautos.com	firstautoworld.com	4autos.com

When the Internet first began, some individuals realized that major corporations would soon want to register their names. Since the registration was easy and cheap, people registered names they thought would ultimately be used by someone else.

At first, some companies paid high fees to buy their names from the registrants. But one company, Intermatic, filed a lawsuit instead of paying. The owner of the mark they wanted had registered numerous trademarks, such as britishairways.com and ussteel.com. The court ruled that since Intermatic owned a trademark on the name, the registration of their name by someone else violated that trademark and that Intermatic was entitled to it.

Since then, people have registered names that are not trademarks, such as CalRipkin.com, and have attempted to charge the individuals with those names to buy their domain. In 1998, Congress stepped in and passed the *Anti-Cybersquatting Consumer Protection Act*. This law makes it illegal to register a domain with no legitimate need to use it.

This law helped a lot of companies protect their names, but then some companies started abusing it and tried to stop legitimate users of similar names. This is especially likely against small companies. One organization that has been set up to help small companies protect their domains is the *Domain Name Rights Coalition*. Its website is:

www.domainnamerights.org

For extensive information on domains, refer to the *Domain Manual* at:

www.domainmanual.com

Registering a domain name for your own business is a simple process. There are many companies that offer registration services. For a list of those companies, visit the site of the *Internet Corporation for Assigned Names and Numbers* (ICANN) at **www.icann.org**. You can link directly to any member's site and compare the costs and registration procedures required for the different top-level domains.

Web Pages

There are many new companies eager to help you set up a website. Some offer turnkey sites for a low flat rate. Custom sites can cost tens of thousands of dollars. If you have plenty of capital, you may want to have your site handled by one of these professionals. However, setting up a website is a fairly simple process, and once you learn the basics, you can handle most of it in-house.

If you are new to the Web, you may want to look at the following sites that will familiarize you with the Internet jargon and give you a basic introduction to the Web:

www.learnthenet.com
www.webopedia.com

Site Set-Up There are seven steps to setting up a website—purpose, design, content, structure, programming, testing, and publicity. Whether you do it yourself, hire a professional site designer, or use a college student, the steps toward creating an effective site are the same.

Before beginning your own site, look at other sites—including those of major corporations and small businesses. Look at the sites of all the companies that compete with you. Look at hundreds of sites and click through them to see how they work (or do not work).

Purpose. To know what to include on your site, decide what its purpose will be. Do you want to take orders for your products or services, attract new employees, give away samples, or show off your company headquarters? You might want to do several of these things.

Design. After looking at other sites, you can see that there are numerous ways to design a site. It can be crowded or open and airy, it can have several windows (frames) open at once or just one, and it can allow long scrolling or just click-throughs.

You will have to decide whether the site will have text only; text plus photographs and graphics; or, text plus photos, graphics, and other design elements, such as animation or Java script. Additionally, you will begin to make decisions about colors, fonts, and the basic graphic appearance of the site.

Content. You must create the content for your site. For this, you can use your existing promotional materials, you can write new material just for the website, or you can use a combination of the two. Whatever you choose, remember that the written material should be concise, free of errors, and easy for your target audience to read. Any graphics, including photographs, and written materials not created by you require permission. Obtain such permission from the lawful copyright holder in order to use any copyrighted material. Once you know your site's purpose, look, and content, you can begin to piece the site together.

Structure. You must decide how the content (text plus photographs, graphics, animation, etc.) will be structured, what content will be on which page, and how a user will link from one part of the site to another. For example, your first page may have the business name and then choices to click on, such as *about us*, *opportunities*, *product catalog*, etc. Have those choices connect to another page containing the detailed information so that a user will see the catalog when they click on *product catalog*. Or your site could have a choice to click on a link to another website related to yours.

Programming and setup. When you know nothing about setting up a website, it can seem like a daunting task that will require an expert. However, *programming* here means merely putting a site together. There are inexpensive computer programs available that make it very simple.

Commercial programs such as Microsoft FrontPage, Dreamweaver, Pagemaker, Photoshop, MS Publisher, and PageMill allow you to set up Web pages as easily as laying out a print publication. These programs will convert the text and graphics you create into HTML, the programming language of the Web. Before you choose Web design software and design your site, determine which Web hosting service you will use. Make sure that the design software you use is compatible with the host server's system. The Web host will be the provider who will give you space on their server and who may provide other services to you, such as secure order processing and analysis of your site to see who is visiting and linking to it.

If you have used a page layout program, you can usually get a simple Web page up and running within a day or two. If you do not have much experience with a computer, you might consider hiring a college student to set up a Web page for you.

Testing. Some of the website setup programs allow you to thoroughly check your new site to see if all the pictures are included and all the links are proper. There are also websites you can go to that will check out your site. Some even allow you to improve your site, such as by reducing the size of your graphics so they download faster. Use a major search engine (listed below) to look for companies that can test your site before you launch it on the Web.

Publicity. Once you set up your website, you will want to get people to look at it. *Publicity* means getting your site noticed as much as possible by drawing people to it.

The first thing to do to get noticed is to be sure your site is registered with as many *search engines* as possible. These are pages that people use to find things on the Internet, such as Yahoo and Excite. They do not automatically know about you just because you created a website. You must tell them about your site, and they must examine and catalog it.

For a fee, there are services that will register your site with numerous search engines. If you are starting out on a shoestring, you can easily do it yourself. While there are hundreds of search engines, most people use a dozen or so of the bigger ones. If your site is in a niche area, such as geneology services, then you would want to be listed on any specific geneology search engines. Most businesses should be mainly concerned with getting on the biggest ones. By far the biggest and most successful search engine today is Google (**www.google.com**). Some of the other big ones are:

www.altavista.com	www.infoseek.com
www.dejanews.com	www.lycos.com
www.excite.com	www.netcrawler.com
www.fastsearch.com	www.northernlight.com
www.goto.com	www.webcrawler.com
www.hotbot.com	www.yahoo.com

Most of these sites have a place to click to *add your site* to their system.

There are sites that rate the search engines, help you list on the search engines, or check to see if you are listed. One site is:

www.searchiq.com

A *meta tag* is an invisible subject word added to your site that can be found by a search engine. For example, if you are a pest control company, you may want to list all of the scientific names of the pests you control and all of the treatments you have available—but you may not need them to be part of the visual design of your site. List these words as meta tags when you set up your page so people searching for those words will find your site.

Some companies thought that a clever way to get viewers would be to use commonly searched names, or names of major competitors, as meta tags to attract people looking for those big companies. For example, a small delivery service that has nothing to do with UPS or FedEx might use those company names as meta tags so people looking for them would find the smaller company. While it may sound like a good idea, it has been declared illegal trademark infringement. Today, many companies have computer programs scanning the Internet for improper use of their trademarks.

Once you have made sure that your site is passively listed in all the search engines, you may want to actively promote your site. However, self-promotion is seen as a bad thing on the Internet, especially if its purpose is to make money.

Newsgroups are places on the Internet where people interested in a specific topic can exchange information. For example, expectant mothers have a group where they can trade advice and experiences. If you have a product that would be great for expectant mothers, that would be a good place for it to be discussed. However, if you log into the group and merely announce your product, suggesting people order it from your website, you will probably be *flamed* (sent a lot of hate mail).

If you join the group, however, and become a regular, and in answer to someone's problem, mention that you *saw this product that might help*, your information will be better received. It may seem unethical to plug your product without disclosing your interest, but this is a procedure used by many large companies. They hire people to plug their product (or *rock star*) all over the

Internet. Perhaps it has become an acceptable marketing method and consumers know to take plugs with a grain of salt. Let your conscience be your guide.

Keep in mind that Internet publicity works both ways. If you have a great product and people love it, you will get a lot of business. If you sell a shoddy product, give poor service, and do not keep your customers happy, bad publicity on the Internet can kill your business. Besides being an equalizer between large and small companies, the Internet can be a filtering mechanism between good and bad products.

Advertising

There is no worse breach of Internet etiquette (*netiquette*) than to send advertising by email to strangers. It is called *spamming,* and doing it can have serious consequences.

The *Controlling the Assault of Non-Solicited Pornography And Marketing Act of 2003* (CANSPAM) has put numerous controls on how you can use email to solicit business for your company. Some of the prohibited activities under the Act are:

- false or misleading information in an email;

- deceptive subject heading;

- failure to include a functioning return address;

- mailing to someone who has asked not to receive solicitations;

- failure to include a valid postal address;

- omitting an opt-out procedure;

- failure to clearly mark the email as advertising; and,

- including sexual material without adequate warnings.

Some of the provisions contain criminal penalties as well as civil fines.

For more information on the CANSPAM Act see:
www.gigalaw.com/canspam

For text of the Act plus other Spam laws around the world, see:
www.spamlaws.com

Many states, including California, Colorado, Connecticut, Delaware, Idaho, Illinois, Iowa, Louisiana, Missouri, Nevada, North Carolina, Oklahoma, Pennsylvania, Rhode Island, Tennessee, Virginia, Washington, and West Virginia, have also enacted antispamming legislation. This legislation sets specific requirements for unsolicited bulk email and makes certain practices illegal. Check with an attorney to see if your business practices fall within the legal limits of these laws. Additionally, many Internet Service Providers (ISPs) have restrictions on unsolicited bulk email (spam). Check with your ISP to make sure you do not violate its policies.

Banner ads are the small rectangular ads on many Web pages that usually blink or move. Although most computer users seem to have become immune to them, there is still a big market in the sale and exchange of these ads.

If your site gets enough viewers, people may pay you to place their ads there. Another possibility is to trade ads with another site. In fact, there are companies that broker ad trades among websites. These trades used to be taxable transactions, but since January 5, 2000, such trades are no longer taxable under IRS Notice 2000-6.

Legal Issues

Before you set up a Web page, you should consider the legal issues described below.

Jurisdiction *Jurisdiction* is the power of a court in a particular location to decide a particular case. Usually, you have to have been physically present in a jurisdiction or have done business there before you can be sued there. Since the Internet extends your business's ability to reach people in distant places, there may be instances when you could be subject to legal jurisdiction far from your own state (or country). There are a number of cases that have been decided in this country regarding the Internet and jurisdiction, but very few cases have been decided on this issue outside of the United States.

In most instances, U.S. courts use the pre-Internet test—whether you have been present in another jurisdiction or have had enough contact with someone in the other jurisdiction. The fact that the Internet itself is not a *place* will not shield you from being sued in another state when you have shipped your company's product there, have entered into a contract with a resident of that state, or have defamed a foreign resident with content on your website. The more interactive your site is with consumers, the more you target an audience for your goods in a particular location, and the farther you reach to send your goods out into the world, the more it becomes possible for someone to sue you outside of your own jurisdiction—possibly even in another country.

The law is not even remotely final on these issues. The American Bar Association, among other groups, is studying this topic in detail. At present, no final, global solution or agreement about jurisdictional issues exists.

One way to protect yourself from the possibility of being sued in a distant jurisdiction would be to have a statement on your website indicating that those using the site or doing business with you agree that *jurisdiction for any actions regarding this site* or your company will be in your home county.

For extra protection, you can have a preliminary page that must be clicked before entering your website. However, this may be overkill for a small business with little risk of lawsuits. If you are in any business for which you could have serious liability, review some competitors' sites and see how they handle the liability issue. They often have a place to click for *legal notice* or *disclaimer* on their first page.

You may want to consult with an attorney to discuss the specific disclaimer you will use on your website, where it should appear, and whether you will have users of your site actively *agree* to this disclaimer or just *passively* read it. However, these disclaimers are not enforceable everywhere in the world. Until there is global agreement on jurisdictional issues, this may remain an area of uncertainty for some time to come.

Libel

Libel is any publication that injures the reputation of another. This can occur in print, writing, pictures, or signs. All that is required for *publication* is that you transmit the material to at least one other person. When putting together your website you must keep in mind that it is visible to millions of people all over the planet and that if you libel a person or company you may have to pay damages. Many countries do not have the freedom of speech that we do and a statement that is not libel in the United States may be libelous elsewhere.

Copyright Infringement

It is so easy to copy and *borrow* information on the Internet that it is easy to infringe copyrights without even knowing it. A *copyright* exists for a work as soon as the creator creates it. There is no need to register the copyright or to put a copyright notice on it. So, practically everything on the Internet belongs to someone. Some people freely give their works away. For example, many people have created web artwork (*gifs* and *animated gifs*) that they freely allow people to copy. There are numerous sites that provide hundreds or thousands of free gifs that you can add to your Web pages. Some require you to acknowledge the source, some do not. Always be sure that the works are free for the taking before using them.

Linking and Framing

One way to violate copyright laws is to improperly link other sites to yours, either directly or with framing. *Linking* is when you provide a place on your site to click that takes someone to another site. *Framing* occurs when you set up your site so that when you link to another site, your site is still viewable as a frame around the linked-to site.

While many sites are glad to be linked to others—some, especially providers of valuable information—object. Courts have ruled that linking and framing can be a copyright violation. One rule that has developed states that it is usually okay to link to the first page of a site, but not to link to a page with valuable information deeper within the site. The rationale for this is that the owner of the site wants visitors to go through the various levels of their site (viewing all the ads) before getting the information. By linking to the information, you are giving away their product without the ads.

The problem with linking to the first page of a site is that it may be a tedious or difficult task to find the needed page from there. Many sites are poorly designed and make it nearly impossible to find anything.

The best solution, if you wish to link to another page, is to ask permission. Email the Webmaster or other person in charge of the site, if one is given, and explain what you want to do. If they grant permission, be sure to print out a copy of their email for your records.

Privacy

Since the Internet is such an easy way to share information, there are many concerns that it will cause a loss of individual privacy. The two main concerns arise when you post information that others consider private and when you gather information from customers and use it in a way that violates their privacy.

While public actions of politicians and celebrities are fair game, details about their private lives are sometimes protected by law. Details about persons who are not public figures are often protected. The laws in each state are different and what might be allowable in one state could be illegal in another. If your site will provide any personal information about individuals, discuss the possibility of liability with an attorney.

Several well-known companies have been in the news lately for violations of their customers' privacy. They either shared what the customer was buying or downloading or looked for additional information on the customer's computer. To let customers know that you do not violate certain standards of privacy, you can subscribe to one of the privacy codes that have been promulgated for the Internet. These allow you to put a symbol on your site guaranteeing to your customers that you follow the code.

The following are websites of two of the organizations that offer this service and their fees at the time of this publication.

    www.privacybot.com $100
    www.bbbonline.com $200 to $7,000

Protecting Yourself

The easiest way to protect yourself personally from the various possible types of liability is to set up a corporation or limited liability company to own the website. This is not foolproof protection, since in some cases you could be sued personally as well, but it is one level of protection.

COPPA

If your website is aimed at children under the age of thirteen or if it attracts children of that age, then you must follow the federal *Children Online Privacy Protection Act of 1998* (COPPA). This law requires such websites to:

- give notice on the site of what information is being collected;

- obtain verifiable parental consent to collect the information;

- allow the parent to review the information collected;

- allow the parent to delete the child's information or to refuse to allow the use of the information;

- limit the information collected to only that necessary to participate on the site; and,

- protect the security and confidentiality of the information.

Financial Transactions

In the future, there will be easy ways to exchange money on the Internet. Some companies have already been started that promote their own kinds of electronic money. Whether any of these become universal is yet to be seen.

The existing services for sending money over the Internet, such as PayPal, usually offer more risk and higher fees than traditional credit card processing. Under their service agreements you usually must agree that they can freeze your account at any time and can take money out of your bank account at any time. Some offer no appeal process! Before signing up for any of these services you should read their service agreement carefully and check the Internet for other peoples' experiences with them. For example, for PayPal you can check **www.nopaypal.com**.

For now, the easiest way to exchange money on the Internet is through traditional credit cards. Because of concerns that email can be abducted in transit and read by others, most companies use a *secure* site in which customers are guaranteed that their card data is encrypted before being sent.

When setting up your website, you should ask the provider if you can be set up with a secure site for transmitting credit card data. If they cannot provide it, you will need to contract with another software provider. Use a major search engine listed on page 63 to look for companies that provide credit card services to businesses on the web.

As a practical matter, there is very little to worry about when sending credit card data by email. If you do not have a secure site, another option is to allow purchasers to fax or phone in their credit card data. However, keep in mind that this extra step will lose some business unless your products are unique and your buyers are very motivated.

The least effective option is to provide an order form on the site, which can be printed out and mailed in with a check. Again, your customers must be really motivated or they will lose interest after finding out this extra work is involved.

FTC Rules

Because the Internet is an instrument of interstate commerce, it is a legitimate subject for federal regulation. The Federal Trade Commission (FTC) first said that all of its consumer protection rules applied to the Internet, but lately it has been adding specific rules and issuing publications. The following publications are available from the FTC website at **www.ftc.gov/bcp/menu-internet.htm** or by mail from Consumer Response Center, Federal Trade Commission, 600 Pennsylvania, NW, Room H-130, Washington, DC 20580-0001.

- *Advertising and Marketing on the Internet: The Rules of the Road*

- *Appliance Labeling Rule Homepage*

- *BBB-Online: Code of Online Business Practices*

- *Big Print. Little Print. What's the Deal? How to Disclose the Details*

- *Businessperson's Guide to the Mail and Telephone Order Mdse Rule*

- *Complying with the Telemarketing Sales Rule*

- *Disclosing Energy Efficiency Information: A Guide for Online Sellers of Appliances*

- *Dot Com Disclosures: Information About Online Advertising*

- *Electronic Commerce: Selling Internationally. A Guide for Business*

- *Frequently Asked Questions About the Children's Online Privacy Protection Rule*

- *How to Comply With The Children's Online Privacy Protection Rule*

- *Internet Auctions: A Guide for Buyer and Sellers*

- *Selling on the Internet: Prompt Delivery Rules*

- *TooLate.Com: The Lowdown on Late Internet Shipments*

- *Website Woes: Avoiding Web Service Scams*

- *What's Dot and What's Not: Domain Name Registration Scams*

- *You, Your Privacy Policy & COPPA*

Fraud

Because the Internet is somewhat anonymous, it is a tempting place for those with fraudulent schemes to look for victims. As a business consumer, exercise caution when dealing with unknown or anonymous parties on the Internet.

The U.S. Department of Justice, the FBI, and the National White Collar Crime Center launched the *Internet Fraud Complaint Center* (IFCC). If you suspect that you are the victim of fraud online, whether as a consumer or a business, you can report incidents to the IFCC on their website, **www.ifccfbi.gov**. The IFCC is currently staffed by FBI agents and representatives of the National White Collar Crime Center and will work with state and local law enforcement officials to prevent, investigate, and prosecute high-tech and economic crime online.

10 Health and Safety Laws

As a reaction to the terrible work conditions prevalent in the factories and mills of the nineteenth century industrial age, Congress and the states developed many laws intended to protect the health and safety of the nation's workers. These laws are difficult to understand and often seem to be very unfair to employers. Therefore, this is an area that you need to pay particular attention to as a new business. Failure to do so can result in terrible consequences for you.

Federal Laws

The federal government's laws regarding health and safety of workers are far-reaching and very important to consider in running your business, especially if you are a manufacturer or in the oil and gas, food production, or agriculture industries.

OSHA The point of the *Occupational Safety and Health Administration* (OSHA) is to place the duty on the employer to keep the workplace free from recognized hazards that are likely to cause death or serious bodily injury to workers. The regulations are not as cumbersome for small businesses as for larger enterprises. If you have ten or fewer employees or if you are in certain types of businesses you do not have to keep a record of illnesses, injuries, and exposure to hazardous substances of employees. If you have eleven or more employees, OSHA's rules will apply. One important rule to know is that within forty-eight hours of an on-the-job death of an employee or injury of five or more employees on the job, the area director of OSHA must be contacted.

For more information, write or call an OSHA office.

OSHA Regional Office
525 Griffin Street, Room 602
Dallas, TX 75202
214-767-4731
www.osha.gov

You can obtain copies of OSHA publications, *OSHA Handbook for Small Business* (OSHA 2209) and *OSHA Publications and Audiovisual Programs Catalog* (OSHA 2019), from its website. They also have a poster that is required to be posted in the workplace by all employers. It is available on their website at **www.osha.gov/pls/publications/pubindex.list**.

Hazard Communication Standard

The *Hazard Communication Standard* requires that employees be made aware of the hazards in the workplace. (Title 29, Code of Federal Regulations (C.F.R.), Section (Sec.) 1910.1200.) It is especially applicable to those working with chemicals, but this can even include offices that use copy machines. Businesses using hazardous chemicals must have a comprehensive program for informing employees of the hazards and for protecting them from contamination.

For more information, you can contact OSHA at the previously-mentioned addresses, phone numbers, or websites. They can supply a copy of the regulation and a booklet called *OSHA 3084*, which explains the law.

EPA

The *Worker Protection Standard for Agricultural Pesticides* requires safety training, decontamination sites and, of course, posters. The Environmental Protection Agency will provide information on compliance with this law. It can be reached at 800-490-9198 or at its website at:

www.epa.gov

FDA

The *Pure Food and Drug Act of 1906* prohibits the misbranding or adulteration of food and drugs. It also created the Food and Drug Administration (FDA), which has promulgated tons of regulations and which must give permission before a new drug can be introduced into the market. If you will be dealing with any food or drugs, keep abreast of FDA policies. Its website is **www.fda.gov**. Its small business site is **www.fda.gov/ora/fed_state/small_business/sb_guide/default.htm** and its local small business representative can be reached at:

FDA, Southwest Region
Small Business Representative
7920 Elmbrook Rd., Suite 102
Dallas, TX 75247
Phone: 214-655-8100

Hazardous Materials Transportation

There are regulations that control the shipping and packing of hazardous materials. For more information, contact:

U.S. Department of Transportation
Research and Special Programs Administration
Office of Hazardous Materials Safety
400 Seventh Street, SW
Washington, DC 20590
202-366-8553
http://hazmat.dot.gov

CPSC

The *Consumer Product Safety Commission* has a set of rules that cover the safety of products. The commission feels that because its rules cover products, rather than people or companies, they apply to everyone producing such products. However, federal laws do not apply to small businesses that do not affect interstate commerce. Whether a small business would fall under a CPSC rule would depend on the size and nature of that business.

The CPSC rules are contained in the Code of Federal Regulations, Title 16 in the following parts. These can be found at most law libraries, some public libraries, and on the Internet at **www.access.gpo.gov/nara/cfr/cfr-table-search.html**. The CPSC's site is **www.cpsc.gov**.

PRODUCT	PART
Antennas, CB and TV	1402
Architectural Glazing Material	1201
Articles Hazardous to Children Under 3	1501
Baby Cribs—Full Size	1508
Baby Cribs—Non-Full Size	1509
Bicycle Helmets	1203
Bicycles	1512
Carpets and Rugs	1630, 1631
Cellulose Insulation	1209, 1404

Cigarette Lighters	1210
Citizens Band Base Station Antennas	1204
Coal and Wood Burning Appliances	1406
Consumer Products Containing Chlorofluorocarbons	1401
Electrically Operated Toys	1505
Emberizing Materials Containing Asbestos (banned)	1305
Extremely Flammable Contact Adhesives (banned)	1302
Fireworks	1507
Garage Door Openers	1211
Hazardous Lawn Darts (banned)	1306
Hazardous Substances	1500
Human Subjects	1028
Lawn Mowers—Walk-Behind	1205
Lead-Containing Paint (banned)	1303
Matchbooks	1202
Mattresses	1632
Pacifiers	1511
Patching Compounds Containing Asbestos (banned)	1304
Poisons	1700
Rattles	1510
Self-Pressurized Consumer Products	1401
Sleepwear-Childrens	1615, 1616
Swimming Pool Slides	1207
Toys, Electrical	1505
Unstable Refuse Bins (banned)	1301

Additional Regulations

Every day there are proposals for new laws and regulations. It would be impossible to include every conceivable one in this book. To be up to date on the laws that affect your type of business, join a trade association for your industry and subscribe to newsletters that cover your industry. Attending industry conventions is a good way to learn more and to discover new ways to increase your profits.

Texas Laws

The federal laws discussed previously are by far the most important with regard to the health and safety of your employees. However, you should note that Texas does have laws regarding smoking in certain places.

Smoking Unless you are in a designated smoking area, it is a Class C misdemeanor to smoke in:

- a public primary or secondary school;

- an elevator;

- an enclosed theater or movie house;

- a library;

- a museum;

- a hospital; or,

- a transit system bus or intrastate bus.

If you are operating any of the above, you must equip the area with fire extinguishers and you must display a reasonably sized notice that *smoking is prohibited by state law* in such a place. Failure to do so is punishable by a fine of up to $500.

If you are operating a business that will sell tobacco products, you must comply with Sections 161.081 to 161.0901 of the Texas Health and Safety Code. These sections provide that it is unlawful to sell cigarettes or tobacco products to a person younger than eighteen years of age or to a person who intends to deliver the products to someone under the age of eighteen.

It is a defense to the statute if you check the person's identification and it appears valid, so check ID's. This is even more important because it is a violation of federal law to sell cigarettes or tobacco products to anyone under the age of twenty-seven, unless that person presents an apparently valid identification.

You must also post a sign in a conspicuous location, close to the place where the cigarettes or tobacco products may be purchased, that says:

> PURCHASING OR ATTEMPTING TO PURCHASE TOBACCO PRODUCTS BY A MINOR UNDER 18 YEARS OF AGE IS PROHIBITED BY LAW. SALE OR PROVISION OF TOBACCO PRODUCTS TO A MINOR UNDER 18 YEARS OF AGE IS PROHIBITED BY LAW. UPON CONVICTION, A CLASS C MISDEMEANOR, INCLUDING A FINE OF UP TO $500 MAY BE IMPOSED. VIOLATIONS MAY BE REPORTED TO THE TEXAS COMPTROLLER'S OFFICE BY CALLING 1-800-862-2260.

The comptroller will provide the sign on request to any person who sells cigarettes or tobacco products.

You must provide notice about the illegality of selling cigarettes and tobacco products to persons under the age of eighteen to a new employee. This must be done within seventy-two hours of when he or she begins to work. To comply with the statute, the employee must sign a form stating that the laws were fully explained to the employee, that he or she understands the law, and that he or she, as a condition to continued employment, agrees to abide by the law.

II Employment and Labor Laws

Like health and safety, Congress and the states have also heavily regulated the actions that employers can take with regard to hiring and firing, improper employment practices, and discrimination. Because the penalties can be severe, educate yourself on the proper actions to take and consult a labor and employment lawyer, if necessary, prior to making important employee decisions.

Hiring and Firing Laws

For small businesses, there are not many rules regarding who you may hire or fire. Fortunately, the ancient law that an employee can be fired at any time (or may quit at any time) still prevails for small businesses. But in certain situations, and as you grow, you will come under a number of laws that affect your hiring and firing practices.

One of the most important things to consider when hiring someone is that if you fire them, they may be entitled to unemployment compensation. If so, your unemployment compensation tax rate will go up, which can cost you a lot of money. Therefore, you should only hire people you are sure you will keep and you should avoid situations in which your former employees can make claims against your company.

One way this can be done is by hiring only part-time employees. The drawback to this is that you may not be able to attract the best employees. When hiring dishwashers or busboys, this may not be an issue, but when hiring someone to develop a software product, you do not want them to leave halfway through the development.

A better solution is to screen applicants first and only hire those who you feel certain will work out. Of course, this is easier said than done. Some people interview well but then turn out to be incompetent at the job.

The best record to look for is someone who has stayed a long time at each of their previous jobs. Next best is someone who has not stayed as long (for good reasons) but has always been employed. The worst type of hire would be someone who is or has been collecting unemployment compensation.

The reason those who have collected compensation are a bad risk is that if they collect in the future—even if it is not your fault—your employment of them could make you chargeable for their claim.

Example: You hire someone who has been on unemployment compensation and he or she works out well for a year, but then he or she quits to take another job and is fired after a few weeks. In this situation, you would be chargeable for most of the unemployment claim because his or her last five quarters of work are analyzed. Look for a steady job history.

The competence of an employee is often more important than his or her experience. An employee with years of typing experience may be fast, but may also be unable to figure out how to use your new computer, whereas a competent employee can learn the equipment quickly and eventually gain speed. Of course, common sense is important in all situations.

The bottom line is that you cannot know if an employee will be able to fill your needs from a résumé and interview. Once you have found someone who you think will work out, offer him or her a job with a ninety-day probationary period. If you are not completely satisfied with him or her after the ninety days, offer to extend the probationary period for an additional ninety days rather than end the relationship immediately. Of course, all of this should be in writing.

Background Checks

Checking references is important, but beware that a former boss may be a good friend or even a relative. It has always been considered acceptable to exaggerate on résumés, but in recent years some applicants have been found to be completely fabricating sections of their education and experience.

Polygraph Tests

Under the federal *Employee Polygraph Protection Act*, you cannot require an employee or prospective employee to take a polygraph test, unless you are in the armored car, security alarm system, guard, or pharmaceutical business.

Drug Tests

Under the *Americans with Disabilities Act* (ADA), drug testing can only be required of applicants who have been offered jobs conditioned upon passing the drug test. Texas law requires that employers with fifteen or more employees and those that carry worker's compensation insurance adopt a policy designed to eliminate drug abuse in the workplace. They must distribute a written copy of the policy to every employee. (TX Labor Code, Sec. 411.091.)

Firing

In most cases, unless you have a contract with an employee for a set time period, you can fire him or her at any time. This is only fair, since the employee can quit at any time. The exceptions to this are: if you fire someone based on illegal discrimination; for filing some sort of health or safety complaint; or, for refusing your sexual advances or those of a coworker.

New Hire Reporting

In order to track down parents who do not pay child support, a federal law requires the reporting of new hires. The *Personal Responsibility and Work Opportunity Reconciliation Act of 1996* (PRWORA) provides that such information must be reported by employers to their state government.

Within twenty days of hiring a new employee, an employer must provide the state with information about the employee, including his or her name, Social Security number, and address. This information can be submitted in several ways, including mail, fax, magnetic tape, or over the Internet. There is a special form that can be used for this reporting. However, an employer can use the **EMPLOYEE'S WITHHOLDING ALLOWANCE CERTIFICATE (IRS FORM W-4)** for this purpose. A copy of the **IRS FORM W-4** is included in Appendix C. (see form 7, p.219.) Since this form must be filled out for all employees anyway, it would be pointless to use a separate form for the new hire reporting. When completed, it may be faxed to the Texas toll-free number, 800-732-5015, or mailed to:

Texas Employer New Hire Reporting Operations Center
P.O. Box 149224
Austin, TX 78714-9224

For more information about the program, you can call 888-TEX-HIRE, write to the above address, or visit them online at **www.newhire.org/tx**.

Employment Agreements

To avoid misunderstanding with employees, you should use an employment agreement or an employee handbook. These can spell out in detail the policies of your company and the rights of your employees. They can protect your trade secrets and spell out clearly that employment can be terminated at any time by either party.

While it may be difficult or awkward to ask an existing employee to sign such an agreement, an applicant hoping you will hire him or her will usually sign whatever is necessary to obtain the job. However, because of the unequal bargaining position, do not use an agreement that would make you look bad if the matter ever went to court.

If having an employee sign an agreement is too awkward, you can usually obtain the same rights by putting the company policies in an employee manual. Each existing and new employee should be given a copy, along with a letter stating that the rules apply to all employees and that by accepting or continuing employment at your company, they agree to abide by the rules. Having an employee sign a receipt for the letter and manual is proof that they received it.

One danger of an employment agreement or handbook is that it may be interpreted to create a long-term employment contract. To avoid this, be sure that you clearly state in the agreement or handbook that the employment is *at will* and can be terminated at any time by either party.

Some other things to consider in an employment agreement or handbook include:

- what the salary and other compensation will be;
- what the hours of employment will be;
- what the probationary period will be;
- that the employee cannot sign any contracts binding the employer; and,
- that the employee agrees to arbitration rather than filing a lawsuit.

Independent Contractors

One way to avoid problems with employees and taxes at the same time is to have all of your work done through independent contractors. This can relieve you of most of the burdens of employment laws, as well as the obligation to pay Social Security and Medicare taxes for the workers.

An independent contractor is, in effect, a separate business that you pay to do a job. You pay them just as you pay any company from which you buy products or services. At the end of the year, if the amount paid exceeds $600, you will issue a 1099 form instead of the W-2 that you issue to employees.

This may seem too good to be true, and in some situations, it is. The IRS does not like independent contractor arrangements because it is too easy for the independent contractors to cheat on their taxes. To limit the use of independent contractors, the IRS has strict regulations on who may and may not be classified as an independent contractor. Also, companies who do not appear to pay enough in wages for their field of business are audited.

The highest at-risk jobs are those that are not traditionally done by independent contractors. For example, you could not get away with hiring a secretary as an independent contractor. One of the most important factors considered in determining if a worker can be an independent contractor is the amount of control the company has over his or her work.

Example 1: If you need someone to paint your building and you agree to pay him or her a certain price to do it according to his or her own methods and schedule, you can pay him or her as an independent contractor. But if you tell him or her when to work, how to do the job, and provide the tools and materials, he or she will be classified as an employee.

Example 2: If you just need some typing done and you take it to a typing service and pick it up when it is ready, you will be safe in treating them as independent contractors. However, if you need someone to come into your office to type on your machine at your schedule, you will probably be required to treat that person as an employee for tax purposes.

The IRS has a form you can use in determining if a person is an employee or an independent contractor called **DETERMINATION OF WORKER STATUS FOR PURPOSE OF FEDERAL EMPLOYMENT TAXES AND INCOME TAX WITHHOLDING (IRS FORM SS-8)**. It is included in Appendix C of this book, along with instructions. (see form 6, p.213.)

Independent Contractors vs Employees

In deciding whether to make use of independent contractors or employees, you should weigh the following advantages and disadvantages.

Advantages.

- Lower taxes. You do not have to pay Social Security, Medicare, unemployment, or other employee taxes.

- Less paperwork. You do not have to handle federal withholding deposits or the monthly employer returns to the state or federal government.

- Less insurance. You do not have to pay workers' compensation insurance, and since the workers are not your employees, you do not have to insure against their possible liabilities.

- More flexibility. You can use independent contractors when you need them and not pay them when business is slow.

Disadvantages.

- ✪ The IRS and state tax offices are strict about when workers can qualify as independent contractors. They will audit companies whose use of independent contractors does not appear to be legitimate.

- ✪ If your use of independent contractors is found to be improper, you may have to pay back taxes and penalties and have problems with your pension plan.

- ✪ While employees usually cannot sue you for their injuries (if you have covered them with workers' compensation), independent contractors can sue you if their injuries were your fault.

- ✪ If you are paying someone to produce a creative work (writing, photography, artwork), you receive less rights to the work of an independent contractor.

- ✪ You have less control over the work of an independent contractor and less flexibility in terminating them if you are not satisfied that the job is being done the way you require.

- ✪ You have less loyalty from an independent contractor who works sporadically for you and possibly others than from your own full-time employees.

For some businesses, the advantages outweigh the disadvantages. For others, they do not. Consider your business plans and the consequences from each type of arrangement. Keep in mind that it will be easier to start with independent contractors and switch to employees than to hire employees and have to fire them to hire independent contractors.

Temporary Workers

Another way to avoid the hassles of hiring employees is to get workers from a temporary agency. In this arrangement, you may pay a higher amount per hour for the work, but the agency will take care of all of the tax and insurance requirements. Since these can be expensive and time-consuming, the extra cost may be well worth it.

Whether or not temporary workers will work for you depends upon the type of business you are in and the tasks you need performed. For jobs such as sales management, you would probably want someone who will stay with you long term and develop relationships with the buyers. For order fulfillment, temporary workers might work out well.

Another advantage of temporary workers is that you can easily stop using those who do not work out well for you, but if you find one who is ideal, you may be able to hire him or her on a full-time basis.

In recent years, a new wrinkle has developed in the temporary worker area. Many large companies are using temps because it is so much cheaper than paying the benefits demanded by full-time employees.

Example: Microsoft Corp. has had as many as 6,000 temporary workers, some of whom work for them for years. Some of the temporary workers recently won a lawsuit declaring that they are really employees and are entitled to the same benefits of other employees (such as pension plans).

The law is not yet settled in this area as to what arrangements will result in a temporary worker being declared an employee. That will take several more court cases, some of which have already been filed. The following are a few things you can do to protect yourself.

- Be sure that any of your benefit plans make it clear that they do not apply to workers obtained through temporary agencies.

- Do not keep the same temporary workers for longer than a year.

- Do not list temporary workers in any employee directories or hold them out to the public as your employees.

- Do not allow them to use your business cards or stationery.

Discrimination Laws

There are numerous federal laws forbidding discrimination based upon race, sex, pregnancy, color, religion, national origin, age, or disability. The laws apply to both hiring and firing, and to employment practices such as salaries, promotions, and benefits. Most of these laws only apply to an employer who has fifteen or more employees for twenty weeks of a calendar year or has federal contracts or subcontracts. Therefore, you most likely will not be required to comply with the law immediately upon opening your business. However, there are similar state laws that may apply to your business.

One exception is the *Equal Pay Act*. It applies to employers with two or more employees and requires that women be paid the same as men in the same type of job.

Employers with fifteen or more employees are required to display a poster regarding discrimination. This poster is available from the Equal Employment Opportunity Commission, 2401 E. Street, N.W., Washington, DC 20506. Employers with 100 or more employees are required to file an annual report with the EEOC.

When hiring employees, some questions are illegal or inadvisable to ask. The following subjects should not be included on your employment application or in your interviews, unless the information is somehow directly tied to the duties of the job.

- Do not ask about an applicant's citizenship or place of birth. After hiring an employee, you must ask about his or her right to work in this country.

- Do not ask a female applicant her maiden name. You can ask if she has been known by any other name in order to do a background check.

- Do not ask if applicants have children, plan to have them, or have child care. You can ask if an applicant will be able to work the required hours.

- Do not ask if the applicant has religious objections for working Saturday or Sunday. You can mention if the job requires such hours and ask whether the applicant can meet this job requirement.

- Do not ask an applicant's age. You can ask if an applicant is eighteen or over, or for a liquor-related job, if he or she is twenty-one or over.

- Do not ask an applicant's weight.

- Do not ask if an applicant has AIDS or is HIV positive.

- Do not ask if the applicant has filed a workers' compensation claim.

- Do not ask about the applicant's previous health problems.

- Do not ask if the applicant is married or whether his or her spouse would object to the job, hours, or duties.

- Do not ask if the applicant owns a home, furniture, or car, as it is considered racially-discriminatory.

- Do not ask if the applicant has ever been arrested. You can ask if the applicant has ever been *convicted* of a crime.

The most recent and perhaps most onerous law is the *Americans with Disabilities Act* (ADA). Under this law, employers who do not make *reasonable accommodations for disabled employees* will face fines of up to $100,000, as well as other civil penalties and civil damage awards.

The ADA currently applies to employers with fifteen or more employees. Employers who need more than fifteen employees might want to consider contracting with independent contractors to avoid problems with this law, particularly if the number of employees is only slightly larger than fifteen.

To find out how this law affects your business, read the *ADA Technical Assistance Manual,* available at:
www.usdoj.gov/crt/ada/taman2.html

Tax benefits. There are three types of tax credits to help small businesses with the burden of these laws.

- Businesses can deduct up to $15,000 a year for making their premises accessible to the disabled and can depreciate the rest. (Internal Revenue Code (IRC), Section 190.)

- Small businesses (under $1,000,000 in revenue and under thirty employees) can get a tax credit each year for 50% of the cost of making their premises accessible to the disabled, but this only applies to the amount between $250 and $10,250.

- Small businesses can get a credit of up to 40% of the first $8,500 of wages paid to certain new employees who qualify through the **PRE-SCREENING NOTICE AND CERTIFICATION REQUEST FOR THE WORK OPPORTUNITY AND WELFARE-TO WORK CREDITS (IRS FORM 8850)**. (see form 12, p.237.)

Records. To protect against potential claims of discrimination, all employers should keep detailed records showing reasons for hiring or not hiring applicants and for firing employees.

Texas Law

Texas has its own laws regarding discrimination in employment practices. The Texas Commission on Human Rights Act prohibits discrimination or classification based upon race, color, disability, religion, sex, national origin, or age of the employee. An employer who violates this law can be sued and be required to pay back pay, damages, and punitive damages. (Texas Labor Code, Sections 21.2580, *et seq.*, and 21.2585.)

Sexual Harassment

In today's employment climate, any employer must pay attention to state and federal laws regarding sexual harassment in the workplace.

Federal Law

In the 1980s, the Equal Employment Opportunity Commission interpreted *Title VII* of the *Civil Rights Act of 1964* to forbid sexual harassment. After that, the courts took over and reviewed all types of conduct in the workplace. The numerous lawsuits that followed revealed a definite trend toward expanding the definition of sexual harassment and favoring employees.

The EEOC has held the following in sexual harassment cases.

- The victim and the harasser may be a woman or a man.

- The victim does not have to be of the opposite sex.

- The harasser can be the victim's supervisor, an agent of the employer, a supervisor in another area, a coworker, or a nonemployee.

- The victim does not have to be the person harassed but could be anyone affected by the offensive conduct.

- Unlawful sexual harassment may occur without economic injury to or discharge of the victim.

- The harasser's conduct must be unwelcome.

- An employer can be held liable for sexual harassment of an employee by a supervisor, even if the employer was unaware of the supervisor's conduct.

Some of the actions that have been considered harassment are:

- displaying sexually explicit posters in the workplace;

- requiring female employees to wear revealing uniforms;

- rating of sexual attractiveness of female employees as they passed male employees' desks;

- continued sexual jokes and innuendos;

- demands for sexual favors from subordinates;

- unwelcomed sexual propositions or flirtation;

- unwelcomed physical contact; and,

- whistling or leering at members of the opposite sex.

The law in the area of sexual harassment is still developing, so it is difficult to make clear rules of conduct.

Some things a business can do to protect against claims of sexual harassment include the following.

- Distribute a written policy against all kinds of sexual harassment to all employees.

- Encourage employees to report all incidents of sexual harassment.

- Insure there is no retaliation against those who complain.

- Make clear that your policy is *zero tolerance*.

- Explain that sexual harassment includes both requests for sexual favors and a work environment that some employees may consider hostile.

- Allow employees to report harassment to someone other than their immediate supervisor in case that person is involved in the harassment.

- Promise as much confidentiality as possible to complainants.

Texas Law While most regulation of sexual harassment comes under the federal laws discussed above, Texas law does provide that it is a Class A misdemeanor for a public servant to intentionally subject another to sexual harassment.

Wage and Hour Laws

The *Fair Labor Standards Act* (FLSA) applies to all employers who are engaged in *interstate commerce* or in the production of goods for interstate commerce (anything that will cross the state line) and all employees of hospitals, schools, residential facilities for the disabled or aged, or public agencies. It also applies to all employees of enterprises that gross $500,000 or more per year.

While many small businesses might not think they are engaged in interstate commerce, the laws have been interpreted so broadly that nearly any use of the mails, interstate telephone service, or other interstate services, however minor, is enough to bring a business under the law.

Minimum Wage The federal wage and hour laws are contained in the federal Fair Labor Standards Act. The current minimum wage is $5.15. In certain circumstances a wage of $4.25 may be paid to employees under twenty years of age for a ninety-day training period.

For employees who regularly receive more than $30 a month in tips, the minimum wage is $2.13 per hour. But if the employee's tips do not bring him or her up to the full $5.15 minimum wage, then the employer must make up the difference.

Overtime The general rule is that employees who work more than forty hours a week must be paid time-and-a-half for hours worked over forty. However, there are many exemptions to this general rule based on salary and position. These exceptions were completely revised in 2004 and an explanation of the changes, including a tutorial video, are available at **www.dol.gov/esa**. For answers to questions about the law, call the Department of Labor at 866-487-9243.

Exempt Employees While nearly all businesses are covered, certain employees are exempt from the FLSA. Exempt employees include employees that are considered executives, administrative, and managerial, professionals, computer professionals, and outside salespeople.

Whether or not one of these exceptions applies to a particular employee is a complicated legal question. Thousands of court cases have been decided on this issue but they have given no clear answers. In one case a person could be determined to be exempt because of his or her duties, but in another, a person with the same duties could be found not exempt.

One thing that is clear is that the determination is made on the employee's function and not just the job title. You cannot make a secretary exempt by calling him or her a manager if most of his or her duties are clerical. For more information, contact:

U. S. Department of Labor
Wage and Hour Division
200 Constitution Avenue., N.W. Room S-3325
Washington, DC 20210
866-4USA-DOL
www.dol.gov/esa

On the Internet you can obtain information on the Department of Labor's *Small Business Handbook* at:
www.dol.gov/asp/programs/handbook/main.htm

Texas Law Texas also has a *Minimum Wage Act*. However, by complying with the federal law described above, you are complying with the Texas Minimum Wage Act, as Section 62 of the Texas Labor Code makes it a violation of state law if you fail to pay the minimum wage proscribed under federal law. In addition, Section 61 of the Texas Labor Code makes it a criminal violation if you fail to properly pay wages owed to your employees.

Pension and Benefit Laws

There are no laws requiring small businesses to provide any types of special benefits to employees. Such benefits are given to attract and keep good employees. The main concern with pension plans is that if you do start one, it must comply with federal tax laws.

Holidays

There are no federal or Texas laws that require that employees be given holidays off. You can require them to work Thanksgiving and Christmas and dock their pay or fire them for failing to show up. Of course, you will not have much luck keeping employees with such a policy.

Most companies give full time employees a certain number of paid holidays, such as: New Year's Day (January 1); Memorial Day (last Monday in May); Fourth of July; Labor Day (first Monday in September); Thanksgiving (fourth Thursday in November); and Christmas (December 25). Some employers include other holidays such as Martin Luther King, Jr.'s birthday; President's Day; and Columbus Day. If one of the holidays falls on a Saturday or Sunday, many employers give the preceding Friday or following Monday off.

Sick Days

There is no federal or Texas law mandating that an employee be paid for time that he or she is home sick. It seems to be that the larger the company, the more paid sick leave is allowed. Part-time workers rarely get sick leave and small business sick leave is usually limited for the simple reason that they cannot afford to pay for time that employees do not work.

Some small companies have an official policy of no paid sick leave, but when an important employee misses a day because he or she is clearly sick, it is paid.

Breaks

There are no federal or Texas laws requiring coffee breaks or lunch breaks. However, it is common sense that employees will be more productive if they have reasonable breaks for nourishment or to use the toilet facilities.

Pension Plans and Retirement Accounts

Few small new businesses can afford to provide pension plans for their employees. The first concern of a small business is usually how the owner can shelter income in a pension plan without having to set up a pension plan for an employee. Under most pension plans this is not allowed.

IRA. Anyone with $3,000 of earnings can put up to that amount in an Individual Retirement Account (IRA). Unless the person or his or her spouse are covered by a company pension plan and have income over a certain amount, the amount put into the account is fully tax deductible.

ROTH IRA. Contributions to a Roth IRA are not tax deductible; however, when the money is taken out, it is not taxable. People who expect to still have taxable income when they withdraw from their IRA can benefit from these.

SEP IRA, SAR-SEP IRA, SIMPLE IRA. With these types of retirement accounts, a person can put a much greater amount into a retirement plan and deduct it from his or her taxable income. Employees must also be covered by such plans, but certain employees are exempt so it is sometimes possible to use these for the owners alone. The best source for more information is a mutual fund company (such as *Vanguard, Fidelity, Dreyfus,* etc.) or a local bank, which can set up the plan and provide you with all of the rules. These have an advantage over qualified plans since they do not have the high annual fees.

Qualified Retirement Plans. Qualified retirement plans are 401(k) plans, Keogh plans, and corporate retirement plans. These are covered by ERISA, the *Employee Retirement Income Security Act*, which is a complicated law meant to protect employee pension plans. Congress did not want employees who contributed to pension plans all their lives ending up with nothing when the plan goes bankrupt.

The law is complicated and the penalties severe. However, many banks and mutual funds have created *canned plans*, which can be used instead of drafting one from scratch. Still the fees for administering them are steep. Check with a bank or mutual fund for details.

Family and Medical Leave Law

To assist business owners in deciding what type of leave to offer their employees, Congress passed the *Family and Medical Leave Act of 1993* (FMLA). This law requires an employee to be given up to twelve weeks of unpaid leave when:

- the employee or employee's spouse has a child;

- the employee adopts a child or takes in a foster child;

- the employee needs to care for an ill spouse, child, or parent; or,

- the employee becomes seriously ill.

The law only applies to employers with fifty or more employees. Also, the top ten percent of an employer's salaried employees can be denied this leave because of the disruption in business their loss could cause.

Texas Law There is no Texas law requiring family or medical leave.

Child Labor Laws

The federal *Fair Labor Standards Act* also contains rules regarding the hiring of children. The basic rules are that children under sixteen years old may not be hired at all except in a few jobs, such as acting and newspaper delivery. Those under eighteen may not be hired for dangerous jobs. Children may not work more than three hours a day/eighteen hours a week in a school week, or more than eight hours a day/forty hours a week in a nonschool week. If you plan to hire children, you should check the federal Fair Labor Standards Act, which is in United States Code (USC), Title 29 and also the related regulations, which are in Code of Federal Regulations (C.F.R.), Title 29.

Texas Law Texas also has a set of child labor laws that are found in Chapter 51 of the Texas Labor Code.

Child Labor. In addition to federal laws, the following rules apply to child labor in Texas.

- Children of any age may work:

    - as performers in a motion picture or a theatrical, radio, or television production;

    - in nonhazardous occupations;

    - under the direct supervision of a child's parent or an adult having custody of the child;

- in a business or enterprise owned or operated by a child's parent or custodian;

- delivering newspapers;

- in agriculture during a period when a child is not legally required to be in school;

- in school or court supervised employment; or,

- casual employment with the permission of a parent or adult custodian.

✪ Except as described above, it is unlawful for a child under the age of fourteen to be employed for any purpose.

Children's Hours. Texas also places limits on the number of hours a child may work. Absent a hardship exemption granted by the Texas Employment Commission, no child fifteen years of age or younger may work more than eight hours a day or more than 48 hours in one week. Further, no child fifteen years of age or younger may work between the hours of 10 p.m. and 5 a.m. when school is scheduled the next day, or between the hours of 12 a.m. and 5 a.m. on a day that is not followed by a school day or a day during summer vacation if the child is not enrolled in summer school.

Immigration Laws

In 1986, a law was passed by Congress that imposes strict penalties for any business that hires aliens who are not eligible to work. Under this law you must verify both the identity and the employment eligibility of anyone you hire by using the **EMPLOYMENT ELIGIBILITY VERIFICATION (FORM I-9)**. (see form 4, p.201.) Both you and the employee must fill out the form and you must check an employee's identification cards or papers.

Fines for hiring illegal aliens range from $250 to $2,000 for the first offense and up to $10,000 for the third offense. Failure to maintain the proper paperwork may result in a fine of up to $1,000. The law does not apply to independent contractors with whom you may contract and it does not penalize you if the employee used fake identification.

There are also penalties that apply to employers of four or more persons for discriminating against eligible applicants because they appear foreign or because of their national origin or citizenship status.

In Appendix B there is a sample filled-in **FORM I-9**. Appendix C has a list of acceptable documentation, a blank form, and instructions. (see form 4, p.201.)

For more information, download the *Handbook for Employers* from the USCIS website at:
> http://uscis.gov/graphics/lawsregs/handbook/hand_emp.pdf

The *Illegal Immigration Reform and Immigrant Responsibility Act of 1996* (IIRIRA) required changes in the rules for filling out **FORM I-9**, but as of early 2004, final versions of the rules had not yet been promulgated. The interim rule made the following changes to the requirements:

- remove documents 2, 3, 8, and 9 from column A;

- allow document 4 only for aliens authorized to work for a specific employer; and,

- new rules for employees who do not have their original documents.

However, no new forms or instructions have been made available and employers are not yet being prosecuted for violations of these changes. Employers can receive updates to these laws by fax. To receive them, send your name, address, and fax number to 202-305-2523.

Foreign employees. If you wish to hire employees who are foreign citizens and are not able to provide the documentation explained above, they must first obtain a work visa. Work visas for foreigners are not easy to get. Millions of people around the globe would like to come to the U.S. to work and the laws are designed to keep most of them out to protect the jobs of American citizens.

Whether or not a person can get a work visa depends on whether there is a shortage of U.S. workers available to fill the job. For jobs requiring few or no skills, it is practically impossible to get a visa. For highly skilled jobs, such as nurses, physical therapists, and for those of exceptional ability, such as Nobel Prize winners and Olympic medalists, obtaining a visa is fairly easy.

There are several types of visas and different rules for different countries. For example, NAFTA has made it easier for some types of workers to enter the U.S. from Canada and Mexico. For some positions, the shortage of workers is assumed. For others, a business must first advertise a position available in the U.S. Only after no qualified persons apply, can it hire someone from another country.

The visa system is complicated and subject to regular change. If you wish to hire a foreign worker, you should consult with an immigration specialist or a book on the subject.

Hiring *Off the Books*

Because of the taxes, insurance, and red tape involved with hiring employees, some new businesses hire people *off the books*. They pay them in cash and never admit they are employees. While the cash paid in wages would not be deductible, they consider this a smaller cost than compliance. Some even use off the books receipts to cover it.

Except when your spouse or child is giving you some temporary help, this is a terrible idea. Hiring people off the books can result in civil fines, loss of insurance coverage, and even criminal penalties. When engaged in dangerous work like roofing or using power tools, you are risking millions of dollars in potential liability if a worker is killed or seriously injured.

It may be more costly and time consuming to comply with the employment laws, but if you are concerned with long-term growth with less risk, it is the wiser way to go.

Federal Contracts

Companies that do work for the federal government are subject to several laws.

The *Davis-Bacon Act* requires contractors engaged in U.S. government construction projects to pay wages and benefits that are equal to or better than the prevailing wages in the area.

The *McNamara-O'Hara Service Contract Act* sets wages and other labor standards for contractors furnishing services to agencies of the U.S. government.

The *Walsh-Healey Public Contracts Act* requires the Department of Labor to settle disputes regarding manufacturers supplying products to the U.S. government.

Miscellaneous Laws

In addition to the laws previously discussed, there are additional laws employers should know.

Affirmative Action   In most cases, the federal government does not yet tell employers who they must hire. This would be especially true for new small businesses. The only situation where a small business would need to comply with affirmative action requirements would be if it accepted federal contracts or subcontracts. These requirements could include the hiring of minorities or of Vietnam veterans.

Layoffs   Companies with 100 or more full-time employees at one location are subject to the *Worker Adjustment and Retraining Notification Act*. This law requires a sixty-day notification prior to certain lay-offs and has other strict provisions.

Unions   The *National Labor Relations Act of 1935* gives employees the right to organize a union or to join one. (29, USC, beginning with Sec. 151.) There are things employers can do to protect themselves, but you should consult a labor attorney or a book on the subject before taking action that might be illegal and result in fines.

Poster Laws   Poster laws dictate what you may or may not display in the workplace. There are also poster laws that require certain posters to be displayed to inform employees of their rights. Not all businesses are required to display all posters, but the following list should be of help.

✪ All employers must display the wage and hour poster available from:
U. S. Department of Labor
www.dol.gov/esa

✪ Employers with fifteen or more employees for twenty weeks of the year must display the sex, race, religion, and ethnic discrimination poster and the age discrimination poster available from:
EEOC
www.eeoc.gov/publications.html

✪ Employers with federal contracts or subcontracts of $10,000 or mor- must display the sex, race, etc. discrimination poster mentioned above plus a poster regarding Vietnam Era Veterans available from the local federal contracting office.

✪ Employers with government contracts subject to the *Service Contract Act* or the *Public Contracts Act* must display a notice to employees working on government contracts available from:
Employment Standards Division
www.dol.gov/esa

Texas Law   In addition to the miscellaneous federal laws discussed, Texas has some additional laws of which you should be aware.

Restrictions on Retail Employers. (Texas Labor Code, Section 52.001). It is unlawful for a retail employer to require a full-time employee to work seven consecutive days without at least one twenty-four hour period off. Also, a retail employer must accommodate the religious beliefs of full-time employees unless the employer can demonstrate that to do so would constitute an *undue hardship* (disruption to business) on the employer's business.

Restrictions on Blacklisting. (Texas Labor Code, Section 52.031). It is unlawful to *blacklist* an employee, which means to prevent a discharged employee from getting employment. This does not, however, prevent an employer from giving a written, truthful statement about the reason for an employee's discharge from employment.

Coercion of Employee Trade. (Texas Labor Code Section 52.041). It is unlawful for an employer to coerce or require an employee to deal with a person, association, or company, or purchase an article of food, clothing, or other merchandise at a certain place or store. It is an offense under this code section if the employer excludes, punishes, or blacklists an employee for failing to do the above actions.

Restriction on Penalizing an Employee for Complying with a Subpoena. (Texas Labor Code, Section 52.051). It is unlawful to discharge, discipline, or otherwise penalize an employee if the employee complies with a valid subpoena to appear in court.

Denial of Employment Based on Membership in Union. (Texas Labor Code, Section 101.052). It is unlawful to deny employment based on membership or nonmembership in a labor union. This is the so-called *right-to-work* law.

Right to Organize. (Texas Labor Code, Section 101.001). It is unlawful to prevent employees to associate and form trade unions and other organizations for the purpose of protecting themselves in their personal labor and employment.

12 Advertising and Promotion Laws

Because of the unscrupulous and deceptive advertising techniques and multitude of con artists trying to steal from innocent consumers, numerous federal and state statutes have been enacted that make it unlawful to use improper advertising and promotional techniques in soliciting business.

Advertising Laws and Rules

This section discusses various federal and Texas laws and regulations relating to advertising.

Federal Law The federal government regulates advertising through the Federal Trade Commission (FTC). The rules are contained in the Code of Federal Regulations (C.F.R.). You can find these rules in most law libraries and many public libraries. If you plan any advertising that you think may be questionable, you might want to check the rules. As you read the rules discussed, you will probably think of many violations you see every day.

Federal rules do not apply to every business. Small businesses that operate only within the state and do not use the postal service may be exempt. However, many of the federal rules have been adopted into law by the state of Texas.

Therefore, a violation could be prosecuted by the state rather than the federal government. Some of the important rules are summarized below. If you wish, you should obtain copies from your library.

Deceptive pricing. When prices are being compared, it is required that actual and not inflated prices are used.

Example: If an object would usually be sold for $7, you should not first offer it for $10 and then start offering it at 30% off.

It is considered misleading to suggest that a discount from list price is a bargain if the item is seldomly sold at list price. If most surrounding stores sell an item for $7 it is considered misleading to say it has a *retail value of $10*, even if there are some stores elsewhere selling it at that price. (16 C.F.R. Ch. I, Part 233.)

Bait advertising. *Bait advertising* is placing an ad when you do not really want the respondents to buy the product offered but to switch to another item. (16 C.F.R. Ch. I, Part 238.)

Use of free, half-off, and similar words. Use of words such as *free, 1¢ sale* and the like must not be misleading. This means that the *regular price* must not include a mark-up to cover the *free* item. The seller must expect to sell the product without the free item at some time in the future. (16 C.F.R. Ch. I, Part 251.)

Substantiation of claims. The FTC requires that advertisers be able to substantiate their claims. (16 C.F.R. Sec 3.40; 48 F.R. Page 10471.) Some information on this policy is contained on the Internet at:
www.ftc.gov/bcp/guides/ad3subst.htm

Endorsements. Rules forbid endorsements that are misleading. An example is a quote from a film review that is used in such a way as to change the substance of the review. It is not necessary to use the exact words of the person endorsing the product as long as the opinion is not distorted. If a product is changed, an endorsement that does not apply to the new version cannot be used. For some items, such as drugs, claims cannot be used without scientific proof. Endorsements by organizations cannot be used unless one is sure that the membership holds the same opinion. (16 C.F.R. Ch. I, Part 255.)

Unfairness. Any advertising practices that can be deemed to be *unfair* are forbidden by the FTC. (15 USC Sec. 45.) An explanation of this policy is located on the Internet at:

www.ftc.gov/bcp/policystmt/ad-unfair.htm

Negative option plans. When a seller uses a sales system in which the buyer must notify the seller if he or she does not want the goods, the seller must provide the buyer with a form to decline the sale and at least ten days in which to decline. Bonus merchandise must be shipped promptly and the seller must promptly terminate any who so request after completion of the contract. (16 C.F.R. Ch. I, Part 425.)

Food and dietary supplements. Under the *Nutritional Labeling Education Act of 1990*, the FTC and the FDA regulate the packaging and advertising of food and dietary products. Anyone involved in this area should obtain a copy of these rules. (21 USC Sec. 343.) They are located on the Internet at:

www.ftc.gov/bcp/menu-health.htm#bized

Jewelry and precious metals. The FTC has numerous rules governing the sale and advertising of jewelry and precious metals. Anyone in this business should obtain a copy of these rules. (61 F.R. Page 27212.) They are located on the Internet at:

www.ftc.gov/bcp/guides/jewel-gd.htm

Texas Law Texas also has laws that regulate what you can and cannot do when you are advertising your business. Besides being a violation of the Texas *Deceptive Trade Practices Act*, (see p. 114), Section 32.42 of the Texas Penal Code makes it a misdemeanor to intentionally, knowingly, recklessly, or with criminal negligence:

- advertise property or services with the intent not to sell them as advertised, or not to sell as much as the public would reasonably demand at the advertised price, unless the ad adequately describes the time or quantity limit of the sale;

- represent that a product is a particular style, grade, or model if it is another;

- represent the price of property or service falsely or in a misleading way;

- use a false weight or measure or any other device for falsely determining or recording any quality or quantity;

- sell less than the represented quantity of a property or service;

- take more than the represented quantity when the buyer is the one furnishing the weight or measure;

- sell an adulterated or mislabeled commodity;

- pass off property or service as that of another;

- represent that a commodity is original or new if it is deteriorated, altered, rebuilt, reconditioned, reclaimed, used, or secondhand;

- conduct a deceptive sales contest;

- make a materially false or misleading statement about price discounts; or,

- make a false or misleading statement in an advertisement for the purchase or sale of property or services.

It is also illegal to set up or promote a lottery, or sell or a card, stub, ticket, check, or other device designed to serve as evidence of participation in any lottery. A *lottery* is defined as a scheme or procedure where one or more prizes are distributed by chance among persons who have paid for a chance to win anything of value, whether such scheme or procedure is called a pool, lottery, raffle, gift, gift enterprise, sale, policy game or any other name.

There is a limited exception to this rule for charitable organizations, but if you are a for profit business, you should consult an attorney before you operate any kind of promotion or advertising campaign that at all looks like a lottery.

Internet Sales Laws

There are not yet specific laws governing Internet transactions that are different from laws governing other transactions. The FTC feels that its current rules regarding deceptive advertising, substantiation, disclaimers, refunds, and related matters must be followed by Internet businesses and that consumers are adequately protected by them. For some specific guidelines on Internet advertising, see the FTC's site at:

http://ftc.gov/bcp/conline/pubs/buspubs/ruleroad.htm

Home Solicitation Laws

The Federal Trade Commission has rules governing door-to-door sales. In any such sale it is a deceptive trade practice to fail to furnish a receipt explaining the sale (in the language of the presentation) and giving notice that there is a right to back out of the contract within three days, known as a right of *rescission*. The notice must be supplied in duplicate, must be in at least 10-point type, and must be captioned either *Notice of Right to Cancel* or *Notice of Cancellation*. The notice must be worded as follows on the next page.

NOTICE OF CANCELLATION

_____
Date

YOU MAY CANCEL THIS TRANSACTION, WITHOUT ANY PENALTY OR OBLIGATION, WITHIN THREE BUSINESS DAYS FROM THE ABOVE DATE.

IF YOU CANCEL, ANY PROPERTY TRADED IN, ANY PAYMENTS MADE BY YOU UNDER THE CONTRACT OR SALE, AND ANY NEGOTIABLE INSTRUMENT EXECUTED BY YOU WILL BE RETURNED TO YOU WITHIN 10 BUSINESS DAYS FOLLOWING RECEIPT BY THE SELLER OF YOUR CANCELLATION NOTICE, AND ANY SECURITY INTEREST ARISING OUT OF THE TRANSACTION WILL BE CANCELLED.

IF YOU CANCEL, YOU MUST MAKE AVAILABLE TO THE SELLER AT YOUR RESIDENCE, IN SUBSTANTIALLY AS GOOD CONDITION AS WHEN RECEIVED, ANY GOODS DELIVERED TO YOU UNDER THIS CONTRACT OR SALE; OR YOU MAY IF YOU WISH, COMPLY WITH THE INSTRUCTIONS OF THE SELLER REGARDING THE RETURN SHIPMENT OF THE GOODS AT THE SELLER'S EXPENSE AND RISK.

IF YOU DO MAKE THE GOODS AVAILABLE TO THE SELLER AND THE SELLER DOES NOT PICK THEM UP WITHIN 20 DAYS OF THE DATE OF YOUR NOTICE OF CANCELLATION, YOU MAY RETAIN OR DISPOSE OF THE GOODS WITHOUT ANY FURTHER OBLIGATION. IF YOU FAIL TO MAKE THE GOODS AVAILABLE TO THE SELLER, OR IF YOU AGREE TO RETURN THE GOODS AND FAIL TO DO SO, THEN YOU REMAIN LIABLE FOR PERFORMANCE OF ALL OBLIGATIONS UNDER THE CONTRACT.

TO CANCEL THIS TRANSACTION, MAIL OR DELIVER A SIGNED AND DATED COPY OF THIS CANCELLATION NOTICE OR ANY OTHER WRITTEN NOTICE, OR SEND A TELEGRAM, TO [name of seller], AT [address of seller's place of business] NOT LATER THAN MIDNIGHT OF _____ (date).

I HEREBY CANCEL THIS TRANSACTION.

_____   _____
(Buyer's signature)   (Date)

The seller must complete the notice and orally inform the buyer of the right to cancel. He or she cannot misrepresent the right to cancel, assign the contract until the fifth business day, nor include a confession of judgment in the contract. (For more specific details see the rules contained at 16 C.F.R. Ch. I, Part 429.)

Texas Law Chapter 39 of the Texas Business and Commerce Code, titled *Cancellation of Certain Consumer Transactions*, provides rules that are similar to the FTC regulations. Chapter 39 applies to transactions that fit the following criteria:

- one of the parties to the transaction must be a consumer;

- the solicitation of the purchase takes place other than at the merchant's place of business;

- the consumer's agreement to the purchase occurs at a place other than at the merchant's place of business; and,

- the price of the transaction exceeds $25, payable in cash or installments (or $100 if the transaction involves the purchase of real estate, payable in cash or installments).

However, the statute exempts transactions that fit the above criteria if the transactions involve:

- a purchase of farm equipment;

- an insurance sale regulated by Texas insurance law;

- a sale of goods or services made under a previously established revolving credit agreement or after negotiations at the merchant's place of business; or,

- a sale of real estate if the purchaser is represented by an attorney, the transaction is negotiated by a real estate broker.

Right to Cancel. Any sale described above may be cancelled by the consumer any time before midnight of the third business day after the date the consumer signs an agreement or offer to purchase.

Notice by Merchant. In a transaction in which the purchase price exceeds $200, a merchant must provide a consumer with a complete receipt or copy of any contract pertaining to the transaction at the time the contract is signed. The document provided must:

- be in the same language as that used in the sales presentation;

- show the date of the transaction;

- contain the name and the address of the merchant; and,

- contain in immediate proximity to the space reserved in the contract for the signature of the consumer or on the front page of the receipt, if a contract is not used, a statement in bold-faced type of at least 10-point type that states:

> YOU, THE BUYER, MAY CANCEL THIS TRANSACTION AT ANY TIME PRIOR TO MIDNIGHT ON THE THIRD BUSINESS DAY AFTER THE DATE OF THIS TRANSACTION. SEE THE ATTACHED NOTICE OF CANCELLATION FORM FOR AN EXPLANATION OF THIS RIGHT.

Attached to the contract or receipt must be a completed notice of cancellation form in the same language as the contract or receipt. The form must be easily detachable and may be in the same form provided in the FTC regulations discussed previously. See page 108 for the text of that form.

In a transaction in which the purchase price does not exceed $200, a merchant complies with the notice requirements of this law if:

- the consumer may, at any time, cancel the order, refuse to accept delivery of the goods without incurring any obligation to pay for them, or return the goods to the merchant and receive full refund of the amount the consumer has paid and

- the consumer's right to cancel the order, refuse delivery, or return the goods without obligation or charge at any time is clearly and conspicuously set forth on the face or reverse side of the sales ticket.

Refund. The refund must be made to the buyer within ten days. If it is not, the seller may be subject to civil penalties and damages.

Buyer's duty. Within a reasonable time after cancellation and demand by seller, a buyer must return any goods received under the contract. If the seller has not made demand within twenty days, the buyer may keep the goods. If the seller does not refund the buyer's money, the buyer may retain possession of the goods and has a lien on them for the amount due him or her. The buyer must take reasonable care of the goods in his or her possession, but does not have to deliver them to the seller at any place other than the buyer's residence.

Telephone Solicitation Laws

In 2003, the Federal Trade Commission issued new rules regulating telephone solicitation calls. The main provision of these rules allows consumers to be listed on a national *Do Not Call* registry, and any company that calls people on the list is subject to penalties. Other provisions:

- require disclosures of specific information;

- prohibit misrepresentations;

- limit when telemarketers may call consumers;

- require transmission of Caller ID information;

- prohibit abandoned outbound calls, subject to a safe harbor;

- prohibit unauthorized billing;

- set payment restrictions for the sale of certain goods and services; and,

- require that specific business records be kept for two years.

For more information on these rules, visit **www.telemarketing.donotcall.gov**. If you have questions about the rules, call 202-326-3737 or email them at tsrquestions@ftc.gov.

Texas Law Chapters 37, 38, and 44 of the Texas Business and Commerce Code regulate telephone solicitations involving transactions of real or personal property or services related to real or personal property used primarily for personal, family, or household purposes, including cemetery lots and time-shares. Penalties for violations include a fine of up to $10,000, attorney's fees, and court costs. The law contains these main provisions.

Identification. Any person who makes a telephone solicitation call must identify him- or herself by first and last name and the name of the business represented, and provide the purpose of the call immediately upon making contact.

Timing of Calls. Calls must be made between 12 noon and 9 p.m. on Sunday or between 9 a.m. and 9 p.m. on a weekday or Saturday.

Credit Cards. A person who sells consumer goods and services through the use of telephone solicitations may not make or submit a charge to a consumer's credit card account unless:

- the seller is a charity that qualifies for tax exempt treatment by the IRS;

- the seller provides to the consumer a written contract fully describing the goods or services being offered, the total price charged, the name, address, and business phone number of the seller, and receives a signed copy of the contract from the seller; or,

- the seller provides that the consumer may receive a full refund for the return of undamaged and unused goods or a cancellation of services by providing notice to the seller by the seventh day after the date the consumer receives the goods or services. (Then, the seller will process a refund within thirty days after the date the seller receives the returned merchandise or the date the buyer cancels an order to purchase service).

Registration Certificate. In general, businesses that intend to make telephone solicitations must register with the Secretary of State of Texas and obtain a registration certificate. To register, a business must submit a registration form (available from the Secretary of State) and pay a fee of $200. If you intend to make telephone solicitations as a part of your business activities, you should consult Chapter 38 of the Texas Business and Commerce Code to determine if your particular business is covered by the statute because Chapter 38 provides numerous exceptions to the registration requirement.

Do Not Call List. In addition to the Federal laws regulating telemarketing calls, Texas has its own law—the Texas *Telemarketing Disclosure and Privacy Act*—found in Chapter 44 of the Business and Commerce Code. This law allows Texas consumers to register phone numbers on a state *do not call* list. Once the registration becomes effective, telemarketers are prohibited from making sales calls to the registered number, except under certain limited circumstances. If you plan on trying to get business by making phone calls, you need to know the rules. More information can be obtained at **www.texasnocall.com**.

This law also prohibits telemarketers from interfering with or blocking the caller ID functions on their phone lines and from calling mobile phone numbers. Businesses who violate this law can be fined for each violation of the law.

Pricing, Weights, and Labeling

Food Products Beginning in 1994, all food products are required to have labels with information on the product's nutritional values such as calories, fat, and protein. For most products, the label must be in the required format so that consumers can easily compare products. However, if such a format will not fit on the product label, the information may be in another format that is easily readable.

Metric Measures In 1994, federal rules requiring metric measurement of products took effect. Under these rules, metric measures do not have to be the first measurement on the container, but they must be included. Food items that are packaged as they are sold (such as delicatessen items) do not have to contain metric labels.

Texas Law Chapter 13 of the Texas Agricultural Code provides extensive regulation of the use of weights and measures in the computing of charges for the sale of services, items, or commodities. If in your business you intend to sell services, items, or commodities (dealing with things such as milk, cheese, or meat) to the public on the basis of a weight or measure, you should consult the Code in order to ensure that you comply with the applicable regulations or speak with an attorney.

Email Advertising

The *Controlling the Assault of Non-Solicited Pornography And Marketing Act of 2003* (CANSPAM) has put numerous controls on how you can use email to solicit business for your company. Some of the prohibited activities under the Act are:

- false or misleading information in an email;

- deceptive subject heading;

- failure to include a functioning return address;

- mailing to someone who has asked not to receive solicitations;

- failure to include a valid postal address;

- omitting an opt-out procedure;

- failure to clearly mark the email as advertising; and,

- including sexual material without adequate warnings.

Some of the provisions contain criminal penalties as well as civil fines. For more information on the CANSPAM Act see:
www.gigalaw.com/canspam

For text of the Act plus other Spam laws around the world see:
www.spamlaws.com

Deceptive Practices

The Texas *Deceptive Trade Practices Act* (Section 17.41 to Section 17.63 of the Texas Business and Commerce Code) provides that it is unlawful to engage in false, misleading, or deceptive acts or practices in the conduct of trade or commerce. Among other things, the term *false, misleading, or deceptive acts* includes:

- passing off goods or services as those of another;

- representing that goods are original or new if they are deteriorated, reconditioned, reclaimed, used, or secondhand;

- disparaging the goods, services, or business of another by false or misleading representation of facts;

- representing that goods or services are of a particular standard, quality, or grade, or that goods are of a particular style or model, if they are of another;

- advertising goods or services with intent not to sell them as advertised;

- making false or misleading statements of fact concerning the reasons for, existence of, or amount of price reductions;

- advertising any sale by fraudulently representing that a person is going out of business; or,

- using the term *corporation*, *incorporated*, or an abbreviation of either of those terms in the name of a business entity that is not incorporated under the laws of this state or another jurisdiction.

(See Section 17.46 of the Texas Business and Commerce Code for a complete list.)

Whenever the Consumer Protection Division of the Attorney General's office has reason to believe that a person has engaged in, or is about to engage in *false, misleading, or deceptive acts*, it can get a court order to stop the act and obtain a penalty of $2,000 per violation up to $10,000 (or $10,000 per violation up to $100,000 if it is determined that the fraudulent action was targeted at consumers age 65 or over).

Also, a consumer may sue a business and, if he or she wins, may obtain *economic damages*. If the jury or court determines that the fraudulent actions were done *knowingly*, then the consumer may get mental anguish damages as well. Finally, if the jury or court determines that the fraudulent actions were done *intentionally*, the consumer may get triple damages (economic damages and mental anguish).

Obviously, a claim made against you or your business under the *Deceptive Trade Practices Act* is a serious matter. Immediately contact an attorney to help you assess your rights and obligations.

13: Payment and Collection

Depending on the business you are in, you may be paid by cash, checks, credit cards, or some sort of financing arrangement, such as a promissory note or mortgage. Both state and federal laws affect the type of payments you collect. Failure to follow the laws can cost you considerably.

Cash

Cash is probably the easiest form of payment and it is subject to few restrictions. The most important one is that you keep an accurate accounting of your cash transactions and that you report all of your cash income on your tax return. Recent efforts to stop the drug trade have resulted in some serious penalties for failing to report cash transactions and for money laundering. The laws are so sweeping that even if you deal in cash in an ordinary business you may violate the law and face huge fines and imprisonment.

The most important law to be concerned with is the one requiring the filing of the **REPORT OF CASH PAYMENTS OVER $10,000 RECEIVED IN A TRADE OR BUSINESS (IRS FORM 8300).** (see form 11, p.233.) A transaction does not have to happen in one day. If a person brings you smaller amounts of cash that add up to $10,000 and the government can construe them as one transaction, then the form must be filed. Under this law, *cash* also includes travelers' checks and money orders but not cashier's checks or bank checks.

Checks

It is important to accept checks in your business. While there is a small percentage that will be bad, most checks will be good and you will be able to accommodate more customers. To avoid having problems with checks, you should follow the following rules:

- require a picture ID when a customer presents a check;

- do not take temporary checks; and,

- always have the presenter endorse the check.

Bad Checks

It is a Class C misdemeanor (or Class B if the check is issued for payment of child support) for a person to issue or pass a check if the person knows that he or she does not have enough money in his or her account to cover that check and any other outstanding checks. Because it is difficult to prove someone's knowledge in this situation, Section 32.41 of the Texas Penal Code allows that a person shall be deemed to have acted with knowledge if, within thirty days after the check is dishonored by the bank, you (the merchant) provide notice to the person who wrote the bad check that the check bounced and the person does not pay you in full within ten days of such notice.

If you receive a bad check, you will also be able to sue the party who passed you the bad check and possibly any endorsers on the check for your damages. You may also be able to charge an additional $25 *processing fee*.

Refunds after Cashing Check

A popular scam is for a person to purchase something by using a check and then come back the next day demanding a refund. After making the refund, the business discovers the initial payment check bounced. Do not make refunds until checks clear.

Credit Cards

In our buy-now, pay-later society, credit cards can add greatly to your sales potential, especially with large, discretionary purchases. For *MasterCard*, *Visa*, and *Discover*, the fees are about 2%, and this amount is easily paid for by the extra purchases that the cards allow. *American Express* charges 4% to 5% and you may decide this is not worth paying since almost everyone who has an *American Express* card also has another card.

For businesses that have a retail outlet, there is usually no problem getting merchant status. Most commercial banks can handle it. *Discover* can also set you up to accept their card as well as *MasterCard* and *Visa*, and they will wire the money into your bank account daily.

For mail order businesses, especially those operating out of the home, it is much harder to get merchant status. This is because of the number of scams in which large amounts are charged, no products are shipped, and the company folds. One good thing about *American Express* is that they will accept mail order companies operating out of the home. However, not as many people have *American Express* cards as other credit cards.

Some companies open a small storefront (or share one) to get merchant status, then process mostly mail orders. The processors usually do not want to accept you if you will do more than fifty percent mail order; but if you do not have many complaints, you may be allowed to process mostly mail orders. Whatever you do, keep your credit customers happy.

You might be tempted to try to run your charges through another business. This may be okay if you actually sell your products through it; however, if you run your business charges through its account, the other business may lose its merchant status. People who bought a book by mail from you and then have a charge on their statement from a florist shop will probably call the credit card company saying that they never bought anything from the florist shop. Too many transactions like these and the account will be closed.

Financing Laws

Some businesses can make sales more easily if they finance the purchases themselves. If the business has enough capital to do this, it can earn extra profits on the financing terms. Nonetheless, because of abuses, many consumer protection laws have been passed by both the federal and state governments.

Federal Law

Two important federal laws regarding financing are called the *Truth in Lending Act* and the *Fair Credit Billing Act*. These are implemented by what is called *Regulation Z* (commonly known as *Reg. Z*), issued by the Board of Governors of the Federal Reserve System. It is contained in Volume 12 of the Code of Federal Regulations, page 226. This is a very complicated law and some have said that no business can be sure to be in compliance with it.

The regulation covers all transactions in which the following four conditions are met:

1. credit is offered;

2. the offering of credit is regularly done;

3. there is a finance charge for the credit or there is a written agreement with more than four payments; and,

4. the credit is for personal, family, or household purposes.

It also covers credit card transactions in which only the first two conditions are met. It applies to leases if the consumer ends up paying the full value and keeping the item leased. It does not apply to the following transactions:

- transactions with businesses or agricultural purposes;

- transactions with organizations such as corporations or the government;

- transactions of over $25,000 that are not secured by the consumer's dwelling;

- credit involving public utilities;

- credit involving securities or commodities; and,

- home fuel budget plans.

The way for a small business to avoid Reg. Z violations is to avoid transactions that meet the conditions or to make sure all transactions fall under the exceptions. For many businesses this is easy. Instead of extending credit to customers, accept credit cards and let the credit card company extend the credit. However, if your customers usually do not have credit cards or if you are in a business (such as used car sales) that often extends credit, you should consult a lawyer knowledgeable about Reg. Z.

Texas Law Texas has many laws regarding the use of credit and financing arrangements, including:

- the rate of interest that a lender may charge;

- who may be lenders; and,

- false, misleading, or deceptive advertising relating to the making of a loan and other prohibited acts in relation to making a loan (See Chapter 341 of the Texas Finance Code).

Further, anyone engaged in installment sales in Texas should consult the following statutes as applicable.

- Cash Advance Loans (Chapter 342, Texas Finance Code)

- Installment Loans (Chapter 343, Texas Finance Code)

- Secondary Mortgage Loans (Chapter 344, Texas Finance Code)

- Retail Installment Sales (Chapter 345, Texas Finance Code)

- Revolving Credit Accounts (Chapter 346, Texas Finance Code)

- Manufactured Home Credit Transactions (Chapter 347, Texas Finance Code)

- Motor Vehicle Installment Sales (Chapter 348, Texas Finance Code)

Usury

Usury is the charging, receiving, or contracting for interest in excess of the maximum amount allowed by law, whether or not you intend to charge or ever receive usurious interest. When you do not have an agreement with the party you are lending money to, the maximum amount of interest you may charge is 6% beginning on the thirtieth day from the time the principal amount is due and payable. If you have an oral agreement, the maximum amount of interest you may charge is 10%.

For written agreements, Texas employs a very complicated, rate-ceiling mechanism that is difficult to comprehend. Luckily, the statute provides a safe-harbor amount of 18%, which may be charged under a written agreement with a debtor.

The penalty for charging usurious interest is equal to the greater of:

- three times the amount computed by subtracting the amount of interest allowed by law from the total amount of interest contracted for, charged, or received or

- $2,000 or 20% of the amount of principal, whichever is less.

Also, if you charge greater than twice the amount of interest authorized by law, you are also liable for:

- the principal amount on which the interest is charged and received and

- the interest and all other amounts charged and received.

Therefore, if in your business you intend to make loans or sell items on credit, it is very important that you understand the usury laws, as violation of them can be very costly. It is advisable that you consult an attorney to make sure that you understand these difficult laws.

Collections

When trying to collect money you are owed, you need to be careful not to violate any federal or state law regarding collection practices.

Federal Law The *Fair Debt Collection Practices Act of 1977* bans the use of deception, harassment, and other unreasonable acts in the collection of debts. It has strict requirements whenever someone is collecting a debt for someone else. If you are in the collection business, you must get a copy of this law.

The Federal Trade Commission has issued some rules that prohibit deceptive representations, such as pretending to be in the motion picture industry, the government, or a credit bureau and/or using questionnaires that do not say that they are for the purpose of collecting a debt. (16 C.F.R. Ch. I, Part 237.)

Texas Law Chapter 392 of the Texas Finance Code applies to obligations, or alleged obligations, owed by individuals primarily for personal, family, or household purposes and arising from a transaction or alleged transaction. In a debt collection, a debt collector may not use threats, coercion, or attempts to coerce that use any of the following practices:

- using or threatening to use violence or other criminal means to cause harm to a person or property of a person;

- accusing falsely or threatening to accuse falsely a person of fraud or any other crime;

- representing or threatening to represent to any person other than you that you are willfully refusing to pay a nondisputed consumer debt when the debt in fact is in dispute and you have notified the debt collector in writing of the dispute;

- threatening to sell a debt and falsely representing that the result of such a sale would be that the consumer would lose a defense to the consumer debt or would be subject to illegal collection attempts;

- threatening that the debtor will be arrested for nonpayment of a consumer debt without properly bringing a lawsuit;

- threatening to file a criminal action against a debtor when the debtor has not violated a criminal law;

- threatening that nonpayment will result in the seizure, repossession, or sale of the person's property without properly bringing a lawsuit; and,

- threatening to take an action prohibited by law.

Also, a debt collector may not oppress, harass, or abuse a person by:

- using profane or obscene language or language intended be to unreasonably abusive;

- placing telephone calls without disclosing the name of the individual making the call and with the intent to annoy, harass, or threaten a person at the called number;

- causing a person to incur a long distance telephone toll, telegram fee, or other charge by without first disclosing the name of the person making the communication; or,

- causing a telephone to ring repeatedly or continuously, or making repeated or continuous telephone calls, with the intent to harass a person at the called number.

However, a debt collector may:

- inform a debtor that the debtor may be arrested after a proper court proceeding is instituted if the debtor has violated a criminal law;

- threaten to institute civil lawsuits or other judicial proceedings to collect a consumer debt; or,

- exercise or threaten to exercise a statutory or contractual right of seizure, repossession, or sale that does not require a lawsuit.

Section 392.304 makes it illegal to make fraudulent, deceptive, or misleading representation in connection with a debt collection or obtaining information concerning a consumer by employing certain deceptive practices.

A debtor who is a victim of any violation of Chapter 392 may get a court order against the creditor to prevent the violation, may receive actual damages, and in some circumstances may receive attorney's fees as well. Also, a violation of Chapter 392 is also a violation of the Texas *Deceptive Trade Practices Act* (see Chapter 12). This may entitle a victim to up to triple damages. Therefore, most violations, if possible, are brought under the Deceptive Trade Practices Act, as the damages award can be significantly larger.

Also, the Texas attorney general may bring an action under Chapter 392 to restrain a creditor from illegal actions.

14 Business Relations Laws

Procedures and actions taken by merchants over the centuries have been adopted into the statutory legal framework that now affects you as a new business owner. Markets and merchants cannot work together efficiently if there are not rules on which business people can rely. If you are to operate efficiently in your new business venture and therefore make more profit, you should become familiar with these rules as well. Many of these rules also address what you *cannot* do as a business owner, which is probably more important for protecting the health and prosperity of your new business.

The Uniform Commercial Code

The *Uniform Commercial Code* (UCC) is a set of laws regulating numerous aspects of doing business. A national group drafted this set of uniform laws to avoid having a patchwork of different laws around the fifty states. Although some states modified some sections of the laws, the code is basically the same in most of the states. In Texas, the UCC is contained in Chapters 1 through 9 of the Texas Business and Commercial Code. Each chapter is concerned with a different aspect of commercial relations such as sales, warranties, bank deposits, commercial paper, and bulk transfers.

Businesses that wish to know their rights in all types of transactions should obtain a copy of the UCC and become familiar with it. It is especially useful in transactions between merchants. However, the meaning is not always clear from a reading of the statutes. In law school, students usually spend a full semester studying each chapter of this law.

Commercial Discrimination

The *Robinson-Patman Act of 1936* prohibits businesses from injuring competition by offering the same goods at different prices to different buyers. This means that the large chain stores should not be getting a better price than your small shop. It also requires that promotional allowances must be made on proportionally the same terms to all buyers.

Restraining Trade

One of the earliest federal laws affecting business is the *Sherman Antitrust Act of 1890*. The purpose of this law is to protect competition in the marketplace by prohibiting monopolies.

Examples of some things that are prohibited are:

- agreements between competitors to sell at the same prices;
- agreements between competitors on how much will be sold or produced;
- agreements between competitors to divide up a market;
- refusing to sell one product without a second product; or,
- exchanging information among competitors that results in similarity of prices.

As a new business you probably will not be in a position to violate the act, but you should be aware of it in case a larger competitor tries to put you out of business.

Texas Law Under the Texas *Free Enterprise and Antitrust Act of 1983* (Sections 15.01 to 15.40 of the Texas Business and Commerce Code), it is unlawful to:

- have a contract or conspiracy to restrain trade;

- monopolize, attempt to monopolize, or conspire to monopolize any part of trade or commerce; or,

- sell, lease, or contract for the sale or lease of any goods that the purchaser shall not use or goods of a competitor of the purchaser in order to lessen competition.

It is also unlawful to acquire, directly or indirectly, the ownership or assets of a competitor in order to lessen competition.

The attorney general's office may seek a fine for violations in amounts up to $1,000,000 for a company or $100,000 for a person and may obtain a court order to stop the violating actions.

A person whose business is hurt by a violation may seek an injunction, and may receive up to triple damages including attorney's fees. Also, violators may be found guilty of a felony and be subject to a fine of up to $5,000, a three year prison term, or both.

Commercial Bribery

Chapter 32.43 of the Texas Penal Code makes it unlawful for a person to solicit or accept any benefit from another person on the agreement that such benefit will influence the conduct of a fiduciary. A *fiduciary* is a person in a position of trust who has a duty to another person. This includes agents, employees, trustees, guardians, custodians, administrators, executors, conservators, receivers, lawyers, doctors, accountants, appraisers, officers, directors, partners, and managers.

It is also a crime to solicit a person to commit the crime of commercial bribery. The person who makes the bribe and the person who accepts the bribe are equally guilty.

Intellectual Property Protection

As a business owner you should know enough about intellectual property law to protect your own creations and to keep from violating the rights of others. *Intellectual property* is that which is the product of human creativity, such as writings, designs, inventions, melodies, and processes. They are things that can be stolen without being physically taken. For example, if you write a book, someone can steal the words from your book without stealing a physical copy of it.

As the Internet grows, intellectual property is becoming more valuable. Business owners should take the action necessary to protect their company's intellectual property. Additionally, business owners should know intellectual property law to be sure that they do not violate the rights of others. Even an unknowing violation of the law can result in stiff fines and penalties.

The following are the types of intellectual property and the ways to protect them.

Patent A *patent* is protection given to new and useful inventions, discoveries, and designs. To be entitled to a patent, a work must be completely *new* and *unobvious*. A patent is granted to the first inventor who files for the patent. Once an invention is patented, no one else can make use of that invention, even if they discover it independently after a lifetime of research.

A patent protects an invention for twenty years (for designs it is three and a half, seven, or fourteen years). Patents cannot be renewed. The patent application must clearly explain how to make the invention so that when the patent expires, others will be able to freely make and use the invention. Patents are registered with the United States Patent and Trademark Office (USPTO). Examples of things that would be patentable would be mechanical devices or new drug formulas.

Copyright A *copyright* is protection given to *original works of authorship*, such as written works, musical works, visual works, performance works, or computer software programs. A copyright exists from the moment of creation, but one cannot register a copyright until it has been fixed in tangible form. Also, one cannot copyright titles, names, or slogans. A copyright currently gives the author and his or her heirs exclusive right to the work for the life of the author plus seventy years.

Copyrights first registered before 1978 last for ninety-five years. (This was previously seventy-five years but was extended twenty years to match the European system.) Copyrights are registered with the *Register of Copyrights* at the Library of Congress. Examples of works that would be copyrightable are books, paintings, songs, poems, plays, drawings, and films.

Trademark

A *trademark* is protection given to a name or symbol that is used to distinguish one person's goods or services from those of others. It can consist of letters, numerals, packaging, labeling, musical notes, colors, or a combination of these. If a trademark is used on services as opposed to goods, it is called a *service mark*.

A trademark lasts indefinitely if it is used continuously and renewed properly. Trademarks are registered with the United States Patent and Trademark Office and with individual states. (This is explained further in Chapter 3.) Examples of trademarks are the *Chrysler* name on automobiles, the red border on *TIME* magazine, and the shape of the *Coca-Cola* bottle.

Trade Secrets

A *trade secret* is some information or process that provides a commercial advantage that is protected by keeping it a secret. Some examples of trade secrets would be a list of successful distributors, the formula for *Coca-Cola*, or some unique source code in a computer program. Trade secrets are not registered anywhere. They are protected by the fact that they are not disclosed. They are protected only for as long as they are kept secret. If you independently discover the formula for *Coca-Cola* tomorrow, you can freely market it. (But you cannot use the trademark *Coca-Cola* on your product to market it.)

Non-Protectable Creations

Some things are just not protectable. Such things as ideas, systems, and discoveries are not allowed any protection under any law. If you have a great idea, such as selling packets of hangover medicine in bars, you cannot stop others from doing the same thing. If you invent a new medicine, you can patent it; if you pick a distinctive name for it, you can register it as a trademark; if you create a unique picture or instructions for the package, you can copyright them. But you cannot stop others from using your basic business idea of marketing hangover medicine in bars.

Notice the subtle differences between the protective systems available. If you invent something two days after someone else does, you cannot even use it yourself if the other person has patented it. But if you write the same poem as someone else and neither of you copied the other, both of you can copyright the poem. If you patent something, you can have the exclusive rights to it for the term of the patent, but you must disclose how others can make it after the patent expires. However, if you keep it a trade secret, you have exclusive rights as long as no one learns the secret.

We are in a time of transition of the law of intellectual property. Every year new changes are made in the laws and new forms of creativity win protection. For more information, consult a new edition of a book on these types of property.

15 Endless Laws

The state of Texas and the federal government have numerous laws and rules that apply to every aspect of every type of business. There are laws governing even such things as fence posts, hosiery, rabbit raising, refund policies, frozen desserts, and advertising. Every business is affected by one or another of these laws.

Some activities are covered by both state and federal laws. In such cases, you must obey the stricter of the rules. In addition, more than one agency of the state or federal government may have rules governing your business. Each of these may have the power to investigate violations and impose fines or other penalties.

Penalties for violations of these laws can range from a warning to a criminal fine and even jail time. In some cases, employees can sue for damages. Since *ignorance of the law is no excuse*, it is your duty to learn which laws apply to your business or risk these penalties.

Very few people in business know the laws that apply to their businesses. If you take the time to learn them, you can become an expert in your field and avoid problems with regulators. You can also fight back if one of your competitors uses some illegal method to compete with you.

The laws and rules that affect the most businesses are explained in this section. Following that is a list of more specialized laws. You should read through this list and see which ones may apply to your business. Then go to your public library or law library and read them. Some may not apply to your phase of the business, but if any of them do apply, you should make copies to keep on hand.

Federal Laws

The federal laws that are most likely to affect small businesses are rules of the Federal Trade Commission (FTC). The FTC has some rules that affect many businesses, such as the rules about labeling, warranties, and mail order sales. Other rules affect only certain industries.

If you sell goods by mail you should send for their booklet, *A Business Guide to the Federal Trade Commission's Mail or Telephone Order Merchandise Rule*. If you are going to be involved in a certain industry such as those listed below, or using warranties or your own labeling, you should ask for their latest information on the subject. The address is:

Federal Trade Commission
Washington, DC 20580

The rules of the FTC are contained in the Code of Federal Regulations (C.F.R.) in Title 16. Some of the industries covered are:

INDUSTRY	PART
Adhesive Compositions	235
Aerosol Products Used for Frosting Cocktail Glasses	417
Automobiles (New car fuel economy advertising)	259
Barber Equipment and Supplies	248
Binoculars	402
Business Opportunities and Franchises	436
Cigarettes	408
Decorative Wall Paneling	243
Dog and Cat Food	241
Dry Cell Batteries	403
Extension Ladders	418
Fallout Shelters	229
Feather and Down Products	253

Fiber Glass Curtains	413
Food (Games of Chance)	419
Funerals	453
Gasoline (Octane posting)	306
Gasoline	419
Greeting Cards	244
Home Entertainment Amplifiers	432
Home Insulation	460
Hosiery	22
Household Furniture	250
Jewelry	23
Ladies' Handbags	247
Law Books	256
Light Bulbs	409
Luggage and Related Products	24
Mail Order Insurance	234
Mail Order Merchandise	435
Men's and Boys' Tailored Clothing	412
Metallic Watch Band	19
Mirrors	21
Nursery	18
Ophthalmic Practices	456
Photographic Film and Film Processing	242
Private Vocational and Home Study Schools	254
Radiation Monitoring Instruments	232
Retail Food Stores (Advertising)	424
Shell Homes	230
Shoes	231
Sleeping Bags	400
Tablecloths and Related Products	404
Television Sets	410
Textile Wearing Apparel	423
Textiles	236
Tires	228
Used Automobile Parts	20
Used Lubricating Oil	406
Used Motor Vehicles	455
Waist Belts	405
Watches	245
Wigs and Hairpieces	252

Some other federal laws that affect businesses are as follows:

- *Alcohol Administration Act*
- *Child Protection and Toy Safety Act (1969)*
- *Clean Water Act*
- *Comprehensive Smokeless Tobacco Health Education Act (1986)*
- *Consumer Credit Protection Act (1968)*
- *Consumer Product Safety Act (1972)*
- *Energy Policy and Conservation Act*
- *Environmental Pesticide Control Act of 1972*
- *Fair Credit Reporting Act (1970)*
- *Fair Packaging and Labeling Act (1966)*
- *Flammable Fabrics Act (1953)*
- *Food, Drug, and Cosmetic Act*
- *Food Safety Enforcement Enhancement Act of 1997*
- *Fur Products Labeling Act (1951)*
- *Hazardous Substances Act (1960)*
- *Hobby Protection Act*
- *Insecticide, Fungicide, and Rodenticide Act*
- *Magnuson-Moss Warranty Act*
- *Nutrition Labeling and Education Act of 1990*

- *Poison Prevention Packaging Act of 1970*
- *Solid Waste Disposal Act*
- *Textile Fiber Products Identification Act*
- *Toxic Substance Control Act*
- *Wool Products Labeling Act* (1939)

Texas Laws

Texas also has laws that regulate hundreds of different types of business and occupations. See the discussion of state regulated occupations and businesses in Chapter 6 for an overview of certain state regulations and a helpful reference to further information.

Following is a list of laws that are most likely to affect small businesses.

NOTE: *Citations refer to Civil Statutes (CS) or Various Texas Codes.*

Adult day care facilities	Hum. Resources Code Chapter 103
Air conditioning	Occupations Code, Sec. 1302
Alcoholic beverages	Alcoholic Beverage Code
Ambulance service contracts	Health & Safety Code, Chapter 773
Anatomical gifts	Health & Safety Code, Chapter 692
Aquaculture	Agriculture Code, Chapter 134
Auctions	Occupations Code, Sec. 1802
Bail bondsmen	Occupations Code, Sec. 1704
Banking	Finance Code
Boiler safety	Health & Safety Code, Chapter 755
Boxing & wrestling	Occupations Code, Sec. 2052
Burial contracts	Finance Code, Chapter 154
Cemeteries	Health & Safety Code, Chapters 711–712
Charitable telephone solicitation	C.S. 9023
Citrus	Agriculture Code
Condominiums	Property Code, Chapters 81–82
Cosmetics	Health & Safety Code, Chapter 431
Credit cards	Finance Code

Credit service organizations	Finance Code, Chapter 393
Dairies	Food, Drug & Commodities Act, Health & Safety Code, Chapter 431
Dog racing & horseracing	C.S. 179e
Drinking water	Health & Safety Code, Chapter 341
Drugs	Health & Safety Code, Chapters 431, 481
Eggs & poultry	Health & Safety Code, Chapter 431, 433
Electrical	Utilities Code
Elevators	Health & Safety Code, Chapter 754
Energy conservation standards	Government Code, Chapter 447
Explosives	Local Govt. Code, Chapter 235
Fences and livestock at large	Agriculture Code, Chapter 143
Fireworks	Occupations Code, Sec. 2154
Food	Health & Safety Code, Chapter 431
Frozen desserts	Health & Safety Code, Chapter 440
Fruits & vegetables	Health & Safety Code, Chapter 431 Agriculture Code
Gambling	Penal Code 47.01 & 47.02, Occupations Code, Sec. 2002 & 2003
Gas, liquefied petroleum	Natural Resources Code
Hazardous waste	Health & Safety Code, Chapter 361
Health care	Health & Safety Code, Chapter 221
Health maintenance organizations	Insurance Code, Sec. 20A, 843
Health spas	Occupations Code, Sec. 702
Home health agencies	Health & Safety Code, Chapter 142
Honey	Agriculture Code, Chapter 131
Hospices	Health & Safety Code, Chapter 142
Insurance	Insurance Code
Invention development	C.S. 9020
Landfills	Health & Safety 361.531 *et seq.*
Landlord & tenant	Property Code, Chapter 91,92
Lead acid batteries	Health & Safety Code, beginning with Chapter 361.451
Liquor	*See Alcoholic Beverages*
Livestock caretakers	Agriculture Code, Chapter 161
Lottery	Govt. Code, Chapter 466
Meats	Health & Safety Code, Chapters 431–433
Mental health	Health & Safety Code, Chapter 531, 571
Metal recyclers	C.S. 9009b
Milk & milk products	Health & Safety Code, Chapter 431

Mines & minerals	Natural Resources Code, Chapter 53
Mobile homes	Occupations Code, Sec. 1201
Motor vehicle lemon law	C.S. 4413(36), Occupations Code, Sec. 2301
Motor vehicles	Occupations Code, Sec. 2301, Transportation Code
Multi-level marketing	Business & Commerce Code, Section 17.46
Newsprint recycling	Health & Safety Code 361.430
Nursing homes	Health & Safety Code, Chapter 242
Obscene language	Penal Code 21.08, 43.21
Oil & gas	Natural Resources Code
Outdoor advertising	Transportation Code, Chapter 391, Local Ordinances
Pari-mutual wagering	C.S. 179e (*Texas Racing Act*)
Plants & nurseries	Agriculture Code, Chapter 71
Plumbing	C.S., beginning with 6243-101 Occupations Code, Sec. 1301
Prostitution	Penal Code 43.01
Pyramid schemes	Business & Commerce Code, Sec. 17.461
Radiation	Health & Safety Code Chapter 401, 436
Real estate brokers and salespersons	Occupations Code, Sec. 1101
Rental housing	Prop. Code, Chapter 91 & 92
Restaurants	Health & Safety Code 437, 438, Local Ordinances
Secondhand dealers	Occupations Code, Sec. 1805
Timber and lumber	Natural Resources Code, Chapter 151
Time shares	Property Code, Chapter 221
Tobacco	Health & Safety Code, Sec. 161.081 *et seq.*
Tourism	Government Code 481
Viticulture	Agriculture Code, Chapter 41
Watches, used	Business & Commerce Code, Sec. 17.18
Weapons and firearms	Penal Code, Chapter 46

16: Bookkeeping and Accounting

It is beyond the scope of this book to explain all the intricacies of setting up a business's bookkeeping and accounting systems. However, if you do not set up an understandable bookkeeping system, your business will undoubtedly fail.

Without accurate records of where your income is coming from and where it is going, you will be unable to increase your profits, lower your expenses, obtain needed financing, or make the right decisions in all areas of your business. The time to decide how you will handle your bookkeeping is when you open your business, not a year later when it is tax time.

Initial Bookkeeping

If you do not understand business taxation, you should pick up a good book on the subject as well as the IRS tax guide for your type of business (proprietorship, partnership, or corporation). The IRS tax book for small businesses is Publication 334, *Tax Guide for Small Businesses*. There are also instruction booklets for each type of business's form, Schedule C for proprietorships, Form 1120 or 1120S for C corporations and S corporations, and 1165 for partnerships and businesses that are taxed like partnerships (LLCs and LLPs).

Keep in mind that the IRS does not give you the best advice for saving on taxes and does not give you the other side of contested issues. For that you need a private tax guide or advisor.

The most important thing to do is to set up your bookkeeping so that you can easily fill out your monthly, quarterly, and annual tax returns. The best way to do this is to get copies of the returns, note the totals that you will need to supply, and set up your bookkeeping system to group those totals.

For example, for a sole proprietorship you will use *Schedule C* to report business income and expenses to the IRS at the end of the year. Use the categories on that form to sort your expenses. To make your job especially easy, every time you pay a bill, put the category number on the check.

Accountants

Most likely your new business will not be able to afford hiring an accountant to handle your books, but that is good. Doing them yourself will force you to learn about business accounting and taxation. The worst way to run a business is to know nothing about the tax laws and turn everything over to an accountant at the end of the year to find out what is due.

You should know the basics of tax law before making basic decisions such as whether to buy or rent equipment or premises. You should understand accounting so you can time your financial affairs appropriately. If you were a boxer who only needed to win fights, you could turn everything over to an accountant. If your business needs to buy supplies, inventory, or equipment and provides goods or services throughout the year, you need to at least have a basic understanding of the system you are working within.

Once you can afford an accountant, weigh the cost against your time and the risk that you will make an error. Even if you think you know enough to do your own corporate tax return, you might take it to an accountant one year to see if you have been missing any deductions that you did not know about. You might decide that the money saved is worth the cost of the accountant's services.

Computer Programs

Today, every business should keep its books by computer. There are inexpensive programs, such as *Quicken*, that can instantly provide you with reports of your income and expenses and the right figures to plug into your tax returns. Most programs offer a tax program each year that will take all of your information and print it out on the current year's tax forms.

Tax Tips

Here are a few tax tips that may help businesses save money.

- Usually when you buy equipment for a business you must amortize the cost over several years. That is, you do not deduct the entire cost when you buy it, but take, say, 25% of the cost off your taxes each year for four years. (The time is determined by the theoretical usefulness of the item.) However, small businesses are allowed to write off the entire cost of a limited amount of items under Internal Revenue Code, Section 179. If you have income to shelter, use it.

- Owners of S corporations do not have to pay Social Security or Medicare taxes on the part of their profits that is not considered salary. As long as you pay yourself a reasonable salary, other money you take out is not subject to these taxes.

- Do not neglect to deposit withholding taxes for your own salary or profits. Besides being a large sum to come up with at once in April, there are penalties that must be paid for failure to do so.

- Be sure to keep track of, and remit, your employees' withholding. You will be personally liable for them even if your business is a corporation.

- If you keep track of your use of your car for business, you can deduct mileage (see IRS guidelines for the amount, as it can change each year). If you use your car for business a considerable amount of time, you may be able to depreciate it.

- If your business is a corporation and if you designate the stock as *section 1244 stock*, then if the business fails you are able to get a much better deduction for the loss.

- By setting up a retirement plan, you can exempt up to 20% of your salary from income tax. But do not use money you might need later. There are penalties for taking it out of the retirement plan.

- When you buy things that will be resold or made into products that will be resold (*i.e.*, you are buying from a wholesaler), you do not have to pay sales tax on those purchases.

17 Paying Federal Taxes

As we all know, the federal government levies many different types of taxes on individuals and businesses. It is very important that you consult an accountant or attorney to properly comply with and take advantage of the incredibly complex federal tax code and regulations. The following discusses several of the most important federal taxes that will most likely affect your new business.

Federal Income Tax

The manner in which each type of business pays taxes is as follows.

Proprietorship   An individual reports profits and expenses on Schedule C attached to the usual Form 1040 and pays tax on all of the net income of the business. Each quarter, Form ES-1040 must be filed along with payment of one-quarter of the amount of income tax and Social Security taxes estimated to be due for the year.

Partnership   A partnership files a return showing the income and expenses but pays no tax. Each partner is given a form showing his or her share of the profits or losses and reports these on Schedule E of Form 1040. Each quarter, Form ES-1040 must be filed by each partner along with payment of one-quarter of the amount of income tax and Social Security taxes estimated to be due for the year.

C Corporation

A regular corporation is a separate taxpayer and pays tax on its profits after deducting all expenses, including officers' salaries. If dividends are distributed, they are paid out of after-tax dollars and the shareholders pay tax a second time when they receive the dividends. If a corporation needs to accumulate money for investment, it may be able to do so at lower tax rates than the shareholders. But if all profits will be distributed to shareholders, the double-taxation may be excessive unless all income is paid as salaries. A C corporation files Form 1120.

S Corporation

A small corporation has the option of being taxed like a partnership. If Form 2553 is filed by the corporation and accepted by the Internal Revenue Service, the S corporation will only file an informational return listing profits and expenses. Then each shareholder will be taxed on a proportional share of the profits (or be able to deduct a proportional share of the losses). Unless a corporation will make a large profit that will not be distributed, S status is usually best in the beginning.

An S corporation files Form 1120S and distributes Form K-1 to each shareholder. If any money is taken out by a shareholder that is not listed as wages subject to withholding, then the shareholder will usually have to file Form ES-1040 each quarter, along with payment of the estimated withholding on the withdrawals.

Limited Liability Company

Limited liability companies and professional limited liability companies are allowed by the IRS to elect to be taxed either as a partnership or a corporation. To make this election you file IRS Form 8832, Entity Classification Election, with the IRS.

Tax Workshops and Booklets

The IRS conducts workshops to inform businesses about the tax laws. (Do not expect in-depth study of the loopholes.) For more information call the IRS at 800-829-1040 or visit its website at **www.irs.gov**.

Federal Withholding, Social Security, and Medicare Taxes

If you need basic information on business tax returns, the IRS publishes a rather large booklet that answers most questions and is available for free. Call, write, or go online and obtain Publication No. 334, *Tax Guide for Small Business*. You should be able to find an IRS toll-free number in the phone book under U. S.

Government/Internal Revenue Service. If you want more creative answers and tax saving information, find a good local accountant or tax attorney. To get started you will need the following.

Employer Identification Number

If you are a sole proprietor with no employees, you can use your Social Security number for your business. If you have employees or are a corporation or partnership, you must obtain an *employer identification number*, by filing **APPLICATION FOR EMPLOYER IDENTIFICATION NUMBER (IRS FORM SS-4)**. (see form 5, p.205.) In about three weeks you will get your number, which you will need to open bank accounts for the business. A sample filled-in form may be found in Appendix B. A blank form with instructions is in Appendix C.

If you need a number quickly, you may obtain one by telephone by calling 800-829-4933, Monday through Friday, between 7:30 a.m. and 5:30 p.m. local time. You must have your **IRS FORM SS-4** filled out before you call and you will still need to mail or fax the form with your number on it. You can fax it to 215-516-3990 between 10:00 a.m. and 5:30 p.m. If you mail it in, send it to:

Internal Revenue Service Center
Attn: EIN Operations
Philadelphia, PA 19255

Employee's Withholding Allowance Certificate

You must have each employee fill out an **EMPLOYEE'S WITHHOLDING ALLOWANCE CERTIFICATE (IRS FORM W-4)** to calculate the amount of federal taxes to be deducted and to obtain their Social Security numbers. (The number of allowances on this form is used with IRS Circular E, Publication 15, to figure out the exact deductions.) A sample filled-in form may be found in Appendix B. A blank form is in Appendix C. (see form 7, p.219.)

Federal Tax Deposit Coupon

After making withholdings from employees' wages, you must deposit them at a bank that is authorized to accept such funds. If, at the end of any month, you have over $1,000 in withheld taxes (including your contribution to FICA), you must make a deposit prior to the 15th of the following month. If, on the 3rd, 7th, 11th, 19th, 22nd, or 25th of any month, you have over $3,000 in withheld taxes, you must make a deposit within three banking days. The deposit is made using the coupons in the Form 8109 booklet supplied by the IRS.

Estimated Tax Payment Voucher

Sole proprietors and partners often take money from their businesses without the formality of withholding. However, they are still required to make deposits of income and FICA taxes each quarter. If more than $500 is due in April on a person's 1040 form, then not enough money was withheld each quarter and a penalty is assessed unless the person falls into an exception.

The quarterly withholding is submitted on Form 1040-ES on the 15th of April, June, September, and January of each year. If these days fall on a weekend, then the due date is the following Monday. The worksheet with Form 1040-ES can be used to determine the amount to pay.

NOTE: *One of the exceptions to the rule is that if you withhold the same amount as last year's tax bill, you do not have to pay a penalty. This is usually a lot easier than filling out the 1040-ES worksheet.*

Employer's Quarterly Tax Return

Each quarter you must file Form 941, reporting your federal withholding and FICA taxes. If you owe more than $1,000 at the end of the quarter, you are required to make a deposit at the end of the month in which you have $1,000 in withholding. The deposits are made to the Federal Reserve Bank or an authorized financial institution on Form 501. Most banks are authorized to accept deposits. If you owe more than $3,000 for any month, you must make a deposit at any point in the month in which you owe $3,000. After you file **IRS Form SS-4**, the 941 forms will be sent to you automatically if you checked the box saying that you expect to have employees.

Wage and Tax Statement

At the end of each year, you are required to issue a W-2 form to each employee. This form shows the amount of wages paid to the employee during the year, as well as the amounts withheld for taxes, Social Security, Medicare, and other deductions.

Miscellaneous Income

If you pay at least $600 to a person other than an employee (such as an independent contractor), you must file a Form 1099 for that person, along with Form 1096, which is a summary sheet. Many people are not aware of this law and fail to file these forms, but they are required for such things as services, royalties, rents, awards, and prizes that you pay to individuals (but not to corporations). The rules for this are quite complicated, so either obtain *Package 1099* from the IRS or consult your accountant.

Earned Income Credit

Persons who are not liable to pay income tax may have the right to a check from the government because of the *Earned Income Credit*. You are required to notify your employees of this. You can satisfy this requirement with one of the following:

- a W-2 Form with the notice on the back;

- a substitute for the W-2 with a notice on it;

- a copy of Notice 797; or,

- a written statement with the wording from Notice 797.

A Notice 797 can be obtained by calling 800-829-3676.

Excise Taxes

Excise taxes are taxes on certain activities or items. Most federal excise taxes have been eliminated since World War II, but a few remain.

Some of the things that are subject to federal excise taxes are tobacco and alcohol, gasoline, tires and inner tubes, some trucks and trailers, firearms, ammunition, bows, arrows, fishing equipment, the use of highway vehicles of over 55,000 pounds, aircraft, wagering, telephone and teletype services, coal, hazardous wastes, and vaccines. If you are involved with any of these, you should obtain from the IRS publication No. 510, *Information on Excise Taxes*.

Unemployment Compensation Tax

You must pay federal unemployment taxes if you paid wages of $1,500 in any quarter, or if you had at least one employee for twenty calendar weeks. The federal tax amount is 0.8% of the first $7,000 of wages paid each employee. If more than $100 is due by the end of any quarter (if you paid $12,500 in wages for the quarter), then IRS Form 508 must be filed with an authorized financial institution or the Federal Reserve Bank in your area. You will receive IRS Form 508 when you obtain your employer identification number.

At the end of each year, you must file IRS Form 940 or IRS Form 940EZ. This is your annual report of federal unemployment taxes. You will receive an original form from the IRS.

18: Paying Texas Taxes

The State of Texas levies many different taxes upon the companies that operate within its borders. The most important taxes are discussed in this chapter, but you should also consult the helpful information provided by the Comptroller of the State of Texas at **www.cpa.state.tx.us**.

Sales and Use Tax

If you sell taxable items (*tangible* and *intangible* personal property or taxable services) in Texas, you must collect state sales or use tax (6.25% of the sales price) plus the appropriate local sales or use taxes (no more than 2%). You are responsible for collecting the correct amount of state and local sales or use tax. You may also be responsible for collecting a transit use tax. Prior to selling any product or service for which sales tax would be due, you must apply to the Comptroller for a **Texas Application for Sales Tax Permit, Use Tax Permit and/or Telecommunications Infrastructure Fund Assessment Set-Up**. (see form 8, p.221.)

Along with tangible and intangible personal property, Texas also taxes the sale of *taxable services*. The following services are considered taxable services and therefore you must collect sales and use tax when you provide them:

- amusement services (*e.g.*, admission to movie theaters, antique shows, sporting events, carnivals, golf courses, etc.);

- cable television services;

- computer programming;

- credit reporting services;

- data processing services;

- debt collection services;

- information services (*e.g.*, syndicated news reports, financial reporting, or investment research);

- insurance services;

- Internet;

- Internet access services;

- motor vehicle parking and storage services;

- non-residential real property repair, restoration or remodeling;

- personal property maintenance (*e.g.*, shoe shining, dog grooming);

- personal property remodeling or repairing (*e.g.*, appliance repair and furniture refurbishing);

- personal services (*e.g.*, laundry, dry cleaning, carpet cleaning, massage therapists, escort services);

- real property services (*e.g.*, extermination and pest control, garbage and waste collection, custodial services);

- security services;

- taxable labor (*e.g.*, the manufacture, assembly or fabrication of products);

- telecommunication services (*e.g.,* conveyance, routing or reception of sounds, data, signals or other information using wires, cable, radio waves, microwaves, satellites, fiber optics, or any other method); and,

- telephone answering services.

The tax due is calculated on the full price charged to the customer and then collected and paid to the comptroller. If you fail to collect the tax, you are still liable for the amount that should have been collected.

Goods or taxable services purchased for *resale* by the purchaser are not subject to the tax. Therefore, if you are selling goods as a wholesaler, then you do not have to collect the tax. However, you may only do this if the purchaser presents you with a *resale certificate,* which evidences the fact that the purchaser is purchasing the goods for resale in its own business. You can obtain a resale certificate from the comptroller if you will be buying products for resale.

Many entities are exempt from paying sales tax, such as certain charities. However, these entities must present you with an exemption certificate before you are authorized to not collect the tax.

Franchise Tax

Texas levies a tax on all corporations and limited liability companies that are formed in Texas or are formed outside Texas but are doing business in Texas. The calculation is complicated and should be done each year by your accountant.

For most corporations and limited liability companies, the tax will be equal to 4.5% of the corporation or limited liability company's net taxable income. However, if you do not have any net taxable income, you may still have to pay a tax equal to .25% of your net taxable capital. Also, if you have receipts from operations outside of Texas, then you will probably not be taxed on all of your net taxable income.

The franchise tax for new corporations and limited liability companies is due eighty-nine days after the one year anniversary of the formation of the new company. For all other entities, the tax is due on May 15th of each year. If you owe less than $100 in tax, then you are exempted from paying the tax, but you must still file an annual report.

Unemployment Taxes

All employers in the state of Texas must register with the Texas Workforce Commission by completing and filing a **STATUS REPORT (FORM C-1)**. (see form 10, p.229.) All employers that pay $1,500 in wages in a calendar quarter or have one or more employees during twenty different weeks in a calendar year must pay the Texas unemployment tax. The tax rate that an employer must pay is calculated based on the industry in which the employer operates and the history of the employer with regard to unemployment claims made by former employees of the employer.

If you are subject to paying the unemployment tax, you are also required by law to display certain information posters in your workplace. Helpful information, including information regarding the obtaining of the required posters, is contained at the Texas Workforce Commission's website at:

www.twc.state.tx.us

Local Property Taxes

Property taxes account for most of the funding of local services in Texas, including schools, police and fire protection, and road servicing. These taxes are levied by local jurisdictions, not the State of Texas. Property values are assessed by the appraisal district in each county and a tax is calculated based on the particular taxing authority's tax rate multiplied by the assessed value. January 1st is the magic day for local property taxes because you are taxed on the property that you own as of January 1st of each year.

When you start a new business, you must give a report, called a *rendition*, to the taxing authority of the jurisdiction in which your business resides. The rendition contains all of the *personal property* used in conducting the business. If the total taxable value of the *personal property* used in your business in a particular jurisdiction is less than $500, then you are exempt from taxation by the taxing authorities of that particular jurisdiction. The tax appraiser will assess a tax based on the value of the personal property listed in the rendition.

The taxing authorities have the power to enter your business to determine if the personal property listed on your rendition matches the personal property on the business premises. Failure to report your personal property correctly can lead to penalties and fines.

Tax bills are typically mailed to property owners after October 1st of each year. Payment is due by the following January 31st. Failure to pay by that date will lead to penalties and interest being assessed against you, and eventually can lead to litigation, a lien being placed against your property, and ultimately foreclosure and sale of your property.

Other Texas Taxes

Texas also imposes the following specialized taxes.

- Amusement Tax
- Battery Sales Tax
- Boat and Boat Motor Sales Tax
- Cement Production Tax
- Cigarette, Cigar, and Tobacco Products Tax
- Coin-Operated Machines Tax
- Crude Oil and Natural Gas Tax
- Fireworks Tax
- Fuels Tax
- Hotel Occupancy Tax
- Minerals Tax
- Mixed Beverage Gross Receipts Tax
- Motor Vehicle Sales Tax

If you think your business may be subject to one of these taxes, consult the comptroller's website at **www.cpa.state.tx.us** for more information.

19 Out-of-State Taxes

As a Texas business, if you operate your business outside of the borders of the state of Texas, you not only have to comply with Texas and federal tax laws, but also with the laws of the states and other countries in which you do business. This can prove to be very complicated.

State Sales Taxes

In 1992, the United States Supreme Court struck a blow for the rights of small businesses by ruling that state tax authorities cannot force them to collect sales taxes on interstate mail orders (*Quill Corporation v. North Dakota*). Unfortunately, the court left open the possibility that Congress could allow interstate taxation of mail order sales, and since then several bills have been introduced that would do so.

At present, companies are only required to collect sales taxes for states in which they *do business*. Exactly what business is enough to trigger taxation is a legal question and some states try to define it as broadly as possible.

If you have an office in a state, clearly you are doing business there and any goods shipped to consumers in the state are subject to sales taxes. If you have a full-time employee working in the state much of the year, many states will consider you to be doing business there. In some states attending a two-day trade show is enough business to trigger taxation for the entire year for every order shipped to the state. One loophole that often works is to be represented at shows by persons who are not your employees.

Because the laws are different in each state you will have to do some research on a state-by-state basis to find out how much business you can do in a state without being subject to their taxation. You can request a state's rules from its department of revenue, but keep in mind that what a department of revenue wants the law to be is not always what the courts will rule that it is.

Business Taxes

Even worse than being subject to a state's sales taxes is to be subject to their income or other business taxes. For example, California charges every company doing business in the state a minimum $800 a year fee and charges income tax on a portion of the company's worldwide income. Doing a small amount of business in the state is clearly not worth getting mired in California taxation.

For this reason some trade shows have been moved from the state and this has resulted in a review of the tax policies and some *safe-harbor* guidelines to advise companies on what they can do without becoming subject to taxation.

Write to the department of revenue of any state with which you have business contacts to see what might trigger your taxation.

Internet Taxes

State revenue departments are drooling at the prospect of taxing commerce on the Internet. Theories have already been proposed that websites available to state residents mean a company is doing business in a state. Fortunately, Congress has passed a moratorium on taxation of the Internet.

Canadian Taxes

The Canadian government expects American companies that sell goods by mail order to Canadians to collect taxes for them and file returns with Revenue Canada, their tax department. Those who receive an occasional unsolicited order are not expected to register and Canadian customers who order things from the U.S. pay the tax plus a $5 fee upon receipt of the goods. But companies that solicit Canadian orders are expected to be registered if their worldwide income is $30,000 or more per year. In some cases a company may be required to post a bond and to pay for the cost of Canadian auditors visiting its premises and auditing its books. For these reasons you may notice that some companies decline to accept orders from Canada.

20 The End...and The Beginning

If you have read through this whole book, you know more about the rules and laws for operating a Texas business than most people in business today. However, after learning about all the governmental regulations, you may become discouraged. You are probably wondering how you can keep track of all the laws and how you will have any time left to make money after complying with the laws. It is not that bad. People are starting businesses every day and they are making money.

Congratulations on deciding to start a business in Texas! If you have any unusual experiences along the way, drop us a line at the following address. The information may be useful for a future book.

Sphinx Publishing
P.O. Box 4410
Naperville, IL 60567-4410

Glossary

A

acceptance. Agreeing to the terms of an offer and creating a contract.

affirmative action. Hiring an employee to achieve a balance in the workplace and avoid existing or continuing discrimination based on minority status.

alien. A person who is not a citizen of the country.

articles of incorporation. The document that sets forth the organization of a corporation.

B

bait advertising. Offering a product for sale with the intention of selling another product.

bulk sales. Selling substantially all of a company's inventory.

C

C corporation. A corporation that pays taxes on its profits.

collections. The collection of money owed to a business.

common law. Laws that are determined in court cases rather than statutes.

consideration. The exchange of value or promises in a contract.

contract. An agreement between two or more parties.

copyright. Legal protection given to *original works of authorship*.

corporation. An artificial *person* that is set up to conduct a business owned by shareholders and run by officers and directors.

D

deceptive pricing. Pricing goods or services in a manner intended to deceive the customers.

discrimination. The choosing among various options based on their characteristics.

domain name. The address of a website.

E

employee. Person who works for another under that person's control and direction.

endorsements. Positive statements about goods or services.

excise tax. A tax paid on the sale or consumption of goods or services.

express warranty. A specific guarantee of a product or service.

F

fictitious name. A name used by a business that is not its personal or legal name.

G

general partnership. A business that is owned by two or more persons.

goods. Items of personal property.

guarantee/guaranty. A promise of quality of a good or service.

I

implied warranty. A guaranty of a product or service that is not specifically made, but can be implied from the circumstances of the sale.

independent contractor. Person who works for another as a separate business, not as an employee.

intangible property. Personal property that does not have physical presence, such as the ownership interest in a corporation.

intellectual property. Legal rights to the products of the mind, such as writings, musical compositions, formulas, and designs.

L

liability. The legal responsibility to pay for an injury.

limited liability company. An entity recognized as a legal *person* that is set up to conduct a business owned and run by members.

limited liability partnership. An entity recognized as a legal *person* that is set up to conduct a business owned and run by members that is set up for professionals such as attorneys or doctors.

limited partnership. A business that is owned by two or more persons of which one or more is liable for the debts of the business and one or more has no liability for the debts.

limited warranty. A guaranty covering certain aspects of a good or service.

M

merchant. A person who is in business.

merchant's firm offer. An offer by a business made under specific terms.

N

nonprofit corporation. An entity recognized as a legal *person* that is set up to run an operation in which none of the profits are distributed to controlling members.

O

occupational license. A government-issued permit to transact business.

offer. A proposal to enter into a contract.

overtime. Hours worked in excess of forty hours in one week or eight hours in one day.

P

partnership. A business formed by two or more persons.

patent. Protection given to inventions, discoveries, and designs.

personal property. Any type of property other than land and the structures attached to it.

pierce the corporate veil. When a court ignores the structure of a corporation and holds its owners responsible for its debts or liabilities.

professional association. An entity recognized as a legal *person* that is set up to conduct a business of professionals such as doctors and other health care professionals.

proprietorship. A business that is owned by one person.

R

real property. Land and the structures attached to it.

resident alien. A person who is not a citizen of the country but who may legally reside and work there.

S

S corporation. A corporation in which the profits are taxed to the shareholders.

sale on approval. Selling an item with the agreement that it may be brought back and the sale cancelled.

sale or return. An agreement whereby goods are to be purchased or returned to the vendor.

securities. Interests in a business such as stocks or bonds.

sexual harassment. Activity that causes an employee to feel or be sexually threatened.

shares. Units of stock in a corporation.

statute of frauds. Law that requires certain contracts to be in writing.

stock. Ownership interests in a corporation.

sublease. An agreement to rent premises from an existing tenant.

T

tangible property. Physical personal property such as desks and tables.

trade secret. Commercially valuable information or process that is protected by being kept a secret.

trademark. A name or symbol used to identify the source of goods or services.

U

unemployment compensation. Payments to a former employee who was terminated from a job for a reason not based on his or her fault.

usury. Charging an interest rate higher than that allowed by law.

W

withholding. Money taken out of an employee's salary and remitted to the government.

workers compensation. Insurance program to cover injuries or deaths of employees.

Appendix A: Business Start-Up Checklist

This checklist will help you to organize your start-up procedures. Refer to the text of the chapters if you have any questions on the items appearing here.

BUSINESS START-UP CHECKLIST

- ☐ Make your plan
    - ☐ Obtain and read all relevant publications on your type of business
    - ☐ Obtain and read all laws and regulations affecting your business
    - ☐ Calculate whether your plan will produce a profit
    - ☐ Plan your sources of capital
    - ☐ Plan your sources of goods or services
    - ☐ Plan your marketing efforts
- ☐ Choose your business name
    - ☐ Check other business names and trademarks
    - ☐ Register your name, trademark, etc.
- ☐ Choose the business form
    - ☐ Prepare and file organizational papers
    - ☐ Prepare and file fictitious name if necessary
- ☐ Choose the location
    - ☐ Check competitors
    - ☐ Check zoning
- ☐ Obtain necessary licenses
    - ☐ City?   ☐ State?
    - ☐ County?   ☐ Federal?
- ☐ Choose a bank
    - ☐ Checking
    - ☐ Credit card processing
    - ☐ Loans
- ☐ Obtain necessary insurance
    - ☐ Worker's Comp   ☐ Automobile
    - ☐ Liability   ☐ Health
    - ☐ Hazard   ☐ Life/disability
- ☐ File necessary federal tax registrations
- ☐ File necessary state tax registrations
- ☐ Set up a bookkeeping system
- ☐ Plan your hiring
    - ☐ Obtain required posters
    - ☐ Obtain or prepare employment application
    - ☐ Obtain new hire tax forms
    - ☐ Prepare employment policies
    - ☐ Determine compliance with health and safety laws
- ☐ Plan your opening
    - ☐ Obtain all necessary equipment and supplies
    - ☐ Obtain all necessary inventory
    - ☐ Do all necessary marketing and publicity
    - ☐ Obtain all necessary forms and agreements
    - ☐ Prepare your company policies on refunds, exchanges, returns

Appendix B: Sample Filled-in Forms

The following forms are selected filled-in forms for demonstration purposes. Most have a corresponding blank form in Appendix C. The form numbers in this appendix correspond to the form numbers in Appendix C. If there is no blank for a particular form, it is because you must obtain it from a government agency. If you need instructions for these forms as you follow how they are filled out, they can be found in Appendix C, or in those pages in the chapters that discuss those forms.

**FORM 2: Assumed Name Certificate for Filing
       with the Secretary of State** 173

**FORM 3: Application for Registration
       of Trademark or Service Mark** 175

**FORM 4: Employment Eligibility Verification
       (IRS Form I-9)** 178

**FORM 5: Application for Employer Identification Number
       (IRS Form SS-4)** 179

FORM 7: EMPLOYEE'S WITHHOLDING ALLOWANCE CERTIFICATE
(IRS FORM W-4). 180

FORM 8: TEXAS APPLICATION FOR SALES TAX PERMIT,
USE TAX PERMIT AND/OR TELECOMMUNICATIONS
INFRASTRUCTURE FUND ASSESSMENT SET-UP 182

Office of the Secretary of State
Corporations Section
P.O. Box 13697
Austin, Texas 78711-3697

ASSUMED NAME CERTIFICATE
FOR FILING WITH THE SECRETARY OF STATE

1. The name of the corporation, limited liability company, limited partnership, or registered limited liability partnership as stated in its articles of incorporation, articles of organization, certificate of limited partnership, application for certificate of authority or comparable document is

   ABC, Inc

2. The assumed name under which the business or professional service is or is to be conducted or rendered is

   Joe's Grocery Store

3. The state, country, or other jurisdiction under the laws of which it was incorporated, organized or associated is   Texas   and the

   address of its registered or similar office in that jurisdiction is

   123 Main Street, San Antonio, TX 78205

4. The period, not to exceed 10 years, during which the assumed name will be used is

   10 years

5. The entity is a (check one):
   A.
   [X] Business Corporation   [ ] Non-Profit Corporation
   [ ] Professional Corporation   [ ] Professional Association
   [ ] Limited Liability Company   [ ] Limited Partnership
   [ ] Registered Limited Liability Partnership

   B. If the entity is some other type business, professional or other association that is incorporated, please specify below (e.g., bank, savings and loan association, etc.)

   N/A

6. If the entity is required to maintain a registered office in Texas, the address of the registered office is   123 Main Street, San Antonio, TX 78205

   and the name of its registered agent at such address is   *Joe Smith*

   The address of the principal office (if not the same as the registered office) is

7. If the entity is not required to or does not maintain a registered office in Texas, the office address in Texas is _N/A_

and if the entity is not incorporated, organized or associated under the laws of Texas, the address of its place of business in Texas is _N/A_

and the office address elsewhere is _N/A_

8. The county or counties where business or professional services are being or are to be conducted or rendered under such assumed name are (if applicable, use the designation "ALL" or "ALL EXCEPT")

    Bexar County

9. The undersigned, if acting in the capacity of an attorney-in-fact of the entity, certifies that the entity has duly authorized the attorney-in-fact in writing to execute this document.

    By _Joe Smith_
    Signature of officer, general partner, manager, representative or attorney-in-fact of the entity

NOTE

This form is designed to meet statutory requirements for filing with the secretary of state and is not designed to meet filing requirements on the county level. Filing requirements for assumed name documents to be filed with the county clerk differ. Assumed name documents filed with the county clerk are to be executed and acknowledged by the filing party, which requires that the document be notarized.

Form No. 503
Revised 9/99

Office of the Secretary of State
Corporations Section
P.O. Box 13697
Austin, Texas 78711-3697

APPLICATION FOR REGISTRATION OF TRADEMARK OR SERVICE MARK

The undersigned applicant has adopted and used, and is now using, a certain trademark or service mark in Texas and hereby makes application for registration of such mark, in accordance with Chapter 16 of the Texas Business & Commerce Code.

1. Applicant: ABC Inc.

2. Address: 123 Main Street

   City: San Antonio   State: TX   Zip: 78205

3. Applicant is incorporated or organized as a Corporation
   and is incorporated or organized under the laws of Texas

4. Describe the mark (words and/or design) SHOWN ON THE ATTACHED DRAWING SHEET:

   The words "Joe's Grocery" surrounded by a circle

5. Description of goods or services in connection with which the mark is being used: (BE SPECIFIC)

   food, beer, wine, cigarettes, drinks

6. The manner in which the mark is being used (labels, tags on the goods, etc; OR brochures, newspapers advertising the services, etc.): (A SAMPLE IS ATTACHED)

   in-store signs, advertising in the newspaper and on television

7. Number and title of the class of goods or services: _____
   (Do not list more than one class. See instruction 7.)

8. Date mark first used by applicant (BOTH A & B MUST BE COMPLETED):

   (a) **Anywhere:** (Month) 1 2 /(Day) 0 1 /(Year) 1 9 9 4
   (b) **In Texas:** (Month) 1 2 /(Day) 0 1 /(Year) 1 9 9 4

9. Applicant hereby appoints the Secretary of State of Texas as its agent for service of process only in suits relating to the registration which may be issued if the applicant is or becomes a nonresident individual, partnership or association or foreign corporation, limited partnership, or limited liability company without a certificate of authority to do business in this state or cannot be found in this state.

10. Applicant is the owner of the mark and, to the best of the applicant's knowledge, no other person is entitled to use the mark in this state in the identical form used by applicant, or in a form that is likely, when used in connection with the goods or services, to cause confusion or mistake, or to deceive, because of its resemblance to the mark used by the applicant.

11. ☒ A drawing of the mark is enclosed.

12. ☐ Two examples of advertising are enclosed (if mark is used in connection with services). OR
    ☐ Two actual tags, labels, or actual product packaging are enclosed (if mark is used in connection with a distributed product).

Executed on this __1st__ **day of** __January__, 2005.

ABC, Inc.
(Name of Applicant)

Joe Smith
(Signature of Applicant)

President
(Title)

♦ 177

TRADEMARK DRAWING SHEET

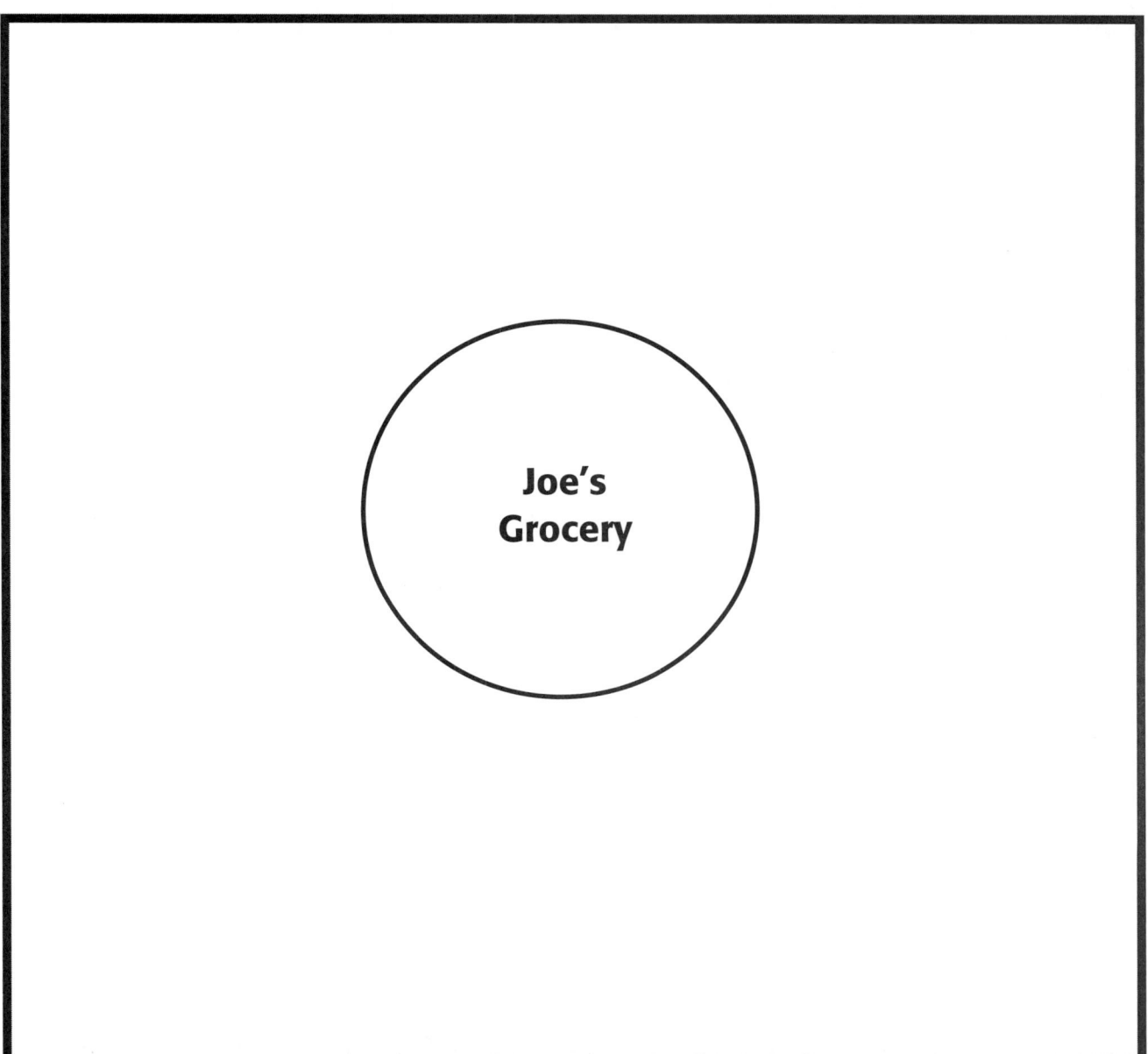

Drawing Instructions:

The applicant also must submit with the application a "drawing sheet" that shows the mark exactly as it appears in the specimen accompanying the application and exactly as it is described in paragraph 4 of the application. If the mark includes a design, a drawing of the entire proposed mark (in clean, uniform black lines) must be attached to the application. If the mark described in the application consists only of a word, letter or numeral, or any combination thereof, and if the mark is not depicted in a special form, the mark may be typed in capital letters on the drawing sheet.

The Office of the Secretary of State does not discriminate on the basis of race, color, national origin, sex, religion, age or disability in employment or the provision of services.

U.S. Department of Justice
Immigration and Naturalization Service

OMB No. 1115-0136

Employment Eligibility Verification

Please read instructions carefully before completing this form. The instructions must be available during completion of this form. **ANTI-DISCRIMINATION NOTICE:** It is illegal to discriminate against work eligible individuals. Employers CANNOT specify which document(s) they will accept from an employee. The refusal to hire an individual because of a future expiration date may also constitute illegal discrimination.

Section 1. Employee Information and Verification. To be completed and signed by employee at the time employment begins.

Print Name: Last	First	Middle Initial	Maiden Name
Smith,	Joe	T.	N/A

Address (Street Name and Number)	Apt. #	Date of Birth (month/day/year)
123 Main Street		1/1/72

City	State	Zip Code	Social Security #
San Antonio	TX	78205	111-22-3333

I am aware that federal law provides for imprisonment and/or fines for false statements or use of false documents in connection with the completion of this form.

I attest, under penalty of perjury, that I am (check one of the following):
☐ A citizen or national of the United States
☐ A Lawful Permanent Resident (Alien # A_____)
☐ An alien authorized to work until ___/___/___
(Alien # or Admission #) _____

Employee's Signature	Date (month/day/year)
Joe T. Smith	1/1/04

Preparer and/or Translator Certification. (To be completed and signed if Section 1 is prepared by a person other than the employee.) I attest, under penalty of perjury, that I have assisted in the completion of this form and that to the best of my knowledge the information is true and correct.

Preparer's/Translator's Signature	Print Name

Address (Street Name and Number, City, State, Zip Code)	Date (month/day/year)

Section 2. Employer Review and Verification. To be completed and signed by employer. Examine one document from List A OR examine one document from List B and one from List C, as listed on the reverse of this form, and record the title, number and expiration date, if any, of the document(s)

List A	OR	List B	AND	List C
Document title: _____		_____		_____
Issuing authority: _____		_____		_____
Document #: _____		_____		_____
Expiration Date (if any): ___/___/___		___/___/___		___/___/___
Document #: _____				
Expiration Date (if any): ___/___/___				

CERTIFICATION - I attest, under penalty of perjury, that I have examined the document(s) presented by the above-named employee, that the above-listed document(s) appear to be genuine and to relate to the employee named, that the employee began employment on (month/day/year) ___/___/___ and that to the best of my knowledge the employee is eligible to work in the United States. (State employment agencies may omit the date the employee began employment.)

Signature of Employer or Authorized Representative	Print Name	Title

Business or Organization Name	Address (Street Name and Number, City, State, Zip Code)	Date (month/day/year)

Section 3. Updating and Reverification. To be completed and signed by employer.

A. New Name (if applicable)	B. Date of rehire (month/day/year) (if applicable)

C. If employee's previous grant of work authorization has expired, provide the information below for the document that establishes current employment eligibility.

Document Title: _____ Document #: _____ Expiration Date (if any): ___/___/___

I attest, under penalty of perjury, that to the best of my knowledge, this employee is eligible to work in the United States, and if the employee presented document(s), the document(s) I have examined appear to be genuine and to relate to the individual.

Signature of Employer or Authorized Representative	Date (month/day/year)

Form **SS-4**
(Rev. December 2001)
Department of the Treasury
Internal Revenue Service

Application for Employer Identification Number
(For use by employers, corporations, partnerships, trusts, estates, churches, government agencies, Indian tribal entities, certain individuals, and others.)
▶ See separate instructions for each line. ▶ Keep a copy for your records.

EIN

OMB No. 1545-0003

Type or print clearly.

1 Legal name of entity (or individual) for whom the EIN is being requested
ABC, Inc

2 Trade name of business (if different from name on line 1)
Joe's Grocery

3 Executor, trustee, "care of" name

4a Mailing address (room, apt., suite no. and street, or P.O. box)
123 Main Street

5a Street address (if different) (Do not enter a P.O. box.)

4b City, state, and ZIP code
San Antonio, TX 78205

5b City, state, and ZIP code

6 County and state where principal business is located
Bexar County

7a Name of principal officer, general partner, grantor, owner, or trustor
Joe Smith

7b SSN, ITIN, or EIN
111-22-3333

8a Type of entity (check only one box)
☐ Sole proprietor (SSN) _____
☐ Partnership
☐ Corporation (enter form number to be filed) ▶ _____
☐ Personal service corp.
☐ Church or church-controlled organization
☐ Other nonprofit organization (specify) ▶ _____
☒ Other (specify) ▶ Business Corporation

☐ Estate (SSN of decedent) _____
☐ Plan administrator (SSN) _____
☐ Trust (SSN of grantor) _____
☐ National Guard   ☐ State/local government
☐ Farmers' cooperative ☐ Federal government/military
☐ REMIC   ☐ Indian tribal governments/enterprises
Group Exemption Number (GEN) ▶ _____

8b If a corporation, name the state or foreign country (if applicable) where incorporated
State: Texas
Foreign country: N/A

9 Reason for applying (check only one box)
☒ Started new business (specify type) ▶ grocery store
☐ Hired employees (Check the box and see line 12.)
☐ Compliance with IRS withholding regulations
☐ Other (specify) ▶

☐ Banking purpose (specify purpose) ▶ _____
☐ Changed type of organization (specify new type) ▶ _____
☐ Purchased going business
☐ Created a trust (specify type) ▶ _____
☐ Created a pension plan (specify type) ▶ _____

10 Date business started or acquired (month, day, year)
1/1/05

11 Closing month of accounting year
December

12 First date wages or annuities were paid or will be paid (month, day, year). **Note:** *If applicant is a withholding agent, enter date income will first be paid to nonresident alien. (month, day, year)* . . . . ▶ 1/15/05

13 Highest number of employees expected in the next 12 months. **Note:** *If the applicant does not expect to have any employees during the period, enter "-0-."* . . . . ▶

Agricultural	Household	Other
0	0	0

14 Check **one** box that best describes the principal activity of your business.
☐ Construction   ☐ Rental & leasing   ☐ Transportation & warehousing   ☐ Health care & social assistance   ☐ Wholesale-agent/broker
☐ Real estate   ☐ Manufacturing   ☐ Finance & insurance   ☐ Accommodation & food service   ☐ Wholesale-other   ☐ Retail
                                                                            ☒ Other (specify) grocery store

15 Indicate principal line of merchandise sold; specific construction work done; products produced; or services provided.
groceries

16a Has the applicant ever applied for an employer identification number for this or any other business? . . . . . ☐ Yes ☒ No
Note: *If "Yes," please complete lines 16b and 16c.*

16b If you checked "Yes" on line 16a, give applicant's legal name and trade name shown on prior application if different from line 1 or 2 above.
Legal name ▶   Trade name ▶

16c Approximate date when, and city and state where, the application was filed. Enter previous employer identification number if known.
Approximate date when filed (mo., day, year) | City and state where filed | Previous EIN

Third Party Designee

Complete this section **only** if you want to authorize the named individual to receive the entity's EIN and answer questions about the completion of this form.

Designee's name

Designee's telephone number (include area code)
(   )

Address and ZIP code

Designee's fax number (include area code)
(   )

Under penalties of perjury, I declare that I have examined this application, and to the best of my knowledge and belief, it is true, correct, and complete.

Name and title (type or print clearly) ▶ Joe T. Smith, President

Applicant's telephone number (include area code)
(210) 555-1111

Signature ▶ *Joe T. Smith*   Date ▶ 1/10/05

Applicant's fax number (include area code)
(210) 555-1112

For Privacy Act and Paperwork Reduction Act Notice, see separate instructions.   Cat. No. 16055N   Form **SS-4** (Rev. 12-2001)

Form W-4 (2004)

Purpose. Complete Form W-4 so that your employer can withhold the correct Federal income tax from your pay. Because your tax situation may change, you may want to refigure your withholding each year.

Exemption from withholding. If you are exempt, complete only lines 1, 2, 3, 4, and 7 and sign the form to validate it. Your exemption for 2004 expires February 16, 2005. See **Pub. 505**, Tax Withholding and Estimated Tax.

Note: *You cannot claim exemption from withholding if: (a) your income exceeds $800 and includes more than $250 of unearned income (e.g., interest and dividends) and (b) another person can claim you as a dependent on their tax return.*

Basic instructions. If you are not exempt, complete the **Personal Allowances Worksheet** below. The worksheets on page 2 adjust your withholding allowances based on itemized deductions, certain credits, adjustments to income, or two-earner/two-job situations. Complete all worksheets that apply. **However, you may claim fewer (or zero) allowances.**

Head of household. Generally, you may claim head of household filing status on your tax return only if you are unmarried and pay more than 50% of the costs of keeping up a home for yourself and your dependent(s) or other qualifying individuals. See line **E** below.

Tax credits. You can take projected tax credits into account in figuring your allowable number of withholding allowances. Credits for child or dependent care expenses and the child tax credit may be claimed using the **Personal Allowances Worksheet** below. See **Pub. 919**, How Do I Adjust My Tax Withholding? for information on converting your other credits into withholding allowances.

Nonwage income. If you have a large amount of nonwage income, such as interest or dividends, consider making estimated tax payments using **Form 1040-ES**, Estimated Tax for Individuals. Otherwise, you may owe additional tax.

Two earners/two jobs. If you have a working spouse or more than one job, figure the total number of allowances you are entitled to claim on all jobs using worksheets from only one Form W-4. Your withholding usually will be most accurate when all allowances are claimed on the Form W-4 for the highest paying job and zero allowances are claimed on the others.

Nonresident alien. If you are a nonresident alien, see the **Instructions for Form 8233** before completing this Form W-4.

Check your withholding. After your Form W-4 takes effect, use Pub. 919 to see how the dollar amount you are having withheld compares to your projected total tax for 2004. See Pub. 919, especially if your earnings exceed $125,000 (Single) or $175,000 (Married).

Recent name change? If your name on line 1 differs from that shown on your social security card, call 1-800-772-1213 to initiate a name change and obtain a social security card showing your correct name.

Personal Allowances Worksheet (Keep for your records.)

- **A** Enter "1" for **yourself** if no one else can claim you as a dependent . . . . **A** _1_
- **B** Enter "1" if:
  - You are single and have only one job; or
  - You are married, have only one job, and your spouse does not work; or
  - Your wages from a second job or your spouse's wages (or the total of both) are $1,000 or less.
  . . **B** _1_
- **C** Enter "1" for your **spouse**. But, you may choose to enter "-0-" if you are married and have either a working spouse or more than one job. (Entering "-0-" may help you avoid having too little tax withheld.) . . . . . **C** _1_
- **D** Enter number of **dependents** (other than your spouse or yourself) you will claim on your tax return . . . . **D** _2_
- **E** Enter "1" if you will file as **head of household** on your tax return (see conditions under **Head of household** above) . **E** ___
- **F** Enter "1" if you have at least $1,500 of **child or dependent care expenses** for which you plan to claim a credit . . **F** ___
  (**Note:** *Do not include child support payments. See Pub. 503, Child and Dependent Care Expenses, for details.*)
- **G** **Child Tax Credit** (including additional child tax credit):
  - If your total income will be less than $52,000 ($77,000 if married), enter "2" for each eligible child.
  - If your total income will be between $52,000 and $84,000 ($77,000 and $119,000 if married), enter "1" for each eligible child plus "1" **additional** if you have four or more eligible children. **G** _1_
- **H** Add lines A through G and enter total here. **Note:** *This may be different from the number of exemptions you claim on your tax return.* ▶ **H** _6_

For accuracy, complete all worksheets that apply.
- If you plan to **itemize or claim adjustments to income** and want to reduce your withholding, see the **Deductions and Adjustments Worksheet** on page 2.
- If you have **more than one job** or are **married and you and your spouse both work** and the combined earnings from all jobs exceed $35,000 ($25,000 if married) see the **Two-Earner/Two-Job Worksheet** on page 2 to avoid having too little tax withheld.
- If **neither** of the above situations applies, **stop here** and enter the number from line H on line 5 of Form W-4 below.

Cut here and give Form W-4 to your employer. Keep the top part for your records.

Form W-4
Department of the Treasury
Internal Revenue Service

Employee's Withholding Allowance Certificate

▶ Your employer must send a copy of this form to the IRS if: (a) you claim more than 10 allowances or (b) you claim "Exempt" and your wages are normally more than $200 per week.

OMB No. 1545-0010

2004

| 1 | Type or print your first name and middle initial: Joe T. | Last name: Smith | 2 | Your social security number: 111 22 3333 |

Home address (number and street or rural route): 123 Main Street

City or town, state, and ZIP code: San Antonio, Texas 72805

3 ☐ Single ☒ Married ☐ Married, but withhold at higher Single rate.
Note: *If married, but legally separated, or spouse is a nonresident alien, check the "Single" box.*

4 If your last name differs from that shown on your social security card, check here. You must call 1-800-772-1213 for a new card. ▶ ☐

| 5 | Total number of allowances you are claiming (from line **H** above **or** from the applicable worksheet on page 2) | **5** | 6 |
| 6 | Additional amount, if any, you want withheld from each paycheck . . . . | **6** | $ 0 |

7 I claim exemption from withholding for 2004, and I certify that I meet **both** of the following conditions for exemption:
- Last year I had a right to a refund of **all** Federal income tax withheld because I had **no** tax liability **and**
- This year I expect a refund of **all** Federal income tax withheld because I expect to have **no** tax liability.

If you meet both conditions, write "Exempt" here . . . . ▶ | **7** | |

Under penalties of perjury, I certify that I am entitled to the number of withholding allowances claimed on this certificate, or I am entitled to claim exempt status.

Employee's signature
(Form is not valid unless you sign it.) ▶ *Joe T. Smith*   Date ▶ 1/1/05

| 8 | Employer's name and address (Employer: Complete lines 8 and 10 only if sending to the IRS.) ABC, Inc./123 Main Street/ San Antonio, TX 78205 | 9 Office code (optional) 74 | 10 Employer identification number (EIN) 111111 |

For Privacy Act and Paperwork Reduction Act Notice, see page 2.   Cat. No. 10220Q   Form **W-4** (2004)

Form W-4 (2004) Page **2**

Deductions and Adjustments Worksheet

Note: *Use this worksheet only if you plan to itemize deductions, claim certain credits, or claim adjustments to income on your 2004 tax return.*

1 Enter an estimate of your 2004 itemized deductions. These include qualifying home mortgage interest, charitable contributions, state and local taxes, medical expenses in excess of 7.5% of your income, and miscellaneous deductions. (For 2004, you may have to reduce your itemized deductions if your income is over $142,700 ($71,350 if married filing separately). See **Worksheet 3** in Pub. 919 for details.) . . . **1** $ _____

2 Enter: { $9,700 if married filing jointly or qualifying widow(er)
$7,150 if head of household
$4,850 if single
$4,850 if married filing separately } . . . . **2** $ _____

3 **Subtract** line 2 from line 1. If line 2 is greater than line 1, enter "-0-" . . . . **3** $ _____
4 Enter an estimate of your 2004 adjustments to income, including alimony, deductible IRA contributions, and student loan interest **4** $ _____
5 **Add** lines 3 and 4 and enter the total. (Include any amount for credits from **Worksheet 7** in Pub. 919) .. **5** $ _____
6 Enter an estimate of your 2004 nonwage income (such as dividends or interest) . . . . **6** $ _____
7 **Subtract** line 6 from line 5. Enter the result, but not less than "-0-" . . . . **7** $ _____
8 **Divide** the amount on line 7 by $3,000 and enter the result here. Drop any fraction . . . . . **8** _____
9 Enter the number from the **Personal Allowances Worksheet,** line H, page 1 . . . . **9** _____
10 **Add** lines 8 and 9 and enter the total here. If you plan to use the **Two-Earner/Two-Job Worksheet,** also enter this total on line 1 below. Otherwise, **stop here** and enter this total on Form W-4, line 5, page 1 .. **10** _____

Two-Earner/Two-Job Worksheet (See **Two earners/two jobs** on page 1.)

Note: *Use this worksheet only if the instructions under line H on page 1 direct you here.*

1 Enter the number from line H, page 1 (or from line 10 above if you used the **Deductions and Adjustments Worksheet**) **1** _____
2 Find the number in **Table 1** below that applies to the **LOWEST** paying job and enter it here . . . .. **2** _____
3 If line 1 is **more than or equal to** line 2, subtract line 2 from line 1. Enter the result here (if zero, enter "-0-") and on Form W-4, line 5, page 1. **Do not** use the rest of this worksheet . . . . **3** _____

Note: *If line 1 is **less than** line 2, enter "-0-" on Form W-4, line 5, page 1. Complete lines 4-9 below to calculate the additional withholding amount necessary to avoid a year-end tax bill.*

4 Enter the number from line 2 of this worksheet . . . . **4** _____
5 Enter the number from line 1 of this worksheet . . . . **5** _____
6 **Subtract** line 5 from line 4 . . . . **6** _____
7 Find the amount in **Table 2** below that applies to the **HIGHEST** paying job and enter it here . . . .. **7** $ _____
8 **Multiply** line 7 by line 6 and enter the result here. This is the additional annual withholding needed .. **8** $ _____
9 Divide line 8 by the number of pay periods remaining in 2004. For example, divide by 26 if you are paid every two weeks and you complete this form in December 2003. Enter the result here and on Form W-4, line 6, page 1. This is the additional amount to be withheld from each paycheck . . . . **9** $ _____

Table 1: Two-Earner/Two-Job Worksheet

Married Filing Jointly			Married Filing Jointly			All Others	
If wages from **HIGHEST** paying job are-	AND, wages from **LOWEST** paying job are-	Enter on line 2 above	If wages from **HIGHEST** paying job are-	AND, wages from **LOWEST** paying job are-	Enter on line 2 above	If wages from **LOWEST** paying job are-	Enter on line 2 above
$0 - $40,000	$0 - $4,000	0	$40,001 and over	31,001 - 38,000	6	$0 - $6,000	0
	4,001 - 8,000	1		38,001 - 44,000	7	6,001 - 11,000	1
	8,001 - 17,000	2		44,001 - 50,000	8	11,001 - 18,000	2
	17,001 and over	3		50,001 - 55,000	9	18,001 - 25,000	3
				55,001 - 65,000	10	25,001 - 31,000	4
$40,001 and over	$0 - $4,000	0		65,001 - 75,000	11	31,001 - 44,000	5
	4,001 - 8,000	1		75,001 - 85,000	12	44,001 - 55,000	6
	8,001 - 15,000	2		85,001 - 100,000	13	55,001 - 70,000	7
	15,001 - 22,000	3		100,001 - 115,000	14	70,001 - 80,000	8
	22,001 - 25,000	4		115,001 and over	15	80,001 - 100,000	9
	25,001 - 31,000	5				100,001 and over	10

Table 2: Two-Earner/Two-Job Worksheet

Married Filing Jointly		All Others	
If wages from **HIGHEST** paying job are-	Enter on line 7 above	If wages from **HIGHEST** paying job are-	Enter on line 7 above
$0 - $60,000	$470	$0 - $30,000	$470
60,001 - 110,000	780	30,001 - 70,000	780
110,001 - 150,000	870	70,001 - 140,000	870
150,001 - 270,000	1,020	140,001 - 320,000	1,020
270,001 and over	1,090	320,001 and over	1,090

Privacy Act and Paperwork Reduction Act Notice. We ask for the information on this form to carry out the Internal Revenue laws of the United States. The Internal Revenue Code requires this information under sections 3402(f)(2)(A) and 6109 and their regulations. **Failure to provide a properly completed form will result in your being treated as a single person who claims no withholding allowances; providing fraudulent information may also subject you to penalties.** Routine uses of this information include giving it to the Department of Justice for civil and criminal litigation, to cities, states, and the District of Columbia for use in administering their tax laws, and using it in the National Directory of New Hires. We may also disclose this information to Federal and state agencies to enforce Federal nontax criminal laws and to combat terrorism.

You are not required to provide the information requested on a form that is subject to the Paperwork Reduction Act unless the form displays a valid OMB control number. Books or records relating to a form or its instructions must be retained as long as their contents may become material in the administration of any Internal Revenue law. Generally, tax returns and return information are confidential, as required by Code section 6103.

The time needed to complete this form will vary depending on individual circumstances. The estimated average time is: **Recordkeeping,** 46 min.; **Learning about the law or the form,** 13 min.; **Preparing the form,** 59 min. If you have comments concerning the accuracy of these time estimates or suggestions for making this form simpler, we would be happy to hear from you. You can write to the Tax Products Coordinating Committee, Western Area Distribution Center, Rancho Cordova, CA 95743-0001. **Do not** send Form W-4 to this address. Instead, give it to your employer.

AP-201-3
(Rev.1-03/7)

TEXAS APPLICATION FOR SALES TAX PERMIT, USE TAX PERMIT AND/OR TELECOMMUNICATIONS INFRASTRUCTURE FUND ASSESSMENT SET-UP

- TYPE OR PRINT
- Do NOT write in shaded areas.

Page 1

SOLE OWNER IDENTIFICATION

1. Name of sole owner *(First, middle initial, and last name)*

2. Social security number (SSN)
   2 - -
   ☐ Check here if you DO NOT have a SSN.

3. Taxpayer number for reporting any Texas tax OR Texas identification number if you now have or have ever had one.

NON-SOLE OWNER IDENTIFICATION --- ALL SOLE OWNERS SKIP TO ITEM 9. ---

4. Business organization type
   - ☐ Texas registered limited liability partnership (PR)
   - ☐ Texas limited liability company (CL)
   - ☐ Non-Texas limited liability company (CI)
   - ☐ Estate (ES)
   - ☐ Non-Texas registered limited liability partnership (PS)
   - ☒ Texas profit corporation (CT)
   - ☐ Non-Texas profit corporation (CF)
   - ☐ Professional corporation (CP)
   - ☐ General partnership (PG)
   - ☐ Texas nonprofit corporation (CN)
   - ☐ Non-Texas nonprofit corporation (CM)
   - ☐ Professional association (AP)
   - ☐ Limited partnership (PL or PF)
   - ☐ Trust (FM) Please submit a copy of the trust agreement with this application
   - ☐ Other *(explain)*

5. Legal name of partnership, company, corporation, association, trust, or other
   ABC, Inc.

6. Taxpayer number for reporting any Texas tax OR Texas identification number if you now have or have ever had one. **none**

7. Federal employer's identification number (FEIN) assigned by the Internal Revenue Service ..... 1 **74** - **111111**

8. ☐ Check here if you do not have an FEIN. 3

BUSINESS INFORMATION

9. Mailing address
   Street number, P.O. Box, or rural route and box number
   123 Main Street
   City: **San Antonio** State/province: **TX** ZIP code: **78205** County *(or country, if outside the U.S.)*: **Bexar**

10. Name of person to contact regarding day to day business operations
    Joe Smith Daytime phone: **210 / 555 - 1111**

11. Principal type of business
    - ☐ Agriculture
    - ☐ Transportation
    - ☒ Retail Trade
    - ☐ Real Estate
    - ☐ Mining
    - ☐ Communications *(See Item 38)*
    - ☐ Finance
    - ☐ Services
    - ☐ Construction
    - ☐ Utilities
    - ☐ Insurance
    - ☐ Public Administration
    - ☐ Manufacturing
    - ☐ Wholesale Trade
    - ☐ Other *(explain)*

12. Primary business activities and type of products or services to be sold
    grocery store   SIC

TAXPAYER INFORMATION

If you are a SOLE OWNER, skip to Item 18.

13. If the business is a Texas profit corporation, nonprofit corporation, professional corporation, or limited liability company, enter the charter number and date. ..... Charter number __ Month Day Year

14. If the business is a non-Texas profit corporation, nonprofit corporation, professional corporation, or limited liability company, enter the state or country of incorporation, charter number and date, Texas Certificate of Authority number and date.
    State/country of inc. __ Charter number __ Month Day Year __ Texas Certificate of Authority number __ Month Day Year

15. If the business is a corporation, have you been involved in a merger within the last seven years? ... ☐ YES ☐ NO   *If "YES," attach a detailed explanation.*

16. If the business is a limited partnership or registered limited liability partnership, enter the home state and registered identification number. ..... State __ Number __

17. General partners, principal members/officers, managing directors or managers *(Attach additional sheets, if necessary.)*

    Name: **Joe Smith**   Title: **president**   Phone: **210 / 555 - 1111**
    Home address: **123 Main Street**   City: **San Antonio**   State: **TX**   ZIP code: **78205**
    SSN or FEIN: **111-22-3333**   Percent of ownership: **100** %   County: **Bexar**
    Position held: ☐ Partner ☒ Officer ☐ Director ☒ Corporate Stockholder ☒ Record keeper

    Name: __   Title: __   Phone: __ / __ - __
    Home address: __   City: __   State: __   ZIP code: __
    SSN or FEIN: __   Percent of ownership: __ %   County: __
    Position held: ☐ Partner ☐ Officer ☐ Director ☐ Corporate Stockholder ☐ Record keeper

AP-201-4
(Rev.1-03/7)

♦ 183

TEXAS APPLICATION FOR SALES TAX PERMIT, USE TAX PERMIT AND/OR TELECOMMUNICATIONS INFRASTRUCTURE FUND ASSESSMENT SET-UP

- *TYPE OR PRINT*
- *Do NOT write in shaded areas.*

Page 2

18. Legal name of entity *(Same as Item 1 OR Item 5)*
Acme Services, LLC

BUSINESS LOCATION

19. Is your business located outside Texas? ☐ YES ☒ NO
If "YES," **skip to Item 28**

20. Business location name and address *(Attach additional sheets for each additional location.)*
Business location name:

Street and number *(Do not use P.O. Box. or rural route)*: 123 Main Street
City: San Antonio
State: TX
ZIP code: 78205
County: Bexar

Physical location *(If business location address is a rural route and box number, provide directions)*:
Business location phone: 210 / 555 - 1111

21. Is your business located inside the boundaries of an incorporated city? ☒ YES ☐ NO
If "YES," indicate city: San Antonio

Answer the questions below about the above location by checking "YES" or "NO."

22. Is your business located inside a metropolitan transit authority/city transit department (MTA/CTD)? ☒ YES ☐ NO
23. Is your business located inside a special purpose district (SPD)? ☐ YES ☒ NO
24. Will you deliver in your own vehicles, provide taxable services, or have sales/service representatives going from this location to customers located in:
- another city? ☐ YES ☒ NO
- another county? ☐ YES ☒ NO
- another MTA/CTD? ☐ YES ☒ NO
- another SPD? ☐ YES ☒ NO

25. Will you ship from this location to other customers via common carrier? ☐ YES ☒ NO
26. Are you a seller with no established place of business selling at a temporary location (trade show, event, or door to door)? ☐ YES ☒ NO
27. Will you have out-of-state suppliers shipping taxable items directly to customers' locations in Texas? ☐ YES ☒ NO

SALES AND USE TAX

28. If you sell fireworks, are you a ☐ Distributor ☐ Jobber ☐ Manufacturer ☐ Retailer
29. Do you sell, lease, or rent off-road, heavy duty diesel powered construction equipment? ☐ YES ☒ NO
30. Check the box that best represents your anticipated quarterly state sales tax collections: ☐ less than $250 (Y) ☐ $250-$1,500 (Q) ☐ greater than $1,500 (M)
31. Enter the date of the first business operation in the above location that is subject to sales or use tax, or the date you plan to start such business operation. *(Date cannot be more than 90 days in the future.)*
month day year: 01 01 2005

32. Is your business operated all year? ☒ YES ☐ NO
If "NO," list the months you will operate.

33. Will you sell any type of alcoholic beverages? ☒ YES ☐ NO
If "YES," indicate the type of permit you will hold: ☐ mixed beverage ☒ beer and wine

34. Brief description of your business activities **for this location**, and the primary products or services to be sold. SIC
grocery store, food, drinks, cigarettes, beer, wine

35. Will you be required to report interest earned on sales tax? *(See "Specific Instructions")* ☐ YES ☐ NO
36. Are you located out of state with representation in Texas? ☐ YES ☒ NO
If "YES," complete Item 37. **If "NO," skip to Item 38.**

37. List names and addresses of all representatives, agents, salespersons, canvassers, or solicitors in Texas. *(Attach additional sheets, if necessary.)*
Name *(First, middle initial, last)*: N/A
Street: | City: | State: | ZIP code:

38. Location of all distribution points, warehouses, or offices in Texas *(Attach additional sheets, if necessary.)*
Street: N/A | City: | State: TX | ZIP code:
Street: | City: | State: TX | ZIP code:

AP-201-5
(Rev.1-03/7)

TEXAS APPLICATION FOR SALES TAX PERMIT, USE TAX PERMIT AND/OR TELECOMMUNICATIONS INFRASTRUCTURE FUND ASSESSMENT SET-UP

- TYPE OR PRINT
- Do NOT write in shaded areas.

Page 3

39. Legal name of entity *(Same as Item 1 OR Item 5)*
ABC, Inc.

TIF ASSESSMENT / 9-1-1

40. Do you receive compensation for providing telecommunications services? ☐ YES ☒ NO

    If "YES," you are responsible for the Telecommunications Infrastructure Fund (TIF) assessment and should complete Items 41-42.

    If "NO," skip to Item 43.

41. Date of the first business operation that is subject to the Telecommunications Infrastructure Fund assessment in Texas or the date you plan to start such business operation.

42. Telecommunications provider type .... ☐ Telecommunications Utility (24) ☐ Commercial Mobile Service Provider (25)

43. 9-1-1 emergency communications fees you collect under Health & Safety Code, Chapter 771. *(Check all that apply.)*
    ☐ 9-1-1 (Wireless) Emergency Service Fee (91)   ☐ 9-1-1 Emergency Service Fee (92)   ☐ 9-1-1 Equalization Surcharge (93)

For Comptroller Use Only
Tax type/reason
☐ 00991   2 0
Reference no.

PREVIOUS OWNER INFORMATION

If you purchased an existing business or business assets, complete Items 44-47.

44. Previous owner's trade name.
N/A

    Previous owner's taxpayer number *(if available)*

45. Previous owner's legal name, address and phone number, if available.
    Name
    Phone *(Area code and number)*
    Address *(Street and number)*   City   State   ZIP code

46. Check each of the following items you purchased.
    ☐ Inventory   ☐ Corporate stock   ☐ Equipment   ☐ Real estate   ☐ Other assets

47. Purchase price of this business or assets and the date of purchase.
    Purchase price $ _____   Date of purchase ___ month ___ day ___ year

SIGNATURES

48. The sole owner, all general partners, corporation or organization president, vice-president, secretary or treasurer, managing director, or an authorized representative must sign. A representative must submit a written power of attorney. *(Attach additional sheets if necessary.)*

    Date of signature(s) month day year

    I (We) declare that the information in this document and any attachments is true and correct to the best of my (our) knowledge and belief.

    Type or print name and title of sole owner, partner, or officer: **Joe T. Smith, President**
    Drivers license number/state: **123321 / TX**
    sign here ▶ Sole owner, partner, or officer: *Joe T. Smith*

    Type or print name and title of partner or officer:
    Drivers license number/state:
    sign here ▶ Partner or officer:

    Type or print name and title of partner or officer:
    Drivers license number/state:
    sign here ▶ Partner or officer:

YOUR PERMIT MUST BE PROMINENTLY DISPLAYED IN YOUR PLACE OF BUSINESS. THE INFORMATION ON YOUR PERMIT IS PUBLIC INFORMATION.

OPEN RECORDS NOTICE - Your name, address, and telephone number are public information under the Texas Open Records Act, Chapter 552, Government Code.

Field office or section number _____   Employee Name _____   USERID _____   Date _____

Appendix C: Blank Forms

The following forms may be photocopied or removed from this book and used immediately. Some of the tax forms explained in this book are not included here because you should use original returns provided by the IRS (940, 941) or the Texas Department of Revenue.

These forms are included on the following pages:

FORM 1: TAX TIMETABLE 187

FORM 2: ASSUMED NAME CERTIFICATE FOR FILING WITH THE SECRETARY OF STATE 189

FORM 3: APPLICATION FOR REGISTRATION OF TRADEMARK OR SERVICE MARK 193

FORM 4: EMPLOYMENT ELIGIBILITY VERIFICATION (IRS FORM I-9) 201

FORM 5: APPLICATION FOR EMPLOYER IDENTIFICATION NUMBER (IRS FORM SS-4) 205

FORM 6: DETERMINATION OF WORKER STATUS FOR PURPOSES OF FEDERAL EMPLOYMENT TAXES AND INCOME TAX WITHHOLDING (IRS FORM SS-8) 213

FORM 7: EMPLOYEE'S WITHHOLDING ALLOWANCE CERTIFICATE
(IRS FORM W-4)..................................219

FORM 8: TEXAS APPLICATION FOR SALES TAX PERMIT,
USE TAX PERMIT AND/OR TELECOMMUNICATIONS
INFRASTRUCTURE FUND ASSESSMENT SET-UP 221

FORM 9: TEXAS SALES AND USE TAX RETURN (DR-15CS) 227

FORM 10: STATUS REPORT (FORM C-1).......................229

FORM 11: REPORT OF CASH PAYMENTS OVER $10,000 RECEIVED
IN A TRADE OR BUSINESS (IRS FORM 8300) 233

FORM 12: PRE-SCREENING NOTICE AND CERTIFICATION REQUEST
FOR THE WORK OPPORTUNITY
AND WELFARE-TO-WORK CREDITS
(IRS FORM 8850) 237

TAX TIMETABLE

form 1 ◆ 187

	Texas				Federal			
	Sales	Unemployment	Personal property	Franchise	Est. Payment	Annual Return	Form 941*	Misc.
JAN.	20th	31st	31st		15th		31st	31st 940 W-2 508 099
FEB.	20th							28th W-3
MAR.	20th					15th Corp. & Partnership		
APR.	20th	30th			15th	15th Personal	30th	30th 508
MAY	20th			15th				
JUN.	20th				15th			
JUL.	20th	31st					31st	31st 508
AUG.	20th							
SEP.	20th				15th			
OCT.	20th	31st					31st	31st 508
NOV.	20th							
DEC.	20th							

*In addition to form 941, deposits must be made regularly if withholding exceeds $500 in any month

This page intentionally left blank.

form 2 ◆ 189

Office of the Secretary of State
Corporations Section
P.O. Box 13697
Austin, Texas 78711-3697

ASSUMED NAME CERTIFICATE
FOR FILING WITH THE SECRETARY OF STATE

1. The name of the corporation, limited liability company, limited partnership, or registered limited liability partnership as stated in its articles of incorporation, articles of organization, certificate of limited partnership, application for certificate of authority or comparable document is

    _____

2. The assumed name under which the business or professional service is or is to be conducted or rendered is

    _____

3. The state, country, or other jurisdiction under the laws of which it was incorporated, organized or associated is_____and the

    address of its registered or similar office in that jurisdiction is

    _____

4. The period, not to exceed 10 years, during which the assumed name will be used is

    _____

5. The entity is a (check one):
   A.
   ☐ Business Corporation   ☐ Non-Profit Corporation
   ☐ Professional Corporation   ☐ Professional Association
   ☐ Limited Liability Company   ☐ Limited Partnership
   ☐ Registered Limited Liability Partnership

   B. If the entity is some other type business, professional or other association that is incorporated, please specify below (e.g., bank, savings and loan association, etc.)

    _____

6. If the entity is required to maintain a registered office in Texas, the address of the registered office is _____

    _____ and the name of its registered agent

    at such address is

    _____

    The address of the principal office (if not the same as the registered office) is

    _____

7. If the entity is not required to or does not maintain a registered office in Texas, the office address in Texas is_____

and if the entity is not incorporated, organized or associated under the laws of Texas, the address of its place of business in Texas is_____

and the office address elsewhere is_____

8. The county or counties where business or professional services are being or are to be conducted or rendered under such assumed name are (if applicable, use the designation "ALL" or "ALL EXCEPT")

9. The undersigned, if acting in the capacity of an attorney-in-fact of the entity, certifies that the entity has duly authorized the attorney-in-fact in writing to execute this document.

By _____
Signature of officer, general partner, manager, representative or attorney-in-fact of the entity

NOTE

This form is designed to meet statutory requirements for filing with the secretary of state and is not designed to meet filing requirements on the county level. Filing requirements for assumed name documents to be filed with the county clerk differ. Assumed name documents filed with the county clerk are to be executed and acknowledged by the filing party, which requires that the document be notarized.

Form No. 503
Revised 9/99

INSTRUCTIONS

1. A corporation, limited liability company, limited partnership or registered limited liability partnership which regularly conducts business or renders a professional service in this state under a name other than its true name, must file an assumed name certificate with the secretary of state. In addition, an assumed name certificate must be filed with the county clerk in the county in which the registered office is located the with the county clerk in the county which the principal office is located if these are not in the same county.

2. This form is designed to meet minimum statutory filing requirements for filing with the secretary of state; no warranty is made regarding the suitability of this form for any particular purpose. This form and the information provided are not substitutes for the advice of an attorney. <u>Prior to signing, please review carefully the statements set forth in the document. A person commits an offense under section 36.27 of the Business & Commerce Code if the person signs a document the person knows is false in any material respect with the intent that the document be delivered to the secretary of state for filing. The offense is punishable as if it were an offense under section 37.10 of the Penal Code.</u>

3. Send the executed certificate accompanied by the filing fee of $25 to the Secretary of State, Statutory Filings Division, Corporations Section, P.O. Box 13697, Austin, Texas 78711-3697. The delivery address is 1019 Brazos, Austin, Texas 78701. The telephone number is (512) 463-5555, TDD: (800) 735-2989, FAX: (512) 463-5709. Upon filing, the certificate will be placed on record. If a duplicate file-stamped copy is desired, you must submit a duplicate copy of the document for this purpose.

4. Personal checks and MasterCard®, Visa®, and Discover® are accepted in payment of the filing fee. Fees paid by credit card are subject to a statutorily authorized processing cost of 2.1% of the total fees.

5. The information provided in paragraph 6 regarding the registered agent and registered office address in Texas must match the information on file in this office. To verify the information on file, you may contact our Public Information Team at (512) 463-5555 or e-mail at corpinfo@sos.state.tx.us.

6. Whenever an event occurs that causes the information in the assumed name certificate to become materially misleading (e.g. change of registered agent/office or a change of name), a new certificate must be filed within 60 days after the occurrence of the event which necessitates the filing.

7. A registrant that ceases to transact business or render professional services under an assumed name for which a certificate has been filed may file an abandonment of use pursuant to the Texas Business & Commerce Code, section 36.14. (Form 504)

8. Assumed name certificates to be filed with the county clerk must be notarized and contain original signatures; <u>this form does not satisfy county filing requirements</u>. An assumed name certificate to be filed with the county clerk must be sent directly to the appropriate county clerk and not to the secretary of state.

Form No. 503
Revised 9/99

This page intentionally left blank.

Office of the Secretary of State
Corporations Section
P.O. Box 13697
Austin, Texas 78711-3697

APPLICATION FOR REGISTRATION
OF TRADEMARK OR SERVICE MARK

The undersigned applicant has adopted and used, and is now using, a certain trademark or service mark in Texas and hereby makes application for registration of such mark, in accordance with Chapter 16 of the Texas Business & Commerce Code.

1. Applicant:_____

2. Address:_____
   City: _____ State:_____ Zip:_____

3. Applicant is incorporated or organized as a _____
   and is incorporated or organized under the laws of _____

4. Describe the mark (words and/or design) SHOWN ON THE ATTACHED DRAWING SHEET:
   _____
   _____

5. Description of goods or services in connection with which the mark is being used: (BE SPECIFIC)
   _____
   _____
   _____

6. The manner in which the mark is being used (labels, tags on the goods, etc; OR brochures, newspapers advertising the services, etc.): (A SAMPLE IS ATTACHED)
   _____
   _____

7. Number and title of the class of goods or services:_____
   (Do not list more than one class. See instruction 7.)

8. Date mark first used by applicant (BOTH A & B MUST BE COMPLETED):

    (a) Anywhere: (Month) __ __/(Day)__ __/(Year)__ __ __ __
    (b) In Texas: (Month) __ __/(Day)__ __/(Year)__ __ __ __

9. Applicant hereby appoints the Secretary of State of Texas as its agent for service of process only in suits relating to the registration which may be issued if the applicant is or becomes a nonresident individual, partnership or association or foreign corporation, limited partnership, or limited liability company without a certificate of authority to do business in this state or cannot be found in this state.

10. Applicant is the owner of the mark and, to the best of the applicant's knowledge, no other person is entitled to use the mark in this state in the identical form used by applicant, or in a form that is likely, when used in connection with the goods or services, to cause confusion or mistake, or to deceive, because of its resemblance to the mark used by the applicant.

11. ☐ A drawing of the mark is enclosed.

12. ☐ Two examples of advertising are enclosed (if mark is used in connection with services). OR
☐ Two actual tags, labels, or actual product packaging are enclosed (if mark is used in connection with a distributed product).

Executed on this _____ day of _____ , ____ .

_____
(Name of Applicant)

_____
(Signature of Applicant)

_____
(Title)

TRADEMARK DRAWING SHEET

Drawing Instructions:

The applicant also must submit with the application a "drawing sheet" that shows the mark exactly as it appears in the specimen accompanying the application and exactly as it is described in paragraph 4 of the application. If the mark includes a design, a drawing of the entire proposed mark (in clean, uniform black lines) must be attached to the application. If the mark described in the application consists only of a word, letter or numeral, or any combination thereof, and if the mark is not depicted in a special form, the mark may be typed in capital letters on the drawing sheet.

The Office of the Secretary of State does not discriminate on the basis of race, color, national origin, sex, religion, age or disability in employment or the provision of services.

TRADEMARKS

GENERAL INFORMATION

TRADEMARKS and SERVICE MARKS are commonly referred to as brand names, logos or slogans. *Trademarks* are used to identify tangible goods. *Service marks* are used to identify services. The term "mark" is used to refer to both trademarks and service marks. A mark generally does not include "trade names," which are terms used only to identify a business organization, rather than to distinguish the goods or services provided by the business. A company name may be viewed to be merely a trade name, instead of a trademark or service mark, if it is advertised in such a way that it attracts little attention, if it is used in close proximity to an address or phone number, or if it is dominated by the presence of another, indisputable trademark. A trade name, however, may be registered as a trademark if it is shown to function as a trademark.

The registration of the trademark or service mark with the Office of the Secretary of State creates a statewide priority of rights in the mark against any other person who subsequently adopts the same or a confusingly similar mark. Registration also provides "constructive notice" to all persons in the state of Texas of the priority of the registered mark and provides the owner with certain procedural advantages when the owner seeks judicial relief for infringement. For these reasons, it is beneficial for an owner of a mark who does business in Texas to register a trademark or service mark with the secretary of state.

Since identical or confusingly similar marks may not be registered by more than one person, a person planning to use or register a mark should take steps to determine whether others have priority of rights to that mark. One important step is checking the active trademark and service mark registrations on file with the Secretary of State prior to submitting the trademark application.

An application for trademark registration undergoes an examination process similar to the federal trademark registration process. A "Trademark Examiner" (either a Trademark Attorney or Trademark Legal Assistant) reviews the application to ascertain whether the mark proposed for registration is registrable under Chapter 16, Business & Commerce Code [Section 16.08] including whether the mark performs the identifying functions of a trademark or service mark. In addition, the Examiner compares the proposed mark with similar marks previously registered in Texas to determine whether the applicant's mark will cause a likelihood of confusion for consumers with any state registered mark. Texas law, federal statutory law (upon which the Texas trademark statute is based), federal case law, and examining procedures similar to those used by the United States Patent and Trademark Office are used by the secretary of state to conduct the examinations of trademark applications.

If the examiner determines that the application does not meet the standards for registration, a written office action specifying the reasons for denial of registration will be sent to the applicant or the applicant's agent. The applicant is given sixty (60) days within which to amend the application, to provide the information requested, or to respond to the denial. Failure to respond within the time specified will terminate the examination process and will result in abandonment of the application. Upon receipt of the applicant's response, the examiner will re-examine the application. The examination procedures described may be repeated until the application is registered, finally denied, or abandoned by the applicant.

Instructions Page 2

The Trademark Examiners cannot provide legal advice to potential or actual applicants with regard to trademark law applicable to a particular circumstance. Because trademark law is quite complex, the secretary of state recommends that persons seeking to register a mark consult with a private attorney.

REQUIRMENTS FOR REGISTRATION

<u>Mark Must Be In Use</u>: Registration of trademarks and service marks in Texas is based on *actual use* of the mark in Texas commerce. For example, before an application can be submitted to the Office of the Secretary of State, the trademark must be used on a product, or the service mark must be used in association with the services rendered (during advertising or sale), and the goods must be sold or distributed in Texas or the services must be rendered in this state. A proposed mark may not be "reserved" prior to its actual use in Texas commerce or before the submission of a properly completed and filed application. If an application is submitted prior to actual use, the secretary of state will consider it void, registration will be refused, and the processing fee submitted with the application will not be refunded.

<u>Mark Must Be Distinctive</u>: Only distinctive words, names, symbols, devices, or logos are entitled to registration. A designation that is primarily a surname, or that is commonly used in describing the product or service, or that directly describes the qualities or characteristics of a product or service is not distinctive on first use and not entitled to registration. For example, the terms "Food & Beverage On-Line" would not be entitled to registration when used in association with "a news and information service for the food processing industry contained in a database" since such terms would be merely descriptive of such a service. However, sometimes a designation that is not inherently distinctive may acquire distinctiveness through at least five (5) years of continuous and substantially exclusive use.

INSTRUCTIONS FOR APPLICATION (Form 901)

Number 1: The applicant should be the person who owns the trademark or service mark and controls the use of the mark and the quality of the goods/services. If the applicant is an individual sole proprietor doing business under an assumed name ["d/b/a"], then provide the individual's name, followed by the assumed name of the business. If the applicant is an organized entity, such as a corporation, limited liability company, or limited partnership, then provide the legal name of the organized entity as shown in its formation document (e.g., ABC Business Company, Inc.)

Number 2: Provide the mailing address of the applicant. Please note however that during the examination/review process, the Secretary of State will send any correspondence regarding the application to the submitter address provided in the cover letter, envelope, or enclosed check.

Number 3: If the applicant is a corporation, limited partnership, limited liability company or other business entity, please identify the type of business organization and the state of incorporation or organization. If applicant is an individual, you may identify the organizational form as "sole owner/proprietor" and identify the state/country of residence. Out-of-state applicants seeking a trademark or service mark registration should also submit

Instructions Page 3

invoices or other material demonstrating the sale of goods or the rendition of services in Texas commerce.

Number 4: You can only seek to register one mark per application submitted. For example, if the mark includes both words and a logo/design element (a "composite mark"), and the applicant also uses the same words without or apart from the design element, an applicant seeking to register both versions of the mark would need to make two separate applications. A single application may not be used to seek registration of (1) different variations of a term or term; (2) terms appearing either "with or without" an accompanying design logo, or (3) more than one logo/design format. In addition, the applicant should describe the mark exactly as it appears in the specimen and drawing sheet accompanying the application so that there is no doubt what the applicant seeks to register. *Finally, the description in number 4, the drawing of the mark, and the samples of use provided should be consistent.*

Number 5: Describe <u>clearly and concisely</u> the goods or the services currently sold or provided by the applicant. Limit the description of goods or services to those goods or services that are classified under the same class heading. [See instructions for number 7.]

Number 6: The applicant should state the ways in which the mark is used, and/or the medium by which it is communicated to the consuming public. For example: tags or labels attached to the goods; or newspapers, brochures or signs advertising the services. <u>Specimens supporting use for the classification sought and consistent with the methods noted in the application must be submitted with the application.</u>

<u>Appropriate Specimens</u>

Trademark applications: Submit specimens of use such as actual labels or tags affixed to, or containers used with, the goods. A photograph of an actual display that appears in immediate proximity to the goods ("point-of-sale" display) is also an acceptable specimen. *Brochures that advertise the product <u>are not</u> sufficient.*

Service mark applications: Submit actual materials used in selling or advertising the services, such as menus, newspaper advertisements, coupons and the like. Advertising samples submitted (including letterhead or business cards) <u>must</u> contain some understandable reference to the services described in the application.

Number 7: State the class in which the applicant believes the goods or services belong. Texas does not permit multiple class applications. <u>Do not list more than one class</u>. If a mark is used in multiple classes, a separate and complete application is required for each class. Inclusion of more than one class in an application will result in an office action denying registration and requesting amendment of the application.

Many of the classification headings are broad in nature, and are generally not sufficient as a description of goods/services in item number 5 of the application. If you are unsure of the appropriate classification for your goods/services, you may leave this item blank or contact our office for assistance in classification. The classification system is set forth below:

Instructions page 4

Goods

Class 1: Chemicals
Class 2: Paints
Class 3: Cosmetics & Cleaning Preparations
Class 4. Lubricants & Fuels
Class 5: Pharmaceuticals
Class 6: Metal Goods
Class 7: Machinery
Class 8: Hand Tools
Class 9: Electrical & Scientific Apparatus
Class 10: Medical Apparatus
Class 11: Environmental Control Apparatus
Class 12: Vehicles
Class 13: Firearms
Class 14: Jewelry
Class 15: Musical Instruments
Class 16: Paper Goods & Printed Matter
Class 17: Rubber Goods
Class 18: Leather Goods
Class 19: Non-metallic Building Materials
Class 20: Furniture and articles not otherwise classified
Class 21: Housewares & Glass
Class 22: Cordage & Fibers
Class 23: Yarns & Threads
Class 24: Fabrics

Class 25: Clothing
Class 26: Fancy Goods (*e.g.,* buttons, ribbons)
Class 27: Floor Coverings
Class 28: Toys & Sporting Goods
Class 29: Meats & Processed Foods
Class 30: Staple Foods (*e.g.,* coffee, sugar)
Class 31: Natural Agricultural Products
Class 32: Light Beverages
Class 33: Wine & Spirits
Class 34: Smokers' Articles

Services

Class 35: Advertising & Business
Class 36: Insurance & Financial
Class 37: Building Construction & Repair
Class 38: Telecommunications
Class 39: Transportation & Storage
Class 40: Treatment of Materials
Class 41: Education & Entertainment
Class 42: Computer, scientific and legal
Class 43: Hotels and restaurants
Class 44: Medical, beauty and agricultural
Class 45: Personal

Number 8: The applicant should note accurately the date on which the mark was first publicly used to identify the goods or services being marketed. BOTH dates of first use "Anywhere" and in "Texas" MUST be indicated on the application. (If the date of first use was in Texas, both dates will be the same). The month, day and year should be noted for each date of first use, *e.g.,* "November 10, 1983." It is insufficient to simply note the month and the year, if the application is submitted within the same month.

Execution and Delivery Instructions

<u>Completed Application</u>: The application must be <u>typewritten</u> or <u>clearly printed in black ink</u>. Enclose two (2) copies of the application and <u>drawing</u> of the mark and two (2) <u>specimens</u> of use (examples of use listed in item 6).

<u>Signature</u>: The applicant must sign and date the application. The applicant's attorney of record may sign the application only with express authorization pursuant to a power of attorney; however, a copy of the power of attorney is not required to be part of the application. In addition, the application should not be executed <u>before</u> the first date of use of the mark.

<u>Prior to signing, please review carefully the statements set forth in the application. A person commits an offense under Section 16.31, Business & Commerce Code, if the person signs a document that is forged or that the person knows is false in any material respect with the intent</u>

that the document be delivered to the secretary of state for filing. The offense is a Class A misdemeanor. In addition, an application or registration procured by fraud is subject to cancellation pursuant to Sections 16.16 and 16.28, Business & Commerce Code.

Fee: The application processing fee of $50.00 may be paid by personal check, money order, cashier's check, or by credit card. Fees paid by credit card are subject to a statutorily authorized convenience fee of 2.1% of the total fees. Checks should be made payable to the secretary of state. The processing fee is not refundable regardless of whether the application is subsequently registered, denied or abandoned.

Delivery: Documents should be mailed to the address shown in the heading of this form. The delivery address is James Earl Rudder Office Building, 1019 Brazos, Austin, Texas 78701. Responses to office actions may be faxed or mailed. The fax number is (512) 463-5709.

Examination Process

Not all applications submitted to the Secretary of State are approved for registration. If an application is rejected, we will notify the submitter of the objections to registration. If the application for registration is approved, then we will return a file stamped copy of the application for registration and attach a certificate of registration. (See General Information section for further information on the examination process.)

During the course of the examination process, the Secretary of State may require the applicant to disclaim an unregistrable component of a mark that is otherwise registrable. An applicant cannot however disclaim all elements of the mark. A disclaimer is a statement that the applicant does not claim the exclusive right to use a specified element or elements of the mark. Generally, elements that are descriptive or generic of the goods/services would be disclaimed (e.g., an outline of the state, a geographic term of origin, or words that are commonly used to describe the services/goods). A disclaimer may be included in an application or may be added by amendment, e.g., to comply with a requirement by the examining attorney.

The purpose of a disclaimer is to permit the registration of a mark that is registrable as a whole but contains matter that would not be registrable standing alone. As used in trademark registrations, a disclaimer of a descriptive component of a composite mark amounts merely to a statement that, in so far as the particular registration is concerned, no rights are being asserted in the disclaimed component standing alone, but rights are asserted in the composite; and that the particular registration represents only such rights as flow from the use of the composite mark.

Application Check-List:

☐ Two copies of the application, including drawing sheet.
☐ Two appropriate specimens of use.
☐ Application processing fee of $50.00.

Form No. 901
Revised 04/03

form 4 ♦ **201**

U.S. Department of Justice
Immigration and Naturalization Service

OMB No. 1115-0136

Employment Eligibility Verification

Please read instructions carefully before completing this form. The instructions must be available during completion of this form. **ANTI-DISCRIMINATION NOTICE:** It is illegal to discriminate against work eligible individuals. Employers CANNOT specify which document(s) they will accept from an employee. The refusal to hire an individual because of a future expiration date may also constitute illegal discrimination.

Section 1. Employee Information and Verification. To be completed and signed by employee at the time employment begins.

| Print Name: Last | First | Middle Initial | Maiden Name |

Address (Street Name and Number) | Apt. # | Date of Birth (month/day/year)

City | State | Zip Code | Social Security #

I am aware that federal law provides for imprisonment and/or fines for false statements or use of false documents in connection with the completion of this form.

I attest, under penalty of perjury, that I am (check one of the following):
- ☐ A citizen or national of the United States
- ☐ A Lawful Permanent Resident (Alien # A_____)
- ☐ An alien authorized to work until ___/___/___
(Alien # or Admission #) _____

Employee's Signature | Date (month/day/year)

Preparer and/or Translator Certification. (To be completed and signed if Section 1 is prepared by a person other than the employee.) I attest, under penalty of perjury, that I have assisted in the completion of this form and that to the best of my knowledge the information is true and correct.

Preparer's/Translator's Signature | Print Name

Address (Street Name and Number, City, State, Zip Code) | Date (month/day/year)

Section 2. Employer Review and Verification. To be completed and signed by employer. Examine one document from List A OR examine one document from List B and one from List C, as listed on the reverse of this form, and record the title, number and expiration date, if any, of the document(s)

| List A | OR | List B | AND | List C |

Document title: _____

Issuing authority: _____

Document #: _____

Expiration Date (if any): ___/___/___   ___/___/___   ___/___/___

Document #: _____

Expiration Date (if any): ___/___/___

CERTIFICATION - I attest, under penalty of perjury, that I have examined the document(s) presented by the above-named employee, that the above-listed document(s) appear to be genuine and to relate to the employee named, that the employee began employment on (month/day/year) ___/___/___ and that to the best of my knowledge the employee is eligible to work in the United States. (State employment agencies may omit the date the employee began employment.)

Signature of Employer or Authorized Representative | Print Name | Title

Business or Organization Name | Address (Street Name and Number, City, State, Zip Code) | Date (month/day/year)

Section 3. Updating and Reverification. To be completed and signed by employer.

A. New Name (if applicable) | B. Date of rehire (month/day/year) (if applicable)

C. If employee's previous grant of work authorization has expired, provide the information below for the document that establishes current employment eligibility.

Document Title: _____   Document #: _____   Expiration Date (if any): ___/___/___

I attest, under penalty of perjury, that to the best of my knowledge, this employee is eligible to work in the United States, and if the employee presented document(s), the document(s) I have examined appear to be genuine and to relate to the individual.

Signature of Employer or Authorized Representative | Date (month/day/year)

Form I-9 (Rev. 11-21-91)N Page 2

U.S. Department of Justice
Immigration and Naturalization Service

OMB No. 1115-0136
Employment Eligibility Verification

INSTRUCTIONS
PLEASE READ ALL INSTRUCTIONS CAREFULLY BEFORE COMPLETING THIS FORM.

Anti-Discrimination Notice. It is illegal to discriminate against any individual (other than an alien not authorized to work in the U.S.) in hiring, discharging, or recruiting or referring for a fee because of that individual's national origin or citizenship status. It is illegal to discriminate against work eligible individuals. Employers **CANNOT** specify which document(s) they will accept from an employee. The refusal to hire an individual because of a future expiration date may also constitute illegal discrimination.

Section 1 - Employee.
All employees, citizens and noncitizens, hired after November 6, 1986, must complete Section 1 of this form at the time of hire, which is the actual beginning of employment. **The employer is responsible for ensuring that Section 1 is timely and properly completed.**

Preparer/Translator Certification. The Preparer/Translator Certification must be completed if Section 1 is prepared by a person other than the employee. A preparer/translator may be used only when the employee is unable to complete Section 1 on his/her own. However, the employee must still sign Section 1.

Section 2 - Employer.
For the purpose of completing this form, the term "employer" includes those recruiters and referrers for a fee who are agricultural associations, agricultural employers or farm labor contractors.

Employers must complete Section 2 by examining evidence of identity and employment eligibility within three (3) business days of the date employment begins. If employees are authorized to work, but are unable to present the required document(s) within three business days, they must present a receipt for the application of the document(s) within three business days and the actual document(s) within ninety (90) days. However, if employers hire individuals for a duration of less than three business days, Section 2 must be completed at the time employment begins. **Employers must record:** 1) document title; 2) issuing authority; 3) document number, 4) expiration date, if any; and 5) the date employment begins. Employers must sign and date the certification. Employees must present original documents. Employers may, but are not required to, photocopy the document(s) presented. These photocopies may only be used for the verification process and must be retained with the I-9. **However, employers are still responsible for completing the I-9.**

Section 3 - Updating and Reverification.
Employers must complete Section 3 when updating and/or reverifying the I-9. Employers must reverify employment eligibility of their employees on or before the expiration date recorded in Section 1. Employers **CANNOT** specify which document(s) they will accept from an employee.

- If an employee's name has changed at the time this form is being updated/reverified, complete Block A.

- If an employee is rehired within three (3) years of the date this form was originally completed and the employee is still eligible to be employed on the same basis as previously indicated on this form (updating), complete Block B and the signature block.

- If an employee is rehired within three (3) years of the date this form was originally completed and the employee's work authorization has expired **or** if a current employee's work authorization is about to expire (reverification), complete Block B and:
  - examine any document that reflects that the employee is authorized to work in the U.S. (see List A or C),
  - record the document title, document number and expiration date (if any) in Block C, and complete the signature block.

Photocopying and Retaining Form I-9. A blank I-9 may be reproduced, provided both sides are copied. The Instructions must be available to all employees completing this form. Employers must retain completed I-9s for three (3) years after the date of hire or one (1) year after the date employment ends, whichever is later.

For more detailed information, you may refer to the INS Handbook for Employers, (Form M-274). You may obtain the handbook at your local INS office.

Privacy Act Notice. The authority for collecting this information is the Immigration Reform and Control Act of 1986, Pub. L. 99-603 (8 USC 1324a).

This information is for employers to verify the eligibility of individuals for employment to preclude the unlawful hiring, or recruiting or referring for a fee, of aliens who are not authorized to work in the United States.

This information will be used by employers as a record of their basis for determining eligibility of an employee to work in the United States. The form will be kept by the employer and made available for inspection by officials of the U.S. Immigration and Naturalization Service, the Department of Labor and the Office of Special Counsel for Immigration Related Unfair Employment Practices.

Submission of the information required in this form is voluntary. However, an individual may not begin employment unless this form is completed, since employers are subject to civil or criminal penalties if they do not comply with the Immigration Reform and Control Act of 1986.

Reporting Burden. We try to create forms and instructions that are accurate, can be easily understood and which impose the least possible burden on you to provide us with information. Often this is difficult because some immigration laws are very complex. Accordingly, the reporting burden for this collection of information is computed as follows: 1) learning about this form, 5 minutes; 2) completing the form, 5 minutes; and 3) assembling and filing (recordkeeping) the form, 5 minutes, for an average of 15 minutes per response. If you have comments regarding the accuracy of this burden estimate, or suggestions for making this form simpler, you can write to the Immigration and Naturalization Service, HQPDI, 425 I Street, N.W., Room 4307r, Washington, DC 20536. OMB No. 1115-0136.

EMPLOYERS MUST RETAIN COMPLETED FORM I-9
PLEASE DO NOT MAIL COMPLETED FORM I-9 TO INS

LISTS OF ACCEPTABLE DOCUMENTS

LIST A
Documents that Establish Both Identity and Employment Eligibility

1. U.S. Passport (unexpired or expired)

2. Certificate of U.S. Citizenship *(INS Form N-560 or N-561)*

3. Certificate of Naturalization *(INS Form N-550 or N-570)*

4. Unexpired foreign passport, with *I-551 stamp or* attached INS Form I-94 indicating unexpired employment authorization

5. Alien Registration Receipt Card with photograph *(INS Form I-151 or I-551)*

6. Unexpired Temporary Card *(INS Form I-688)*

7. Unexpired Employment Authorization Card *(INS Form I-688A)*

8. Unexpired Reentry Permit *(INS Form I-327)*

9. Unexpired Refugee Travel Document *(INS Form I-571)*

10. Unexpired Employment Authorization Document issued by the INS which contains a photograph *(INS Form I-688B)*

OR

LIST B
Documents that Establish Identity

1. Driver's license or ID card issued by a state or outlying possession of the United States provided it contains a photograph or information such as name, date of birth, sex, height, eye color and address

2. ID card issued by federal, state or local government agencies or entities, provided it contains a photograph or information such as name, date of birth, sex, height, eye color and address

3. School ID card with a photograph

4. Voter's registration card

5. U.S. Military card or draft record

6. Military dependent's ID card

7. U.S. Coast Guard Merchant Mariner Card

8. Native American tribal document

9. Driver's license issued by a Canadian government authority

For persons under age 18 who are unable to present a document listed above:

10. School record or report card

11. Clinic, doctor or hospital record

12. Day-care or nursery school record

AND

LIST C
Documents that Establish Employment Eligibility

1. U.S. social security card issued by the Social Security Administration *(other than a card stating it is not valid for employment)*

2. Certification of Birth Abroad issued by the Department of State *(Form FS-545 or Form DS-1350)*

3. Original or certified copy of a birth certificate issued by a state, county, municipal authority or outlying possession of the United States bearing an official seal

4. Native American tribal document

5. U.S. Citizen ID Card *(INS Form I-197)*

6. ID Card for use of Resident Citizen in the United States *(INS Form I-179)*

7. Unexpired employment authorization document issued by the INS *(other then those listed under List A)*

Illustrations of many of these documents appear in Part 8 of the Handbook for Employers (M-274)

This page intentionally left blank.

Form **SS-4**
(Rev. December 2001)
Department of the Treasury
Internal Revenue Service

Application for Employer Identification Number

(For use by employers, corporations, partnerships, trusts, estates, churches, government agencies, Indian tribal entities, certain individuals, and others.)

▶ See separate instructions for each line. ▶ Keep a copy for your records.

form 5 ♦ 205

EIN

OMB No. 1545-0003

Type or print clearly.

1	Legal name of entity (or individual) for whom the EIN is being requested
2 Trade name of business (if different from name on line 1)	**3** Executor, trustee, "care of" name
4a Mailing address (room, apt., suite no. and street, or P.O. box)	**5a** Street address (if different) (Do not enter a P.O. box.)
4b City, state, and ZIP code	**5b** City, state, and ZIP code
6 County and state where principal business is located	
7a Name of principal officer, general partner, grantor, owner, or trustor	**7b** SSN, ITIN, or EIN

8a Type of entity (check only one box)
☐ Sole proprietor (SSN) _____
☐ Partnership
☐ Corporation (enter form number to be filed) ▶ _____
☐ Personal service corp.
☐ Church or church-controlled organization
☐ Other nonprofit organization (specify) ▶ _____
☐ Other (specify) ▶

☐ Estate (SSN of decedent) _____
☐ Plan administrator (SSN) _____
☐ Trust (SSN of grantor) _____
☐ National Guard   ☐ State/local government
☐ Farmers' cooperative   ☐ Federal government/military
☐ REMIC   ☐ Indian tribal governments/enterprises
Group Exemption Number (GEN) ▶ _____

8b If a corporation, name the state or foreign country (if applicable) where incorporated

State	Foreign country

9 Reason for applying (check only one box)
☐ Started new business (specify type) ▶ _____
☐ Hired employees (Check the box and see line 12.)
☐ Compliance with IRS withholding regulations
☐ Other (specify) ▶

☐ Banking purpose (specify purpose) ▶ _____
☐ Changed type of organization (specify new type) ▶ _____
☐ Purchased going business
☐ Created a trust (specify type) ▶ _____
☐ Created a pension plan (specify type) ▶ _____

10 Date business started or acquired (month, day, year)	**11** Closing month of accounting year

12 First date wages or annuities were paid or will be paid (month, day, year). **Note:** *If applicant is a withholding agent, enter date income will first be paid to nonresident alien. (month, day, year)* . . . . ▶

13 Highest number of employees expected in the next 12 months. **Note:** *If the applicant does not expect to have any employees during the period, enter "-0-."* . . . . ▶

Agricultural	Household	Other

14 Check **one** box that best describes the principal activity of your business.
☐ Construction   ☐ Rental & leasing   ☐ Transportation & warehousing   ☐ Health care & social assistance   ☐ Wholesale–agent/broker
☐ Real estate   ☐ Manufacturing   ☐ Finance & insurance   ☐ Accommodation & food service   ☐ Wholesale–other   ☐ Retail
☐ Other (specify)

15 Indicate principal line of merchandise sold; specific construction work done; products produced; or services provided.

16a Has the applicant ever applied for an employer identification number for this or any other business? . . . . . ☐ Yes ☐ No
Note: *If "Yes," please complete lines 16b and 16c.*

16b If you checked "Yes" on line 16a, give applicant's legal name and trade name shown on prior application if different from line 1 or 2 above.
Legal name ▶   Trade name ▶

16c Approximate date when, and city and state where, the application was filed. Enter previous employer identification number if known.

Approximate date when filed (mo., day, year)	City and state where filed	Previous EIN

Third Party Designee

Complete this section **only** if you want to authorize the named individual to receive the entity's EIN and answer questions about the completion of this form.

Designee's name	Designee's telephone number (include area code) ( )
Address and ZIP code	Designee's fax number (include area code) ( )

Under penalties of perjury, I declare that I have examined this application, and to the best of my knowledge and belief, it is true, correct, and complete.

Name and title (type or print clearly) ▶

Applicant's telephone number (include area code) ( )

Signature ▶   Date ▶

Applicant's fax number (include area code) ( )

For Privacy Act and Paperwork Reduction Act Notice, see separate instructions.   Cat. No. 16055N   Form **SS-4** (Rev. 12-2001)

Do I Need an EIN?

File Form SS-4 if the applicant entity does not already have an EIN but is required to show an EIN on any return, statement, or other document.[1] **See also the separate instructions for each line on Form SS-4.**

IF the applicant...	AND...	THEN...
Started a new business	Does not currently have (nor expect to have) employees	Complete lines 1, 2, 4a-6, 8a, and 9-16c.
Hired (or will hire) employees, including household employees	Does not already have an EIN	Complete lines 1, 2, 4a-6, 7a-b (if applicable), 8a, 8b (if applicable), and 9-16c.
Opened a bank account	Needs an EIN for banking purposes only	Complete lines 1-5b, 7a-b (if applicable), 8a, 9, and 16a-c.
Changed type of organization	Either the legal character of the organization or its ownership changed (e.g., you incorporate a sole proprietorship or form a partnership)[2]	Complete lines 1-16c (as applicable).
Purchased a going business[3]	Does not already have an EIN	Complete lines 1-16c (as applicable).
Created a trust	The trust is other than a grantor trust or an IRA trust[4]	Complete lines 1-16c (as applicable).
Created a pension plan as a plan administrator[5]	Needs an EIN for reporting purposes	Complete lines 1, 2, 4a-6, 8a, 9, and 16a-c.
Is a foreign person needing an EIN to comply with IRS withholding regulations	Needs an EIN to complete a Form W-8 (other than Form W-8ECI), avoid withholding on portfolio assets, or claim tax treaty benefits[6]	Complete lines 1-5b, 7a-b (SSN or ITIN optional), 8a-9, and 16a-c.
Is administering an estate	Needs an EIN to report estate income on Form 1041	Complete lines 1, 3, 4a-b, 8a, 9, and 16a-c.
Is a withholding agent for taxes on non-wage income paid to an alien (i.e., individual, corporation, or partnership, etc.)	Is an agent, broker, fiduciary, manager, tenant, or spouse who is required to file **Form 1042,** Annual Withholding Tax Return for U.S. Source Income of Foreign Persons	Complete lines 1, 2, 3 (if applicable), 4a-5b, 7a-b (if applicable), 8a, 9, and 16a-c.
Is a state or local agency	Serves as a tax reporting agent for public assistance recipients under Rev. Proc. 80-4, 1980-1 C.B. 581[7]	Complete lines 1, 2, 4a-5b, 8a, 9, and 16a-c.
Is a single-member LLC	Needs an EIN to file **Form 8832,** Classification Election, for filing employment tax returns, **or** for state reporting purposes[8]	Complete lines 1-16c (as applicable).
Is an S corporation	Needs an EIN to file **Form 2553,** Election by a Small Business Corporation[9]	Complete lines 1-16c (as applicable).

[1] For example, a sole proprietorship or self-employed farmer who establishes a qualified retirement plan, or is required to file excise, employment, alcohol, tobacco, or firearms returns, must have an EIN. **A partnership, corporation, REMIC (real estate mortgage investment conduit), nonprofit organization (church, club, etc.), or farmers' cooperative must use an EIN for any tax-related purpose even if the entity does not have employees.**

[2] However, **do not** apply for a new EIN if the existing entity only **(a)** changed its business name, **(b)** elected on Form 8832 to change the way it is taxed (or is covered by the default rules), or **(c)** terminated its partnership status because at least 50% of the total interests in partnership capital and profits were sold or exchanged within a 12-month period. (The EIN of the terminated partnership should continue to be used. See Regulations section 301.6109-1(d)(2)(iii).)

[3] Do not use the EIN of the prior business unless you became the "owner" of a corporation by acquiring its stock.

[4] However, IRA trusts that are required to file **Form 990-T,** Exempt Organization Business Income Tax Return, must have an EIN.

[5] A plan administrator is the person or group of persons specified as the administrator by the instrument under which the plan is operated.

[6] Entities applying to be a Qualified Intermediary (QI) need a QI-EIN even if they already have an EIN. **See Rev. Proc. 2000-12.**

[7] See also *Household employer* on page 4. (**Note:** State or local agencies may need an EIN for other reasons, e.g., hired employees.)

[8] Most LLCs **do not** need to file Form 8832. See **Limited liability company (LLC)** on page 4 for details on completing Form SS-4 for an LLC.

[9] An existing corporation that is electing or revoking S corporation status should use its previously-assigned EIN.

Instructions for Form SS-4
(Rev. September 2003)

For use with Form SS-4 (Rev. December 2001)
Application for Employer Identification Number.
Section references are to the Internal Revenue Code unless otherwise noted.

**Department of the Treasury
Internal Revenue Service**

General Instructions

Use these instructions to complete **Form SS-4,** Application for Employer Identification Number. Also see **Do I Need an EIN?** on page 2 of Form SS-4.

Purpose of Form

Use Form SS-4 to apply for an employer identification number (EIN). An EIN is a nine-digit number (for example, 12-3456789) assigned to sole proprietors, corporations, partnerships, estates, trusts, and other entities for tax filing and reporting purposes. The information you provide on this form will establish your business tax account.

*An EIN is for use in connection with your business activities only. Do **not** use your EIN in place of your social security number (SSN).*

Items To Note

Apply online. You can now apply for and receive an EIN online using the internet. See **How To Apply** below.

File only one Form SS-4. Generally, a sole proprietor should file only one Form SS-4 and needs only one EIN, regardless of the number of businesses operated as a sole proprietorship or trade names under which a business operates. However, if the proprietorship incorporates or enters into a partnership, a new EIN is required. Also, each corporation in an affiliated group must have its own EIN.

EIN applied for, but not received. If you do not have an EIN by the time a return is due, write "Applied For" and the date you applied in the space shown for the number. **Do not** show your SSN as an EIN on returns.

If you do not have an EIN by the time a tax deposit is due, send your payment to the Internal Revenue Service Center for your filing area as shown in the instructions for the form that you are filing. Make your check or money order payable to the "United States Treasury" and show your name (as shown on Form SS-4), address, type of tax, period covered, and date you applied for an EIN.

How To Apply

You can apply for an EIN online, by telephone, by fax, or by mail depending on how soon you need to use the EIN. Use only one method for each entity so you do not receive more than one EIN for an entity.

Online. You can receive your EIN by internet and use it immediately to file a return or make a payment. Go to the IRS website at **www.irs.gov/businesses** and click on **Employer ID Numbers** under **topics.**

Telephone. You can receive your EIN by telephone and use it immediately to file a return or make a payment. Call the IRS at **1-800-829-4933.** (International applicants must call 215-516-6999.) The hours of operation are 7:00 a.m. to 10:00 p.m. The person making the call must be authorized to sign the form or be an authorized designee. See **Signature** and **Third Party Designee** on page 6. Also see the **TIP** below.

If you are applying by telephone, it will be helpful to complete Form SS-4 before contacting the IRS. An IRS representative will use the information from the Form SS-4 to establish your account and assign you an EIN. Write the number you are given on the upper right corner of the form and sign and date it. Keep this copy for your records.

If requested by an IRS representative, mail or fax (facsimile) the signed Form SS-4 (including any Third Party Designee authorization) within 24 hours to the IRS address provided by the IRS representative.

*Taxpayer representatives can apply for an EIN on behalf of their client and request that the EIN be faxed to their **client** on the same day.*
Note: *By using this procedure, you are authorizing the IRS to fax the EIN without a cover sheet.*

Fax. Under the Fax-TIN program, you can receive your EIN by fax within 4 business days. Complete and fax Form SS-4 to the IRS using the Fax-TIN number listed on page 2 for your state. A long-distance charge to callers outside of the local calling area will apply. Fax-TIN numbers can only be used to apply for an EIN. **The numbers may change without notice.** Fax-TIN is available 24 hours a day, 7 days a week.

Be sure to provide your fax number so the IRS can fax the EIN back to you. **Note:** By using this procedure, you are authorizing the IRS to fax the EIN without a cover sheet.

Mail. Complete Form SS-4 at least 4 to 5 weeks before you will need an EIN. Sign and date the application and mail it to the service center address for your state. You will receive your EIN in the mail in approximately 4 weeks. See also **Third Party Designee** on page 6.

Call 1-800-829-4933 to verify a number or to ask about the status of an application by mail.

Cat. No. 62736F

Where To Fax or File

If your principal business, office or agency, or legal residence in the case of an individual, is located in:	Call the Fax-TIN number shown or file with the "Internal Revenue Service Center" at:
Connecticut, Delaware, District of Columbia, Florida, Georgia, Maine, Maryland, Massachusetts, New Hampshire, New Jersey, New York, North Carolina, Ohio, Pennsylvania, Rhode Island, South Carolina, Vermont, Virginia, West Virginia	Attn: EIN Operation P. O. Box 9003 Holtsville, NY 11742-9003 Fax-TIN 631-447-8960
Illinois, Indiana, Kentucky, Michigan	Attn: EIN Operation Cincinnati, OH 45999 Fax-TIN 859-669-5760
Alabama, Alaska, Arizona, Arkansas, California, Colorado, Hawaii, Idaho, Iowa, Kansas, Louisiana, Minnesota, Mississippi, Missouri, Montana, Nebraska, Nevada, New Mexico, North Dakota, Oklahoma, Oregon, Puerto Rico, South Dakota, Tennessee, Texas, Utah, Washington, Wisconsin, Wyoming	Attn: EIN Operation Philadelphia, PA 19255 Fax-TIN 215-516-3990
If you have no legal residence, principal place of business, or principal office or agency in any state:	Attn: EIN Operation Philadelphia, PA 19255 Telephone 215-516-6999 Fax-TIN 215-516-3990

How To Get Forms and Publications

Phone. You can order forms, instructions, and publications by phone 24 hours a day, 7 days a week. Call 1-800-TAX-FORM (1-800-829-3676). You should receive your order or notification of its status within 10 workdays.

Personal computer. With your personal computer and modem, you can get the forms and information you need using the IRS website at **www.irs.gov** or File Transfer Protocol at **ftp.irs.gov**.

CD-ROM. For small businesses, return preparers, or others who may frequently need tax forms or publications, a CD-ROM containing over 2,000 tax products (including many prior year forms) can be purchased from the National Technical Information Service (NTIS).

To order **Pub. 1796,** Federal Tax Products on CD-ROM, call **1-877-CDFORMS** (1-877-233-6767) toll free or connect to **www.irs.gov/cdorders**.

Tax Help for Your Business

IRS-sponsored Small Business Workshops provide information about your Federal and state tax obligations. For information about workshops in your area, call 1-800-829-4933.

Related Forms and Publications

The following **forms** and **instructions** may be useful to filers of Form SS-4:

- **Form 990-T,** Exempt Organization Business Income Tax Return
- **Instructions for Form 990-T**
- **Schedule C (Form 1040),** Profit or Loss From Business
- **Schedule F (Form 1040),** Profit or Loss From Farming
- **Instructions for Form 1041 and Schedules A, B, D, G, I, J, and K-1,** U.S. Income Tax Return for Estates and Trusts
- **Form 1042,** Annual Withholding Tax Return for U.S. Source Income of Foreign Persons
- **Instructions for Form 1065,** U.S. Return of Partnership Income
- **Instructions for Form 1066,** U.S. Real Estate Mortgage Investment Conduit (REMIC) Income Tax Return
- **Instructions for Forms 1120 and 1120-A**
- **Form 2553,** Election by a Small Business Corporation
- **Form 2848,** Power of Attorney and Declaration of Representative
- **Form 8821,** Tax Information Authorization
- **Form 8832,** Entity Classification Election

For more **information** about filing Form SS-4 and related issues, see:

- **Circular A,** Agricultural Employer's Tax Guide (Pub. 51)
- **Circular E,** Employer's Tax Guide (Pub. 15)
- **Pub. 538,** Accounting Periods and Methods
- **Pub. 542,** Corporations
- **Pub. 557,** Exempt Status for Your Organization
- **Pub. 583,** Starting a Business and Keeping Records
- **Pub. 966,** Electronic Choices for Paying ALL Your Federal Taxes
- **Pub. 1635,** Understanding Your EIN
- **Package 1023,** Application for Recognition of Exemption Under Section 501(c)(3) of the Internal Revenue Code
- **Package 1024,** Application for Recognition of Exemption Under Section 501(a)

Specific Instructions

Print or type all entries on Form SS-4. Follow the instructions for each line to expedite processing and to avoid unnecessary IRS requests for additional information. Enter "N/A" (nonapplicable) on the lines that do not apply.

Line 1—Legal name of entity (or individual) for whom the EIN is being requested. Enter the legal name of the entity (or individual) applying for the EIN exactly as it appears on the social security card, charter, or other applicable legal document.

Individuals. Enter your first name, middle initial, and last name. If you are a sole proprietor, enter your individual name, not your business name. Enter your business name on line 2. Do not use abbreviations or nicknames on line 1.

Trusts. Enter the name of the trust.

Estate of a decedent. Enter the name of the estate.

Partnerships. Enter the legal name of the partnership as it appears in the partnership agreement.

Corporations. Enter the corporate name as it appears in the corporation charter or other legal document creating it.

Plan administrators. Enter the name of the plan administrator. A plan administrator who already has an EIN should use that number.

Line 2—Trade name of business. Enter the trade name of the business if different from the legal name. The trade name is the "doing business as " (DBA) name.

*Use the full legal name shown on line 1 on all tax returns filed for the entity. (However, if you enter a trade name on line 2 and choose to use the trade name instead of the legal name, enter the trade name on **all returns** you file.) To prevent processing delays and errors, **always** use the legal name only (or the trade name only) on **all** tax returns.*

Line 3—Executor, trustee, "care of" name. Trusts enter the name of the trustee. Estates enter the name of the executor, administrator, or other fiduciary. If the entity applying has a designated person to receive tax information, enter that person's name as the "care of" person. Enter the individual's first name, middle initial, and last name.

Lines 4a-b—Mailing address. Enter the mailing address for the entity's correspondence. If line 3 is completed, enter the address for the executor, trustee or "care of" person. Generally, this address will be used on all tax returns.

*File **Form 8822**, Change of Address, to report any subsequent changes to the entity's mailing address.*

Lines 5a-b—Street address. Provide the entity's physical address **only** if different from its mailing address shown in lines 4a-b. **Do not** enter a P.O. box number here.

Line 6—County and state where principal business is located. Enter the entity's primary **physical** location.

Lines 7a-b—Name of principal officer, general partner, grantor, owner, or trustor. Enter the first name, middle initial, last name, and SSN of **(a)** the principal officer if the business is a corporation, **(b)** a general partner if a partnership, **(c)** the owner of an entity that is disregarded as separate from its owner (disregarded entities owned by a corporation enter the corporation's name and EIN), or **(d)** a grantor, owner, or trustor if a trust.

If the person in question is an **alien individual** with a previously assigned individual taxpayer identification number (ITIN), enter the ITIN in the space provided and submit a copy of an official identifying document. If necessary, complete **Form W-7,** Application for IRS Individual Taxpayer Identification Number, to obtain an ITIN.

You are **required** to enter an SSN, ITIN, or EIN unless the only reason you are applying for an EIN is to make an entity classification election (see Regulations sections 301.7701-1 through 301.7701-3) and you are a nonresident alien with no effectively connected income from sources within the United States.

Line 8a—Type of entity. Check the box that best describes the type of entity applying for the EIN. If you are an alien individual with an ITIN previously assigned to you, enter the ITIN in place of a requested SSN.

*This is not an election for a tax classification of an entity. See **Limited liability company (LLC)** on page 4.*

Other. If not specifically listed, check the "Other" box, enter the type of entity and the type of return, if any, that will be filed (for example, "Common Trust Fund, Form 1065" or "Created a Pension Plan"). Do not enter "N/A." If you are an alien individual applying for an EIN, see the **Lines 7a-b** instructions above.

• **Household employer.** If you are an individual, check the "Other" box and enter "Household Employer" and your SSN. If you are a state or local agency serving as a tax reporting agent for public assistance recipients who become household employers, check the "Other" box and enter "Household Employer Agent." If you are a trust that qualifies as a household employer, you do not need a separate EIN for reporting tax information relating to household employees; use the EIN of the trust.

• **QSub.** For a qualified subchapter S subsidiary (QSub) check the "Other" box and specify "QSub."

• **Withholding agent.** If you are a withholding agent required to file Form 1042, check the "Other" box and enter "Withholding Agent."

Sole proprietor. Check this box if you file Schedule C, C-EZ, or F (Form 1040) and have a qualified plan, or are required to file excise, employment, alcohol, tobacco, or firearms returns, or are a payer of gambling winnings. Enter your SSN (or ITIN) in the space provided. If you are a nonresident alien with no effectively connected income from sources within the United States, you do not need to enter an SSN or ITIN.

Corporation. This box is for any corporation **other than a personal service corporation.** If you check this box, enter the income tax form number to be filed by the entity in the space provided.

*If you entered "1120S" after the "Corporation" checkbox, the corporation **must** file Form 2553 **no later than the 15th day of the 3rd month of the tax year the election is to take effect.***

Until Form 2553 has been received and approved, you will be considered a Form 1120 filer. See the Instructions for Form 2553.

Personal service corp. Check this box if the entity is a personal service corporation. An entity is a personal service corporation for a tax year only if:

- The principal activity of the entity during the testing period (prior tax year) for the tax year is the performance of personal services substantially by employee-owners, and
- The employee-owners own at least 10% of the fair market value of the outstanding stock in the entity on the last day of the testing period.

Personal services include performance of services in such fields as health, law, accounting, or consulting. For more information about personal service corporations, see the Instructions for Forms 1120 and 1120-A and Pub. 542.

Other nonprofit organization. Check this box if the nonprofit organization is other than a church or church-controlled organization and specify the type of nonprofit organization (for example, an educational organization).

*If the organization also seeks tax-exempt status, you **must** file either Package 1023 or Package 1024. See Pub. 557 for more information.*

If the organization is covered by a group exemption letter, enter the four-digit **group exemption number (GEN).** (Do not confuse the GEN with the nine-digit EIN.) If you do not know the GEN, contact the parent organization. Get Pub. 557 for more information about group exemption numbers.

Plan administrator. If the plan administrator is an individual, enter the plan administrator's SSN in the space provided.

REMIC. Check this box if the entity has elected to be treated as a real estate mortgage investment conduit (REMIC). See the Instructions for Form 1066 for more information.

Limited liability company (LLC). An LLC is an entity organized under the laws of a state or foreign country as a limited liability company. For Federal tax purposes, an LLC may be treated as a partnership or corporation or be disregarded as an entity separate from its owner.

By **default,** a domestic LLC with only one member is **disregarded** as an entity separate from its owner and must include all of its income and expenses on the owner's tax return (e.g., **Schedule C (Form 1040)**). Also by default, a domestic LLC with two or more members is treated as a partnership. A domestic LLC may file Form 8832 to avoid either default classification and elect to be classified as an association taxable as a corporation. For more information on entity classifications (including the rules for foreign entities), see the instructions for Form 8832.

*Do not file Form 8832 if the LLC accepts the default classifications above. **However, if the LLC will be electing S Corporation status, it must timely file both Form 8832 and Form 2553.***

Complete Form SS-4 for LLCs as follows:
- A single-member domestic LLC that accepts the default classification (above) does not need an EIN and generally should not file Form SS-4. Generally, the LLC should use the name and EIN of its **owner** for all Federal tax purposes. However, the reporting and payment of employment taxes for employees of the LLC may be made using the name and EIN of **either** the owner or the LLC as explained in Notice 99-6. You can find Notice 99-6 on page 12 of Internal Revenue Bulletin 1999-3 at **www.irs.gov/pub/irs-irbs/irb99-03.pdf. (Note:** If the LLC applicant indicates in box 13 that it has employees or expects to have employees, the owner (whether an individual or other entity) of a single-member domestic LLC will also be assigned its own EIN (if it does not already have one) even if the LLC will be filing the employment tax returns.)
- A single-member, domestic LLC that accepts the default classification (above) and wants an EIN for filing employment tax returns (see above) or non-Federal purposes, such as a state requirement, must check the "Other" box and write "Disregarded Entity" or, when applicable, "Disregarded Entity—Sole Proprietorship" in the space provided.
- A multi-member, domestic LLC that accepts the default classification (above) must check the "Partnership" box.
- A domestic LLC that will be filing Form 8832 to elect corporate status must check the "Corporation" box and write in "Single-Member" or "Multi-Member" immediately below the "form number" entry line.

Line 9—Reason for applying. Check only **one** box. Do not enter "N/A."

Started new business. Check this box if you are starting a new business that requires an EIN. If you check this box, enter the type of business being started. **Do not** apply if you already have an EIN and are only adding another place of business.

Hired employees. Check this box if the existing business is requesting an EIN because it has hired or is hiring employees and is therefore required to file employment tax returns. **Do not** apply if you already have an EIN and are only hiring employees. For information on employment taxes (e.g., for family members), see Circular E.

You may be required to make electronic deposits of all depository taxes (such as employment tax, excise tax, and corporate income tax) using the Electronic Federal Tax Payment System (EFTPS). See section 11, Depositing Taxes, of Circular E and Pub. 966.

Created a pension plan. Check this box if you have created a pension plan and need an EIN for reporting purposes. Also, enter the type of plan in the space provided.

Check this box if you are applying for a trust EIN when a new pension plan is established. In addition, check the "Other" box in line 8a and write "Created a Pension Plan" in the space provided.

Banking purpose. Check this box if you are requesting an EIN for banking purposes only, and enter the banking purpose (for example, a bowling league for depositing dues or an investment club for dividend and interest reporting).

Changed type of organization. Check this box if the business is changing its type of organization. For example, the business was a sole proprietorship and has been incorporated or has become a partnership. If you check this box, specify in the space provided (including available space immediately below) the type of change made. For example, "From Sole Proprietorship to Partnership."

Purchased going business. Check this box if you purchased an existing business. **Do not** use the former owner's EIN unless you became the "owner" of a corporation by acquiring its stock.

Created a trust. Check this box if you created a trust, and enter the type of trust created. For example, indicate if the trust is a nonexempt charitable trust or a split-interest trust.

Exception. Do **not** file this form for certain grantor-type trusts. The trustee does not need an EIN for the trust if the trustee furnishes the name and TIN of the grantor/owner and the address of the trust to all payors. See the Instructions for Form 1041 for more information.

Do not check this box if you are applying for a trust EIN when a new pension plan is established. Check "Created a pension plan."

Other. Check this box if you are requesting an EIN for any other reason; and enter the reason. For example, a newly-formed state government entity should enter "Newly-Formed State Government Entity" in the space provided.

Line 10—Date business started or acquired. If you are starting a new business, enter the starting date of the business. If the business you acquired is already operating, enter the date you acquired the business. If you are changing the form of ownership of your business, enter the date the new ownership entity began. Trusts should enter the date the trust was legally created. Estates should enter the date of death of the decedent whose name appears on line 1 or the date when the estate was legally funded.

Line 11—Closing month of accounting year. Enter the last month of your accounting year or tax year. An accounting or tax year is usually 12 consecutive months, either a calendar year or a fiscal year (including a period of 52 or 53 weeks). A calendar year is 12 consecutive months ending on December 31. A fiscal year is either 12 consecutive months ending on the last day of any month other than December or a 52-53 week year. For more information on accounting periods, see Pub. 538.

Individuals. Your tax year generally will be a calendar year.

Partnerships. Partnerships must adopt one of the following tax years:
- The tax year of the majority of its partners,
- The tax year common to all of its principal partners,
- The tax year that results in the least aggregate deferral of income, or
- In certain cases, some other tax year.

See the Instructions for Form 1065 for more information.

REMICs. REMICs must have a calendar year as their tax year.

Personal service corporations. A personal service corporation generally must adopt a calendar year unless:
- It can establish a business purpose for having a different tax year, or
- It elects under section 444 to have a tax year other than a calendar year.

Trusts. Generally, a trust must adopt a calendar year except for the following:
- Tax-exempt trusts,
- Charitable trusts, and
- Grantor-owned trusts.

Line 12—First date wages or annuities were paid or will be paid. If the business has or will have employees, enter the date on which the business began or will begin to pay wages. If the business does not plan to have employees, enter "N/A."

Withholding agent. Enter the date you began or will begin to pay income (including annuities) to a nonresident alien. This also applies to individuals who are required to file Form 1042 to report alimony paid to a nonresident alien.

Line 13—Highest number of employees expected in the next 12 months. Complete each box by entering the number (including zero ("-0-")) of "Agricultural," "Household," or "Other" employees expected by the applicant in the next 12 months. For a definition of agricultural labor (farmwork), see Circular A.

Lines 14 and 15. Check the **one** box in line 14 that best describes the principal activity of the applicant's business. Check the "Other" box (and specify the applicant's principal activity) if none of the listed boxes applies.

Use line 15 to describe the applicant's principal line of business in more detail. For example, if you checked the "Construction" box in line 14, enter additional detail such as "General contractor for residential buildings" in line 15.

Construction. Check this box if the applicant is engaged in erecting buildings or other structures, (e.g., streets, highways, bridges, tunnels). The term "Construction" also includes special trade contractors, (e.g., plumbing, HVAC, electrical, carpentry, concrete, excavation, etc. contractors).

Real estate. Check this box if the applicant is engaged in renting or leasing real estate to others; managing, selling, buying or renting real estate for others; or providing related real estate services (e.g., appraisal services).

Rental and leasing. Check this box if the applicant is engaged in providing tangible goods such as autos, computers, consumer goods, or industrial machinery and equipment to customers in return for a periodic rental or lease payment.

Manufacturing. Check this box if the applicant is engaged in the mechanical, physical, or chemical transformation of materials, substances, or components into new products. The assembling of component parts of manufactured products is also considered to be manufacturing.

Transportation & warehousing. Check this box if the applicant provides transportation of passengers or cargo; warehousing or storage of goods; scenic or sight-seeing transportation; or support activities related to these modes of transportation.

Finance & insurance. Check this box if the applicant is engaged in transactions involving the creation, liquidation, or change of ownership of financial assets and/or facilitating such financial transactions; underwriting annuities/insurance policies; facilitating such underwriting by selling insurance policies; or by providing other insurance or employee-benefit related services.

Health care and social assistance. Check this box if the applicant is engaged in providing physical, medical, or psychiatric care using licensed health care professionals or providing social assistance activities such as youth centers, adoption agencies, individual/family services, temporary shelters, etc.

Accommodation & food services. Check this box if the applicant is engaged in providing customers with lodging, meal preparation, snacks, or beverages for immediate consumption.

Wholesale–agent/broker. Check this box if the applicant is engaged in arranging for the purchase or sale of goods owned by others or purchasing goods on a commission basis for goods traded in the wholesale market, usually between businesses.

Wholesale–other. Check this box if the applicant is engaged in selling goods in the wholesale market generally to other businesses for resale on their own account.

Retail. Check this box if the applicant is engaged in selling merchandise to the general public from a fixed store; by direct, mail-order, or electronic sales; or by using vending machines.

Other. Check this box if the applicant is engaged in an activity not described above. Describe the applicant's principal business activity in the space provided.

Lines 16a–c. Check the applicable box in line 16a to indicate whether or not the entity (or individual) applying for an EIN was issued one previously. Complete lines 16b and 16c **only** if the "Yes" box in line 16a is checked. If the applicant previously applied for **more than one** EIN, write "See Attached" in the empty space in line 16a and attach a separate sheet providing the line 16b and 16c information for each EIN previously requested.

Third Party Designee. Complete this section **only** if you want to authorize the named individual to receive the entity's EIN and answer questions about the completion of Form SS-4. The designee's authority terminates at the time the EIN is assigned and released to the designee. **You must complete the signature area for the authorization to be valid.**

Signature. When required, the application must be signed by **(a)** the individual, if the applicant is an individual, **(b)** the president, vice president, or other principal officer, if the applicant is a corporation, **(c)** a responsible and duly authorized member or officer having knowledge of its affairs, if the applicant is a partnership, government entity, or other unincorporated organization, or **(d)** the fiduciary, if the applicant is a trust or an estate. Foreign applicants may have any duly-authorized person, (e.g., division manager), sign Form SS-4.

Privacy Act and Paperwork Reduction Act Notice. We ask for the information on this form to carry out the Internal Revenue laws of the United States. We need it to comply with section 6109 and the regulations thereunder which generally require the inclusion of an employer identification number (EIN) on certain returns, statements, or other documents filed with the Internal Revenue Service. If your entity is required to obtain an EIN, you are required to provide all of the information requested on this form. Information on this form may be used to determine which Federal tax returns you are required to file and to provide you with related forms and publications.

We disclose this form to the Social Security Administration for their use in determining compliance with applicable laws. We may give this information to the Department of Justice for use in civil and criminal litigation, and to the cities, states, and the District of Columbia for use in administering their tax laws. We may also disclose this information to Federal and state agencies to enforce Federal nontax criminal laws and to combat terrorism.

We will be unable to issue an EIN to you unless you provide all of the requested information which applies to your entity. Providing false information could subject you to penalties.

You are not required to provide the information requested on a form that is subject to the Paperwork Reduction Act unless the form displays a valid OMB control number. Books or records relating to a form or its instructions must be retained as long as their contents may become material in the administration of any Internal Revenue law. Generally, tax returns and return information are confidential, as required by section 6103.

The time needed to complete and file this form will vary depending on individual circumstances. The estimated average time is:

Recordkeeping	6 min.
Learning about the law or the form	22 min.
Preparing the form	46 min.
Copying, assembling, and sending the form to the IRS	20 min.

If you have comments concerning the accuracy of these time estimates or suggestions for making this form simpler, we would be happy to hear from you. You can write to the Tax Products Coordinating Committee, Western Area Distribution Center, Rancho Cordova, CA 95743-0001. **Do not** send the form to this address. Instead, see **How To Apply** on page 1.

Form **SS-8**
(Rev. June 2003)
Department of the Treasury
Internal Revenue Service

Determination of Worker Status for Purposes of Federal Employment Taxes and Income Tax Withholding

form 6 ◆ 213

OMB No. 1545-0004

Name of firm (or person) for whom the worker performed services	Worker's name

Firm's address (include street address, apt. or suite no., city, state, and ZIP code) | Worker's address (include street address, apt. or suite no., city, state, and ZIP code)

Trade name	Telephone number (include area code) ( )	Worker's social security number

Telephone number (include area code) ( )	Firm's employer identification number	Worker's employer identification number (if any)

If the worker is paid by a firm other than the one listed on this form for these services, enter the name, address, and employer identification number of the payer.

Important Information Needed To Process Your Request

We must have your permission to disclose your name and the information on this form and any attachments to other parties involved with this request. **Do we have your permission to disclose this information?** ☐ Yes ☐ No
If you answered "No" or did not mark a box, we will not process your request and will not issue a determination.

You must answer ALL items OR mark them "Unknown" or "Does not apply." If you need more space, attach another sheet.

A This form is being completed by: ☐ Firm ☐ Worker; for services performed _____ to _____ .
   (beginning date)   (ending date)

B Explain your reason(s) for filing this form (e.g., you received a bill from the IRS, you believe you received a Form 1099 or Form W-2 erroneously, you are unable to get worker's compensation benefits, you were audited or are being audited by the IRS). _____

C Total number of workers who performed or are performing the same or similar services _____ .

D How did the worker obtain the job? ☐ Application ☐ Bid ☐ Employment Agency ☐ Other (specify) _____ .

E Attach copies of all supporting documentation (contracts, invoices, memos, Forms W-2, Forms 1099, IRS closing agreements, IRS rulings, etc.). In addition, please inform us of any current or past litigation concerning the worker's status. If no income reporting forms (Form 1099-MISC or W-2) were furnished to the worker, enter the amount of income earned for the year(s) at issue $ _____ .

F Describe the firm's business. _____

G Describe the work done by the worker and provide the worker's job title. _____

H Explain why you believe the worker is an employee or an independent contractor. _____

I Did the worker perform services for the firm before getting this position? ☐ Yes ☐ No ☐ N/A
   If "Yes," what were the dates of the prior service? _____
   If "Yes," explain the differences, if any, between the current and prior service. _____

J If the work is done under a written agreement between the firm and the worker, attach a copy (preferably signed by both parties). Describe the terms and conditions of the work arrangement. _____

For Privacy Act and Paperwork Reduction Act Notice, see page 5.   Cat. No. 16106T   Form **SS-8** (Rev. 6-2003)

Form SS-8 (Rev. 6-2003) Page **2**

Part I — Behavioral Control

1. What specific training and/or instruction is the worker given by the firm? ⋯
2. How does the worker receive work assignments? ⋯
3. Who determines the methods by which the assignments are performed? ⋯
4. Who is the worker required to contact if problems or complaints arise and who is responsible for their resolution? ⋯
5. What types of reports are required from the worker? Attach examples. ⋯
6. Describe the worker's daily routine (i.e., schedule, hours, etc.). ⋯
7. At what location(s) does the worker perform services (e.g., firm's premises, own shop or office, home, customer's location, etc.)? ⋯
8. Describe any meetings the worker is required to attend and any penalties for not attending (e.g., sales meetings, monthly meetings, staff meetings, etc.). ⋯
9. Is the worker required to provide the services personally? ☐ Yes ☐ No
10. If substitutes or helpers are needed, who hires them? ⋯
11. If the worker hires the substitutes or helpers, is approval required? ☐ Yes ☐ No
    If "Yes," by whom? ⋯
12. Who pays the substitutes or helpers? ⋯
13. Is the worker reimbursed if the worker pays the substitutes or helpers? ☐ Yes ☐ No
    If "Yes," by whom? ⋯

Part II — Financial Control

1. List the supplies, equipment, materials, and property provided by each party:
   The firm ⋯
   The worker ⋯
   Other party ⋯
2. Does the worker lease equipment? ☐ Yes ☐ No
   If "Yes," what are the terms of the lease? (Attach a copy or explanatory statement.) ⋯
3. What expenses are incurred by the worker in the performance of services for the firm? ⋯
4. Specify which, if any, expenses are reimbursed by:
   The firm ⋯
   Other party ⋯
5. Type of pay the worker receives: ☐ Salary ☐ Commission ☐ Hourly Wage ☐ Piece Work ☐ Lump Sum ☐ Other (specify) ⋯
   If type of pay is commission, and the firm guarantees a minimum amount of pay, specify amount $ ⋯
6. Is the worker allowed a drawing account for advances? ☐ Yes ☐ No
   If "Yes," how often? ⋯
   Specify any restrictions. ⋯
7. Whom does the customer pay? ☐ Firm ☐ Worker
   If worker, does the worker pay the total amount to the firm? ☐ Yes ☐ No If "No," explain. ⋯
8. Does the firm carry worker's compensation insurance on the worker? ☐ Yes ☐ No
9. What economic loss or financial risk, if any, can the worker incur beyond the normal loss of salary (e.g., loss or damage of equipment, material, etc.)? ⋯

Form **SS-8** (Rev. 6-2003)

Form SS-8 (Rev. 6-2003) Page **3**

Part III — Relationship of the Worker and Firm

1. List the benefits available to the worker (e.g., paid vacations, sick pay, pensions, bonuses). ⋯⋯⋯⋯⋯⋯⋯⋯⋯⋯⋯⋯⋯

2. Can the relationship be terminated by either party without incurring liability or penalty? ⋯⋯⋯⋯⋯⋯⋯⋯ ☐ Yes ☐ No
   If "No," explain your answer. ⋯⋯

3. Does the worker perform similar services for others? ⋯⋯⋯⋯⋯⋯⋯⋯⋯⋯⋯⋯⋯⋯⋯⋯⋯⋯⋯ ☐ Yes ☐ No
   If "Yes," is the worker required to get approval from the firm? ⋯⋯⋯⋯⋯⋯⋯⋯⋯⋯⋯⋯⋯⋯⋯ ☐ Yes ☐ No

4. Describe any agreements prohibiting competition between the worker and the firm while the worker is performing services or during any later period. Attach any available documentation. ⋯⋯⋯⋯⋯⋯⋯⋯⋯⋯⋯⋯⋯⋯⋯⋯⋯⋯⋯⋯⋯⋯⋯⋯⋯⋯⋯

5. Is the worker a member of a union? ⋯⋯⋯⋯⋯⋯⋯⋯⋯⋯⋯⋯⋯⋯⋯⋯⋯⋯⋯⋯⋯⋯⋯⋯⋯⋯⋯⋯⋯ ☐ Yes ☐ No

6. What type of advertising, if any, does the worker do (e.g., a business listing in a directory, business cards, etc.)? Provide copies, if applicable. ⋯⋯

7. If the worker assembles or processes a product at home, who provides the materials and instructions or pattern? ⋯⋯⋯⋯⋯⋯

8. What does the worker do with the finished product (e.g., return it to the firm, provide it to another party, or sell it)? ⋯⋯⋯⋯

9. How does the firm represent the worker to its customers (e.g., employee, partner, representative, or contractor)? ⋯⋯⋯⋯⋯

10. If the worker no longer performs services for the firm, how did the relationship end? ⋯⋯⋯⋯⋯⋯⋯⋯⋯⋯⋯⋯⋯⋯⋯⋯⋯

Part IV — For Service Providers or Salespersons
Complete this part if the worker provided a service directly to customers or is a salesperson.

1. What are the worker's responsibilities in soliciting new customers? ⋯⋯⋯⋯⋯⋯⋯⋯⋯⋯⋯⋯⋯⋯⋯⋯⋯⋯⋯⋯⋯⋯⋯⋯⋯⋯

2. Who provides the worker with leads to prospective customers? ⋯⋯⋯⋯⋯⋯⋯⋯⋯⋯⋯⋯⋯⋯⋯⋯⋯⋯⋯⋯⋯⋯⋯⋯⋯⋯⋯⋯

3. Describe any reporting requirements pertaining to the leads. ⋯⋯⋯⋯⋯⋯⋯⋯⋯⋯⋯⋯⋯⋯⋯⋯⋯⋯⋯⋯⋯⋯⋯⋯⋯⋯⋯⋯⋯

4. What terms and conditions of sale, if any, are required by the firm? ⋯⋯⋯⋯⋯⋯⋯⋯⋯⋯⋯⋯⋯⋯⋯⋯⋯⋯⋯⋯⋯⋯⋯⋯⋯

5. Are orders submitted to and subject to approval by the firm? ⋯⋯⋯⋯⋯⋯⋯⋯⋯⋯⋯⋯⋯⋯⋯⋯⋯⋯⋯ ☐ Yes ☐ No

6. Who determines the worker's territory? ⋯⋯⋯⋯⋯⋯⋯⋯⋯⋯⋯⋯⋯⋯⋯⋯⋯⋯⋯⋯⋯⋯⋯⋯⋯⋯⋯⋯⋯⋯⋯⋯⋯⋯⋯⋯⋯⋯

7. Did the worker pay for the privilege of serving customers on the route or in the territory? ⋯⋯⋯⋯⋯⋯ ☐ Yes ☐ No
   If "Yes," whom did the worker pay? ⋯⋯⋯
   If "Yes," how much did the worker pay? ⋯⋯⋯⋯⋯⋯⋯⋯⋯⋯⋯⋯⋯⋯⋯⋯⋯⋯⋯⋯⋯⋯⋯⋯ $ ⋯⋯⋯⋯⋯⋯⋯⋯

8. Where does the worker sell the product (e.g., in a home, retail establishment, etc.)? ⋯⋯⋯⋯⋯⋯⋯⋯⋯⋯⋯⋯⋯⋯⋯⋯⋯

9. List the product and/or services distributed by the worker (e.g., meat, vegetables, fruit, bakery products, beverages, or laundry or dry cleaning services). If more than one type of product and/or service is distributed, specify the principal one. ⋯⋯⋯⋯⋯⋯⋯⋯⋯⋯⋯⋯⋯⋯⋯⋯⋯⋯⋯⋯

10. Does the worker sell life insurance full time? ⋯⋯⋯⋯⋯⋯⋯⋯⋯⋯⋯⋯⋯⋯⋯⋯⋯⋯⋯⋯⋯⋯⋯⋯⋯⋯ ☐ Yes ☐ No

11. Does the worker sell other types of insurance for the firm? ⋯⋯⋯⋯⋯⋯⋯⋯⋯⋯⋯⋯⋯⋯⋯⋯⋯⋯⋯ ☐ Yes ☐ No
    If "Yes," enter the percentage of the worker's total working time spent in selling other types of insurance. ⋯⋯⋯ ⋯⋯⋯⋯⋯⋯ %

12. If the worker solicits orders from wholesalers, retailers, contractors, or operators of hotels, restaurants, or other similar establishments, enter the percentage of the worker's time spent in the solicitation. ⋯⋯⋯⋯⋯⋯⋯⋯⋯⋯⋯⋯⋯⋯⋯⋯⋯⋯ %

13. Is the merchandise purchased by the customers for resale or use in their business operations? ⋯⋯⋯⋯⋯⋯ ☐ Yes ☐ No
    Describe the merchandise and state whether it is equipment installed on the customers' premises. ⋯⋯⋯⋯⋯⋯⋯⋯⋯⋯

Part V — Signature (see page 4)

Under penalties of perjury, I declare that I have examined this request, including accompanying documents, and to the best of my knowledge and belief, the facts presented are true, correct, and complete.

Signature ▶ ⋯⋯⋯⋯⋯⋯⋯⋯⋯⋯⋯⋯⋯⋯⋯⋯⋯⋯⋯⋯⋯⋯ Title ▶ ⋯⋯⋯⋯⋯⋯⋯⋯⋯⋯⋯⋯⋯⋯⋯⋯⋯⋯⋯⋯ Date ▶ ⋯⋯⋯⋯⋯⋯⋯⋯
(Type or print name below)

Form **SS-8** (Rev. 6-2003)

General Instructions

Section references are to the Internal Revenue Code unless otherwise noted.

Purpose

Firms and workers file Form SS-8 to request a determination of the status of a worker for purposes of Federal employment taxes and income tax withholding.

A Form SS-8 determination may be requested only in order to resolve Federal tax matters. If Form SS-8 is submitted for a tax year for which the statute of limitations on the tax return has expired, a determination letter will not be issued. The statute of limitations expires 3 years from the due date of the tax return or the date filed, whichever is later.

The IRS does not issue a determination letter for proposed transactions or on hypothetical situations. We may, however, issue an information letter when it is considered appropriate.

Definition

Firm. For the purposes of this form, the term "firm" means any individual, business enterprise, organization, state, or other entity for which a worker has performed services. The firm may or may not have paid the worker directly for these services. **If the firm was not responsible for payment for services, be sure to enter the name, address, and employer identification number of the payer on the first page of Form SS-8 below the identifying information for the firm and the worker.**

The SS-8 Determination Process

The IRS will acknowledge the receipt of your Form SS-8. Because there are usually two (or more) parties who could be affected by a determination of employment status, the IRS attempts to get information from all parties involved by sending those parties blank Forms SS-8 for completion. The case will be assigned to a technician who will review the facts, apply the law, and render a decision. The technician may ask for additional information from the requestor, from other involved parties, or from third parties that could help clarify the work relationship before rendering a decision. The IRS will generally issue a formal determination to the firm or payer (if that is a different entity), and will send a copy to the worker. A determination letter applies only to a worker (or a class of workers) requesting it, and the decision is binding on the IRS. In certain cases, a formal determination will not be issued. Instead, an information letter may be issued. Although an information letter is advisory only and is not binding on the IRS, it may be used to assist the worker to fulfill his or her Federal tax obligations.

Neither the SS-8 determination process nor the review of any records in connection with the determination constitutes an examination (audit) of any Federal tax return. If the periods under consideration have previously been examined, the SS-8 determination process will not constitute a reexamination under IRS reopening procedures. Because this is not an examination of any Federal tax return, the appeal rights available in connection with an examination do not apply to an SS-8 determination. However, if you disagree with a determination and you have additional information concerning the work relationship that you believe was not previously considered, you may request that the determining office reconsider the determination.

Completing Form SS-8

Answer all questions as completely as possible. Attach additional sheets if you need more space. Provide information for all years the worker provided services for the firm. Determinations are based on the entire relationship between the firm and the worker.

Additional copies of this form may be obtained by calling 1-800-829-4933 or from the IRS website at **www.irs.gov**.

Fee

There is no fee for requesting an SS-8 determination letter.

Signature

Form SS-8 must be signed and dated by the taxpayer. A stamped signature will not be accepted.

The person who signs for a corporation must be an officer of the corporation who has personal knowledge of the facts. If the corporation is a member of an affiliated group filing a consolidated return, it must be signed by an officer of the common parent of the group.

The person signing for a trust, partnership, or limited liability company must be, respectively, a trustee, general partner, or member-manager who has personal knowledge of the facts.

Where To File

Send the completed Form SS-8 to the address listed below for the firm's location. However, for cases involving Federal agencies, send Form SS-8 to the Internal Revenue Service, Attn: CC:CORP:T:C, Ben Franklin Station, P.O. Box 7604, Washington, DC 20044.

Firm's location:	Send to:
Alaska, Arizona, Arkansas, California, Colorado, Hawaii, Idaho, Illinois, Iowa, Kansas, Minnesota, Missouri, Montana, Nebraska, Nevada, New Mexico, North Dakota, Oklahoma, Oregon, South Dakota, Texas, Utah, Washington, Wisconsin, Wyoming, American Samoa, Guam, Puerto Rico, U.S. Virgin Islands	Internal Revenue Service SS-8 Determinations P.O. Box 630 Stop 631 Holtsville, NY 11742-0630
Alabama, Connecticut, Delaware, District of Columbia, Florida, Georgia, Indiana, Kentucky, Louisiana, Maine, Maryland, Massachusetts, Michigan, Mississippi, New Hampshire, New Jersey, New York, North Carolina, Ohio, Pennsylvania, Rhode Island, South Carolina, Tennessee, Vermont, Virginia, West Virginia, all other locations not listed	Internal Revenue Service SS-8 Determinations 40 Lakemont Road Newport, VT 05855-1555

Instructions for Workers

If you are requesting a determination for more than one firm, complete a separate Form SS-8 for each firm.

 Form SS-8 is not a claim for refund of social security and Medicare taxes or Federal income tax withholding.

If the IRS determines that you are an employee, you are responsible for filing an amended return for any corrections related to this decision. A determination that a worker is an employee does not necessarily reduce any current or prior tax liability. For more information, call 1-800-829-1040.

Time for filing a claim for refund. Generally, you must file your claim for a credit or refund within 3 years from the date your original return was filed or within 2 years from the date the tax was paid, whichever is later.

Filing Form SS-8 does not prevent the expiration of the time in which a claim for a refund must be filed. If you are concerned about a refund, and the statute of limitations for filing a claim for refund for the year(s) at issue has not yet expired, you should file **Form 1040X,** Amended U.S. Individual Income Tax Return, to protect your statute of limitations. File a separate Form 1040X for each year.

On the Form 1040X you file, do not complete lines 1 through 24 on the form. Write "Protective Claim" at the top of the form, sign and date it. In addition, you should enter the following statement in Part II, Explanation of Changes to Income, Deductions, and Credits: "Filed Form SS-8 with the Internal Revenue Service Office in (Holtsville, NY; Newport, VT; or Washington, DC; as appropriate). By filing this protective claim, I reserve the right to file a claim for any refund that may be due after a determination of my employment tax status has been completed."

Filing Form SS-8 does not alter the requirement to timely file an income tax return. Do not delay filing your tax return in anticipation of an answer to your SS-8 request. In addition, if applicable, do not delay in responding to a request for payment while waiting for a determination of your worker status.

Instructions for Firms

If a **worker** has requested a determination of his or her status while working for you, you will receive a request from the IRS to complete a Form SS-8. In cases of this type, the IRS usually gives each party an opportunity to present a statement of the facts because any decision will affect the employment tax status of the parties. Failure to respond to this request will not prevent the IRS from issuing a determination letter based on the information he or she has made available so that the worker may fulfill his or her Federal tax obligations. However, the information that you provide is extremely valuable in determining the status of the worker.

If **you** are requesting a determination for a particular class of worker, complete the form for **one** individual who is representative of the class of workers whose status is in question. If you want a written determination for more than one class of workers, complete a separate Form SS-8 for one worker from each class whose status is typical of that class. A written determination for any worker will apply to other workers of the same class if the facts are not materially different for these workers. Please provide a list of names and addresses of all workers potentially affected by this determination.

If you have a reasonable basis for not treating a worker as an employee, you may be relieved from having to pay employment taxes for that worker under section 530 of the 1978 Revenue Act. However, this relief provision cannot be considered in conjunction with a Form SS-8 determination because the determination does not constitute an examination of any tax return. For more information regarding section 530 of the 1978 Revenue Act and to determine if you qualify for relief under this section, you may visit the IRS website at **www.irs.gov**.

Privacy Act and Paperwork Reduction Act Notice. We ask for the information on this form to carry out the Internal Revenue laws of the United States. This information will be used to determine the employment status of the worker(s) described on the form. Subtitle C, Employment Taxes, of the Internal Revenue Code imposes employment taxes on wages. Sections 3121(d), 3306(a), and 3401(c) and (d) and the related regulations define employee and employer for purposes of employment taxes imposed under Subtitle C. Section 6001 authorizes the IRS to request information needed to determine if a worker(s) or firm is subject to these taxes. Section 6109 requires you to provide your taxpayer identification number. Neither workers nor firms are required to request a status determination, but if you choose to do so, you must provide the information requested on this form. Failure to provide the requested information may prevent us from making a status determination. If any worker or the firm has requested a status determination and you are being asked to provide information for use in that determination, you are not required to provide the requested information. However, failure to provide such information will prevent the IRS from considering it in making the status determination. Providing false or fraudulent information may subject you to penalties. Routine uses of this information include providing it to the Department of Justice for use in civil and criminal litigation, to the Social Security Administration for the administration of social security programs, and to cities, states, and the District of Columbia for the administration of their tax laws. We may also disclose this information to Federal and state agencies to enforce Federal nontax criminal laws and to combat terrorism. We may provide this information to the affected worker(s) or the firm as part of the status determination process.

You are not required to provide the information requested on a form that is subject to the Paperwork Reduction Act unless the form displays a valid OMB control number. Books or records relating to a form or its instructions must be retained as long as their contents may become material in the administration of any Internal Revenue law. Generally, tax returns and return information are confidential, as required by section 6103.

The time needed to complete and file this form will vary depending on individual circumstances. The estimated average time is: **Recordkeeping,** 22 hrs.; **Learning about the law or the form,** 47 min.; and **Preparing and sending the form to the IRS,** 1 hr., 11 min. If you have comments concerning the accuracy of these time estimates or suggestions for making this form simpler, we would be happy to hear from you. You can write to the Tax Products Coordinating Committee, Western Area Distribution Center, Rancho Cordova, CA 95743-0001. **Do not** send the tax form to this address. Instead, see **Where To File** on page 4.

This page intentionally left blank.

form 7 ♦ 219

Form W-4 (2004)

Purpose. Complete Form W-4 so that your employer can withhold the correct Federal income tax from your pay. Because your tax situation may change, you may want to refigure your withholding each year.

Exemption from withholding. If you are exempt, complete only lines 1, 2, 3, 4, and 7 and sign the form to validate it. Your exemption for 2004 expires February 16, 2005. See **Pub. 505,** Tax Withholding and Estimated Tax.

Note: *You cannot claim exemption from withholding if:* **(a)** *your income exceeds $800 and includes more than $250 of unearned income (e.g., interest and dividends) and* **(b)** *another person can claim you as a dependent on their tax return.*

Basic instructions. If you are not exempt, complete the **Personal Allowances Worksheet** below. The worksheets on page 2 adjust your withholding allowances based on itemized deductions, certain credits, adjustments to income, or two-earner/two-job situations. Complete all worksheets that apply. However, you may claim fewer (or zero) allowances.

Head of household. Generally, you may claim head of household filing status on your tax return only if you are unmarried and pay more than 50% of the costs of keeping up a home for yourself and your dependent(s) or other qualifying individuals. See line **E** below.

Tax credits. You can take projected tax credits into account in figuring your allowable number of withholding allowances. Credits for child or dependent care expenses and the child tax credit may be claimed using the **Personal Allowances Worksheet** below. See **Pub. 919,** How Do I Adjust My Tax Withholding? for information on converting your other credits into withholding allowances.

Nonwage income. If you have a large amount of nonwage income, such as interest or dividends, consider making estimated tax payments using **Form 1040-ES,** Estimated Tax for Individuals. Otherwise, you may owe additional tax.

Two earners/two jobs. If you have a working spouse or more than one job, figure the total number of allowances you are entitled to claim on all jobs using worksheets from only one Form W-4. Your withholding usually will be most accurate when all allowances are claimed on the Form W-4 for the highest paying job and zero allowances are claimed on the others.

Nonresident alien. If you are a nonresident alien, see the **Instructions for Form 8233** before completing this Form W-4.

Check your withholding. After your Form W-4 takes effect, use Pub. 919 to see how the dollar amount you are having withheld compares to your projected total tax for 2004. See Pub. 919, especially if your earnings exceed $125,000 (Single) or $175,000 (Married).

Recent name change? If your name on line 1 differs from that shown on your social security card, call 1-800-772-1213 to initiate a name change and obtain a social security card showing your correct name.

Personal Allowances Worksheet (Keep for your records.)

A Enter "1" for **yourself** if no one else can claim you as a dependent . . . . **A** _____

B Enter "1" if: {
- You are single and have only one job; or
- You are married, have only one job, and your spouse does not work; or
- Your wages from a second job or your spouse's wages (or the total of both) are $1,000 or less.
} . . **B** _____

C Enter "1" for your **spouse.** But, you may choose to enter "-0-" if you are married and have either a working spouse or more than one job. (Entering "-0-" may help you avoid having too little tax withheld.) . . . . **C** _____

D Enter number of **dependents** (other than your spouse or yourself) you will claim on your tax return . . . . . . **D** _____

E Enter "1" if you will file as **head of household** on your tax return (see conditions under **Head of household** above) . **E** _____

F Enter "1" if you have at least $1,500 of **child or dependent care expenses** for which you plan to claim a credit . . **F** _____
(**Note:** *Do not include child support payments. See* **Pub. 503,** *Child and Dependent Care Expenses, for details.*)

G **Child Tax Credit** (including additional child tax credit):
- If your total income will be less than $52,000 ($77,000 if married), enter "2" for each eligible child.
- If your total income will be between $52,000 and $84,000 ($77,000 and $119,000 if married), enter "1" for each eligible child plus "1" **additional** if you have four or more eligible children. . . . . **G** _____

H Add lines A through G and enter total here. **Note:** *This may be different from the number of exemptions you claim on your tax return.* ▶ **H** _____

For accuracy, complete all worksheets that apply. {
- If you plan to **itemize or claim adjustments to income** and want to reduce your withholding, see the **Deductions and Adjustments Worksheet** on page 2.
- If you have **more than one job** or are **married and you and your spouse both work** and the combined earnings from all jobs exceed $35,000 ($25,000 if married) see the **Two-Earner/Two-Job Worksheet** on page 2 to avoid having too little tax withheld.
- If **neither** of the above situations applies, **stop here** and enter the number from line H on line 5 of Form W-4 below.
}

--------- Cut here and give Form W-4 to your employer. Keep the top part for your records. ---------

---

Form **W-4**
Department of the Treasury
Internal Revenue Service

Employee's Withholding Allowance Certificate

▶ Your employer must send a copy of this form to the IRS if: (a) you claim more than 10 allowances or (b) you claim "Exempt" and your wages are normally more than $200 per week.

OMB No. 1545-0010

2004

1 Type or print your first name and middle initial | Last name | **2** Your social security number

Home address (number and street or rural route) | **3** ☐ Single ☐ Married ☐ Married, but withhold at higher Single rate.
Note: *If married, but legally separated, or spouse is a nonresident alien, check the "Single" box.*

City or town, state, and ZIP code | **4** If your last name differs from that shown on your social security card, check here. You must call 1-800-772-1213 for a new card. ▶ ☐

5 Total number of allowances you are claiming (from line **H** above **or** from the applicable worksheet on page 2) | **5** _____

6 Additional amount, if any, you want withheld from each paycheck . . . . | **6** $ _____

7 I claim exemption from withholding for 2004, and I certify that I meet **both** of the following conditions for exemption:
- Last year I had a right to a refund of **all** Federal income tax withheld because I had **no** tax liability **and**
- This year I expect a refund of **all** Federal income tax withheld because I expect to have **no** tax liability.

If you meet both conditions, write "Exempt" here . . . . ▶ **7** _____

Under penalties of perjury, I certify that I am entitled to the number of withholding allowances claimed on this certificate, or I am entitled to claim exempt status.

Employee's signature
(Form is not valid unless you sign it.) ▶ | **Date** ▶

8 Employer's name and address (Employer: Complete lines 8 and 10 only if sending to the IRS.) | **9** Office code (optional) | **10** Employer identification number (EIN)

For Privacy Act and Paperwork Reduction Act Notice, see page 2. | Cat. No. 10220Q | Form **W-4** (2004)

Form W-4 (2004) Page **2**

Deductions and Adjustments Worksheet

Note: *Use this worksheet **only** if you plan to itemize deductions, claim certain credits, or claim adjustments to income on your 2004 tax return.*

1. Enter an estimate of your 2004 itemized deductions. These include qualifying home mortgage interest, charitable contributions, state and local taxes, medical expenses in excess of 7.5% of your income, and miscellaneous deductions. (For 2004, you may have to reduce your itemized deductions if your income is over $142,700 ($71,350 if married filing separately). See **Worksheet 3** in Pub. 919 for details.) ... **1** $ _____

2. Enter:
   - $9,700 if married filing jointly or qualifying widow(er)
   - $7,150 if head of household
   - $4,850 if single
   - $4,850 if married filing separately

   ... **2** $ _____

3. **Subtract** line 2 from line 1. If line 2 is greater than line 1, enter "-0-" ... **3** $ _____
4. Enter an estimate of your 2004 adjustments to income, including alimony, deductible IRA contributions, and student loan interest **4** $ _____
5. **Add** lines 3 and 4 and enter the total. (Include any amount for credits from **Worksheet 7** in Pub. 919) .. **5** $ _____
6. Enter an estimate of your 2004 nonwage income (such as dividends or interest) ... **6** $ _____
7. **Subtract** line 6 from line 5. Enter the result, but not less than "-0-" ... **7** $ _____
8. **Divide** the amount on line 7 by $3,000 and enter the result here. Drop any fraction ... **8** _____
9. Enter the number from the **Personal Allowances Worksheet,** line H, page 1 ... **9** _____
10. **Add** lines 8 and 9 and enter the total here. If you plan to use the **Two-Earner/Two-Job Worksheet,** also enter this total on line 1 below. Otherwise, **stop here** and enter this total on Form W-4, line 5, page 1 ... **10** _____

Two-Earner/Two-Job Worksheet (See **Two earners/two jobs** on page 1.)

Note: *Use this worksheet **only** if the instructions under line H on page 1 direct you here.*

1. Enter the number from line H, page 1 (or from line 10 above if you used the **Deductions and Adjustments Worksheet**) **1** _____
2. Find the number in **Table 1** below that applies to the **LOWEST** paying job and enter it here ... **2** _____
3. If line 1 is **more than or equal to** line 2, subtract line 2 from line 1. Enter the result here (if zero, enter "-0-") and on Form W-4, line 5, page 1. **Do not** use the rest of this worksheet ... **3** _____

Note: *If line 1 is **less than** line 2, enter "-0-" on Form W-4, line 5, page 1. Complete lines 4-9 below to calculate the additional withholding amount necessary to avoid a year-end tax bill.*

4. Enter the number from line 2 of this worksheet ... **4** _____
5. Enter the number from line 1 of this worksheet ... **5** _____
6. **Subtract** line 5 from line 4 ... **6** _____
7. Find the amount in **Table 2** below that applies to the **HIGHEST** paying job and enter it here ... **7** $ _____
8. **Multiply** line 7 by line 6 and enter the result here. This is the additional annual withholding needed .. **8** $ _____
9. Divide line 8 by the number of pay periods remaining in 2004. For example, divide by 26 if you are paid every two weeks and you complete this form in December 2003. Enter the result here and on Form W-4, line 6, page 1. This is the additional amount to be withheld from each paycheck ... **9** $ _____

Table 1: Two-Earner/Two-Job Worksheet

Married Filing Jointly			Married Filing Jointly			All Others	
If wages from **HIGHEST** paying job are-	AND, wages from **LOWEST** paying job are-	Enter on line 2 above	If wages from **HIGHEST** paying job are-	AND, wages from **LOWEST** paying job are-	Enter on line 2 above	If wages from **LOWEST** paying job are-	Enter on line 2 above
$0 - $40,000	$0 - $4,000	0	$40,001 and over	31,001 - 38,000	6	$0 - $6,000	0
	4,001 - 8,000	1		38,001 - 44,000	7	6,001 - 11,000	1
	8,001 - 17,000	2		44,001 - 50,000	8	11,001 - 18,000	2
	17,001 and over	3		50,001 - 55,000	9	18,001 - 25,000	3
				55,001 - 65,000	10	25,001 - 31,000	4
$40,001 and over	$0 - $4,000	0		65,001 - 75,000	11	31,001 - 44,000	5
	4,001 - 8,000	1		75,001 - 85,000	12	44,001 - 55,000	6
	8,001 - 15,000	2		85,001 - 100,000	13	55,001 - 70,000	7
	15,001 - 22,000	3		100,001 - 115,000	14	70,001 - 80,000	8
	22,001 - 25,000	4		115,001 and over	15	80,001 - 100,000	9
	25,001 - 31,000	5				100,001 and over	10

Table 2: Two-Earner/Two-Job Worksheet

Married Filing Jointly		All Others	
If wages from **HIGHEST** paying job are-	Enter on line 7 above	If wages from **HIGHEST** paying job are-	Enter on line 7 above
$0 - $60,000	$470	$0 - $30,000	$470
60,001 - 110,000	780	30,001 - 70,000	780
110,001 - 150,000	870	70,001 - 140,000	870
150,001 - 270,000	1,020	140,001 - 320,000	1,020
270,001 and over	1,090	320,001 and over	1,090

Privacy Act and Paperwork Reduction Act Notice. We ask for the information on this form to carry out the Internal Revenue laws of the United States. The Internal Revenue Code requires this information under sections 3402(f)(2)(A) and 6109 and their regulations. Failure to provide a properly completed form will result in your being treated as a single person who claims no withholding allowances; providing fraudulent information may also subject you to penalties. Routine uses of this information include giving it to the Department of Justice for civil and criminal litigation, to cities, states, and the District of Columbia for use in administering their tax laws, and using it in the National Directory of New Hires. We may also disclose this information to Federal and state agencies to enforce Federal nontax criminal laws and to combat terrorism.

You are not required to provide the information requested on a form that is subject to the Paperwork Reduction Act unless the form displays a valid OMB control number. Books or records relating to a form or its instructions must be retained as long as their contents may become material in the administration of any Internal Revenue law. Generally, tax returns and return information are confidential, as required by Code section 6103.

The time needed to complete this form will vary depending on individual circumstances. The estimated average time is: **Recordkeeping,** 46 min.; **Learning about the law or the form,** 13 min.; **Preparing the form,** 59 min. If you have comments concerning the accuracy of these time estimates or suggestions for making this form simpler, we would be happy to hear from you. You can write to the Tax Products Coordinating Committee, Western Area Distribution Center, Rancho Cordova, CA 95743-0001. **Do not** send Form W-4 to this address. Instead, give it to your employer.

AP-201-3
(Rev.1-03/7)

TEXAS APPLICATION FOR SALES TAX PERMIT, USE TAX PERMIT AND/OR TELECOMMUNICATIONS INFRASTRUCTURE FUND ASSESSMENT SET-UP

- TYPE OR PRINT
- Do NOT write in shaded areas.

Page 1

SOLE OWNER IDENTIFICATION

1. Name of sole owner *(First, middle initial, and last name)*

2. Social security number (SSN)
   2 ___ - ___ - ___
   ☐ Check here if you DO NOT have a SSN.

3. Taxpayer number for reporting any Texas tax OR Texas identification number if you now have or have ever had one.

NON-SOLE OWNER IDENTIFICATION

--- ALL SOLE OWNERS SKIP TO ITEM 9. ---

4. Business organization type
   ☐ Texas registered limited liability partnership (PR)
   ☐ Texas limited liability company (CL)
   ☐ Non-Texas limited liability company (CI)
   ☐ Estate (ES)
   ☐ Non-Texas registered limited liability partnership (PS)
   ☐ Texas profit corporation (CT)
   ☐ Non-Texas profit corporation (CF)
   ☐ Professional corporation (CP)
   ☐ General partnership (PG)
   ☐ Texas nonprofit corporation (CN)
   ☐ Non-Texas nonprofit corporation (CM)
   ☐ Professional association (AP)
   ☐ Limited partnership (PL or PF)
   ☐ Trust (FM) Please submit a copy of the trust agreement with this application
   ☐ Other *(explain)*

5. Legal name of partnership, company, corporation, association, trust, or other

6. Taxpayer number for reporting any Texas tax OR Texas identification number if you now have or have ever had one.

7. Federal employer's identification number (FEIN) assigned by the Internal Revenue Service .... 1 ___ - ___

8. ☐ Check here if you do not have an FEIN. .... 3 ___

BUSINESS INFORMATION

9. Mailing address
   Street number, P.O. Box, or rural route and box number

   City   State/province   ZIP code   County *(or country, if outside the U.S.)*

10. Name of person to contact regarding day to day business operations   Daytime phone ___/___-___

11. Principal type of business
    ☐ Agriculture   ☐ Transportation   ☐ Retail Trade   ☐ Real Estate   ☐ Mining   ☐ Communications *(See Item 38)*
    ☐ Finance   ☐ Services   ☐ Construction   ☐ Utilities   ☐ Insurance   ☐ Public Administration
    ☐ Manufacturing   ☐ Wholesale Trade   ☐ Other *(explain)*

12. Primary business activities and type of products or services to be sold   SIC ___

TAXPAYER INFORMATION

If you are a SOLE OWNER, skip to Item 18.

13. If the business is a Texas profit corporation, nonprofit corporation, professional corporation, or limited liability company, enter the charter number and date. ....   Charter number   Month Day Year

14. If the business is a non-Texas profit corporation, nonprofit corporation, professional corporation, or limited liability company, enter the state or country of incorporation, charter number and date, Texas Certificate of Authority number and date.
    State/country of inc.   Charter number   Month Day Year   Texas Certificate of Authority number   Month Day Year

15. If the business is a corporation, have you been involved in a merger within the last seven years? ... ☐ YES ☐ NO   *If "YES," attach a detailed explanation.*

16. If the business is a limited partnership or registered limited liability partnership, enter the home state and registered identification number. ....   State   Number

17. General partners, principal members/officers, managing directors or managers *(Attach additional sheets, if necessary.)*
    Name   Title   Phone *(Area code and number)* ___/___-___
    Home address   City   State   ZIP code
    SSN or FEIN   Percent of ownership ___%   County *(or country, if outside the U.S.)*
    Position held   ☐ Partner   ☐ Officer   ☐ Director   ☐ Corporate Stockholder   ☐ Record keeper

    Name   Title   Phone *(Area code and number)* ___/___-___
    Home address   City   State   ZIP code
    SSN or FEIN   Percent of ownership ___%   County *(or country, if outside the U.S.)*
    Position held   ☐ Partner   ☐ Officer   ☐ Director   ☐ Corporate Stockholder   ☐ Record keeper

AP-201-4
(Rev.1-03/7)

TEXAS APPLICATION FOR SALES TAX PERMIT, USE TAX PERMIT AND/OR TELECOMMUNICATIONS INFRASTRUCTURE FUND ASSESSMENT SET-UP

- TYPE OR PRINT
- Do NOT write in shaded areas.

Page 2

18. Legal name of entity *(Same as Item 1 OR Item 5)*

BUSINESS LOCATION

19. Is your business located outside Texas? .... ☐ YES ☐ NO
    If "YES," **skip to Item 28**

20. Business location name and address *(Attach additional sheets for each additional location.)*
    Business location name
    Street and number *(Do not use P.O. Box. or rural route)*   City   State   ZIP code   County
    Physical location *(If business location address is a rural route and box number, provide directions)*   Business location phone

21. Is your business located inside the boundaries of an incorporated city? .... ☐ YES ☐ NO
    If "YES," indicate city *(You may need to contact your local city/county planning offices for assistance in determining the city taxing jurisdiction for your business location address entered in Item 20.)*

    Answer the questions below about the above location by checking "YES" or "NO."   ☐ O/L

22. Is your business located inside a metropolitan transit authority/city transit department (MTA/CTD)? .... ☐ YES ☐ NO

23. Is your business located inside a special purpose district (SPD)? .... ☐ YES ☐ NO

24. Will you deliver in your own vehicles, provide taxable services, or have sales/service representatives going from this location to customers located in:
    another city? .... ☐ YES ☐ NO
    another county? .... ☐ YES ☐ NO
    another MTA/CTD? .... ☐ YES ☐ NO
    another SPD? .... ☐ YES ☐ NO

25. Will you ship from this location to other customers via common carrier? .... ☐ YES ☐ NO

26. Are you a seller with no established place of business selling at a temporary location (trade show, event, or door to door)? .... ☐ YES ☐ NO

27. Will you have out-of-state suppliers shipping taxable items directly to customers' locations in Texas? .... ☐ YES ☐ NO

SALES AND USE TAX

28. If you sell fireworks, are you a .... ☐ Distributor .... ☐ Jobber .... ☐ Manufacturer .... ☐ Retailer

29. Do you sell, lease, or rent off-road, heavy duty diesel powered construction equipment? .... ☐ YES ☐ NO

30. Check the box that best represents your anticipated quarterly state sales tax collections: ☐ less than $250 (Y) ☐ $250-$1,500 (Q) ☐ greater than $1,500 (M)

31. Enter the date of the first business operation in the above location that is subject to sales or use tax, or the date you plan to start such business operation. *(Date cannot be more than 90 days in the future.)* ....   month day year

32. Is your business operated all year? .... ☐ YES ☐ NO
    If "NO," list the months you will operate.

33. Will you sell any type of alcoholic beverages? .... ☐ YES ☐ NO
    If "YES," indicate the type of permit you will hold: .... ☐ mixed beverage   ☐ beer and wine

34. Brief description of your business activities **for this location**, and the primary products or services to be sold.   SIC

35. Will you be required to report interest earned on sales tax? *(See "Specific Instructions")* .... ☐ YES ☐ NO

36. Are you located out of state with representation in Texas? .... ☐ YES ☐ NO
    If "YES," complete Item 37. **If "NO," skip to Item 38.**

37. List names and addresses of all representatives, agents, salespersons, canvassers, or solicitors in Texas. *(Attach additional sheets, if necessary.)*
    Name *(First, middle initial, last)*
    Street   City   State   ZIP code

38. Location of all distribution points, warehouses, or offices in Texas *(Attach additional sheets, if necessary.)*
    Street   City   State TX   ZIP code
    Street   City   State TX   ZIP code

AP-201-5
(Rev.1-03/7)

TEXAS APPLICATION FOR SALES TAX PERMIT, USE TAX PERMIT AND/OR TELECOMMUNICATIONS INFRASTRUCTURE FUND ASSESSMENT SET-UP

- TYPE OR PRINT
- Do NOT write in shaded areas.

Page 3

39. Legal name of entity *(Same as Item 1 OR Item 5)*

For Comptroller Use Only
Tax type/reason
☐ ■ 00991   ■ 2 0
Reference no.

month day year

TIF ASSESSMENT / 9-1-1

40. Do you receive compensation for providing telecommunications services? .... ☐ YES   ☐ NO
    If "YES," you are responsible for the Telecommunications Infrastructure Fund (TIF) assessment and should complete Items 41-42.
    If "NO," skip to Item 43.

41. Date of the first business operation that is subject to the Telecommunications Infrastructure Fund assessment in Texas or the date you plan to start such business operation. ....

42. Telecommunications provider type .... ☐ Telecommunications Utility (24) ☐ Commercial Mobile Service Provider (25)

43. 9-1-1 emergency communications fees you collect under Health & Safety Code, Chapter 771. *(Check all that apply.)*
    ☐ 9-1-1 (Wireless) Emergency Service Fee (91)   ☐ 9-1-1 Emergency Service Fee (92)   ☐ 9-1-1 Equalization Surcharge (93)

PREVIOUS OWNER INFORMATION

If you purchased an existing business or business assets, complete Items 44-47.

44. Previous owner's trade name.

    Previous owner's taxpayer number *(if available)*

45. Previous owner's legal name, address and phone number, if available.
    Name
    Phone *(Area code and number)*
    Address *(Street and number)*   City   State   ZIP code

46. Check each of the following items you purchased.
    ☐ Inventory   ☐ Corporate stock   ☐ Equipment   ☐ Real estate   ☐ Other assets

47. Purchase price of this business or assets and the date of purchase.
    Purchase price $ Date of purchase   month day year

SIGNATURES

48. The sole owner, all general partners, corporation or organization president, vice-president, secretary or treasurer, managing director, or an authorized representative must sign. A representative must submit a written power of attorney. *(Attach additional sheets if necessary.)*

    Date of signature(s)
    month day year

    I (We) declare that the information in this document and any attachments is true and correct to the best of my (our) knowledge and belief.

    Type or print name and title of sole owner, partner, or officer   Drivers license number/state   sign here ▶   Sole owner, partner, or officer

    Type or print name and title of partner or officer   Drivers license number/state   sign here ▶   Partner or officer

    Type or print name and title of partner or officer   Drivers license number/state   sign here ▶   Partner or officer

YOUR PERMIT MUST BE PROMINENTLY DISPLAYED IN YOUR PLACE OF BUSINESS. THE INFORMATION ON YOUR PERMIT IS PUBLIC INFORMATION.

OPEN RECORDS NOTICE - Your name, address, and telephone number are public information under the Texas Open Records Act, Chapter 552, Government Code.

Field office or section number _____   Employee Name _____   USERID _____   Date _____

224 ♦

TEXAS APPLICATION

SALES TAX PERMIT

OFF-ROAD, HEAVY DUTY DIESEL
POWERED CONSTRUCTION
EQUIPMENT SURCHARGE

USE TAX PERMIT

FIREWORKS TAX

TELECOMMUNICATIONS
INFRASTRUCTURE FUND
ASSESSMENT

9-1-1 EMERGENCY COMMUNICATIONS

CAROLE KEETON STRAYHORN • TEXAS COMPTROLLER OF PUBLIC ACCOUNTS

GENERAL INSTRUCTIONS

WHO MUST SUBMIT THIS APPLICATION - You must submit this application if:
- you are an individual, partnership, corporation, or organization engaged in business in Texas; AND
- you are selling tangible personal property or providing taxable services in Texas to customers in Texas; and/or
- you acquire tangible personal property or taxable services from out-of-state suppliers that do not hold a Texas permit;
OR
- you sell or resell telecommunications services, such as the electronic transmission of tax returns or other information, the provision of phone service for a charge to tenants or hotel guests, fax services, or paging services, or you are a telecommunications utility or a mobile service provider collecting and paying telecommunications receipts under Texas Tax Code, Chapter 151;
OR
- you are a telecommunications utility, a mobile service provider, or a business service user that provides local exchange access, equivalent local exchange access, wireless telecommunications connections, or intrastate long-distance service, and you are responsible for collecting emergency communications charges and/or surcharges under Texas Health and Safety Code, Chapter 771;
OR
- you collect tax on the retail sale of fireworks. *(You are required to charge both the sales tax and the fireworks tax.)*
OR
- you sell, lease, or rent off-road, heavy duty diesel powered construction equipment. *(You are required to charge both the sales tax and the surcharge.)*

DEFINITIONS -
- **SALES TAX PERMIT:** This permit is required for every individual, partnership, corporation, or organization who makes sales, leases, or rentals of taxable items in Texas. Permits are issued without charge.
- **SALES TAX BOND:** You may need to post a bond or other security for this permit. To determine the amount of bond or security required, complete a "Texas Sales and Use Tax Bond-Security Information," Form 01-707. Submit this application and Form 01-707 to avoid delay in receiving your permit.
- **USE TAX PERMIT:** This permit is required for every individual, partnership, corporation, or organization who makes sales, leases, or rentals of taxable items in Texas but does NOT have a place of business in Texas, AND for out-of-state contractors improving real property in Texas with tangible personal property purchased outside of Texas.
- **ENGAGED IN BUSINESS:** You are engaged in business in Texas if you or your independent salespersons make sales, leases, or rentals, or take orders for tangible personal property, or deliver tangible personal property or perform taxable services; or have lease (personal) property, a warehouse or other location in Texas; or benefit from a location in Texas of authorized installations, servicing or repair facilities; or allow a franchisee or licensee to operate under your trade name if they are required to collect Texas tax.
- **PLACE OF BUSINESS OR BUSINESS LOCATION:** Any store, office, or location where you receive orders for tangible personal property or taxable services or make sales, leases, or rentals of tangible personal property or taxable services at least three times or more in a calendar year. *(See Rule 3.286: State Sales and Use Tax Seller's and Purchaser's Responsibilities.)*

NOTE: *If you have been making sales and have not applied for a permit, you will need to file returns and pay tax, plus applicable penalty and interest, for the period of time that you have been in business.*

FOR ASSISTANCE - If you have any questions about this application, contact your nearest Texas State Comptroller's Office or call us toll free at 1-800-252-5555. The local number in Austin is 512/463-4600. The Tax Help E-mail Address is: tax.help@cpa.state.tx.us

AMERICANS WITH DISABILITIES ACT- In compliance with the Americans with Disabilities Act, this document may be requested in alternative formats by calling toll-free 1-800-252-5555. From a Telecommunications Device for the Deaf (TDD), our hearing impaired taxpayers may call toll free 1-800-248-4099, or they may call via 1-800-RELAY-TX. The Austin TDD number is 512/463-4621.

FEDERAL PRIVACY ACT - Disclosure of your social security number is required and authorized under law, for the purpose of tax administration and identification of any individual affected by applicable law. 42 U.S.C. §405(c)(2)(C)(i); Tex. Govt. Code §§403.011 and 403.078. Release of information on this form in response to a public information request will be governed by the Public Information Act, Chapter 552, Government Code, and applicable federal law.

If you are hiring one or more employees, please contact the Texas Workforce Commission at 512/463-2699 or your local TWC tax office to determine if you are liable for payroll taxes under the Texas Unemployment Compensation Act.

Complete this application and mail to: COMPTROLLER OF PUBLIC ACCOUNTS
111 E. 17th Street
Austin, TX 78774-0100

Under Ch. 559, Government Code, you are entitled to review, request, and correct information we have on file about you, with limited exceptions in accordance with Ch. 552, Government Code. To request information for review or to request error correction, contact us at the address or toll-free number listed on this form.

AP-201-2
(Rev.1-03/7)

SPECIFIC INSTRUCTIONS

Item 35 - You WILL be required to report interest earned on sales tax IF:
- you make retail sales of taxable items on an installment purchase plan or deferred payment plan; **AND**
- you charge interest on the entire balance, including sales tax, on the sale of taxable items made on installment purchases or deferred payment plans; **AND**
- you do your own financing on some accounts on which interest is charged; **AND**
- you include installment payments which were received during a reporting period in "TOTAL SALES" on your sales tax return for that period (i.e., you keep your records on a cash basis of accounting).

NOTE: If any one of the statements above does **NOT** apply to your business, then you will **NOT** be required to report interest earned on sales tax.

Below is a listing of taxes and fees collected by the Comptroller of Public Accounts. If you are responsible for reporting or paying one of the listed taxes or fees, and you **DO NOT HAVE A PERMIT OR AN ACCOUNT WITH US FOR THIS PURPOSE**, please obtain the proper application by calling toll-free 1-800-252-5555, or by visiting your local Enforcement field office.

TAX TYPE(S)

9-1-1 Emergency Service Fee/Equalization Surcharge - If you are a telecommunications utility, a mobile service provider, or a business service user that provides local exchange access, equivalent local exchange access, wireless telecommunications connections, or intrastate long-distance service, and you are responsible for collecting emergency communications charges and/or surcharges, you must complete *Form AP-201*.

Amusement Tax - If you engage in any business dealing with coin-operated machines OR engage in business to own or operate coin-operated machines exclusively on premises occupied by and in connection with the business, you must complete *Form AP-146 or Form AP-147*.

Automotive Oil Sales Fee - If you manufacture and sell automotive oil in Texas; or you import or cause automotive oil to be imported into Texas for sale, use, or consumption; or you sell more than 25,000 gallons of automotive oil annually and you own a warehouse or distribution center located in Texas, you must complete *Form AP-161*.

Battery Sales Fee - If you sell or offer to sell new or used lead acid batteries, you must complete *Form AP-160*.

Cement Production Tax - If you manufacture or produce cement in Texas, or you import cement into Texas and you distribute or sell cement in intrastate commerce or use the cement in Texas, you must complete *Form AP-171*.

Cigarette, Cigar and/or Tobacco Products Tax - If you wholesale, distribute, store, or make retail sales of cigarettes, cigars, and/or tobacco products, you must complete *Form AP-175 or Form AP-193*.

Coastal Protection Fee - If you transfer crude oil and condensate from or to vessels at a marine terminal located in Texas, you must complete *Form AP-159*.

Crude Oil and Natural Gas Production Taxes - If you produce and/or purchase crude oil and/or natural gas, you must complete *Form AP-134*.

Direct Payment Permit - If you annually purchase at least $800,000 worth of taxable items for your own use and not for resale, you must complete *Form AP-101* to qualify for the permit.

Fireworks Tax - If you collect tax on the retail sale of fireworks, you must complete *Form AP-201*. This is in addition to the sales tax permit. You are required to charge both the sales tax and the fireworks tax.

Franchise Tax - If you are a non-Texas corporation or a non-Texas limited liability company without a certificate of authority, you must complete *Form AP-114*.

Fuels Tax - If you are required to be licensed under Texas Fuels Tax Law for the type and class permit required, you must complete *Form AP-133*.

Gross Receipts Tax - If you provide certain services on oil and gas wells OR are a utility company located in an incorporated city or town having a population of more than 1,000 according to the most recent federal census and intend to do business in Texas, you must complete *Form AP-110*.

Off-Road, Heavy Duty Diesel Powered Construction Equipment Surcharge - If you sell, lease or rent off-road, heavy duty diesel powered construction equipment, you must complete *Form AP-201*. This is in addition to the sales tax permit. You are required to charge both the sales tax and the surcharge.

Hotel Occupancy Tax - If you provide sleeping accommodations to the public for a cost of $2 or more per day, you must complete *Form AP-102*.

International Fuel Tax Agreement (IFTA) - If you operate qualified motor vehicles which require you to be licensed under the International Fuel Tax Agreement, you must complete *Form AP-178*.

Manufactured Housing Sales Tax - If you are a manufacturer of manufactured homes or industrialized housing engaged in business in Texas, you must complete *Form AP-118*.

Maquiladora Export Permit - If you are a maquiladora enterprise and wish to make tax-free purchases in Texas for export to Mexico, you must complete *Form AP-153*, to receive the permit.

Motor Vehicle Seller-Financed Sales Tax - If you finance sales of motor vehicles and collect Motor Vehicle Sales Tax in periodic payments, you must complete *Form AP-169*.

Motor Vehicle Gross Rental Tax - If you rent motor vehicles in Texas, you must complete *Form AP-143*.

Petroleum Products Delivery Fee - If you are required to be licensed under Texas Water Code, sec. 26.3574, you must complete *Form AP-154*.

Sales and Use Tax - If you engage in business in Texas; AND you sell or lease tangible personal property or provide taxable services in Texas to customers in Texas; and/or you acquire tangible personal property or taxable services from out-of-state suppliers that do not hold a Texas Sales or Use Tax permit, you must complete *Form AP-201*.

Sulphur Production Tax - If you own, control, manage, lease, or operate a sulphur mine, well, or shaft, or produce sulphur by any method, system, or manner, you must complete *Form AP-171*.

Telecommunications Infrastructure Fund - If you are a telecommunications utility company or a mobile service provider who collects and pays taxes on telecommunications receipts under Texas Tax Code, Chapter 151, you must complete *Form AP-201*.

Texas Customs Broker License - If you have been licensed by the United States Customs Service AND want to issue export certifications, you must complete *Form AP-168*.

This page intentionally left blank.

TEXAS SALES AND USE TAX RETURN

Form 01-114 (Rev.2-04/33)

a. 26100

c. Taxpayer number

d. Filing period

e.

f. Due date

- Do not staple or paper clip.
- Do not write in shaded areas.

SEE INSTRUCTIONS ON REVERSE SIDE

Page 1 of

g. Taxpayer name and mailing address

- Blacken this box if your mailing address has changed. Show changes by the preprinted information. .... 1.
- Blacken this box if you are no longer in business. Write in the date you went out of business. .... 2.
- Blacken this box if one of your locations is out of business or has changed its address. .... 3.

You have certain rights under Ch. 559, Government Code, to review, request, and correct information we have on file about you. Contact us at the address or toll-free number listed on this form.

h. 88   i.

RETURN MUST BE FILED EVEN IF NO TAX IS DUE

l. **NO SALES** - If you had zero to report in Items 1, 2 and 3 for ALL locations for this filing period, blacken this box, sign and date this return and mail it to the Comptroller's office. ▶ 1

j. Are you taking credit to reduce taxes due on this return for taxes you paid in error on your own purchases? (Blacken appropriate box) .... YES 1 / NO 2

k. Did you refund sales tax for items exported outside the U.S. based on a Texas Licensed Customs Broker Export Certificate? (Blacken appropriate box) ..... YES 1 / NO 2

If you answered yes to either question j or k, you must complete Form 01-148 and submit it with your return.

PLEASE PRINT YOUR NUMERALS LIKE THIS   0 1 2 3 4 5 6 7 8 9

6. Physical location (outlet) name and address *(Do not use a P.O. box address.)*   Outlet no.

1. TOTAL SALES *(Whole dollars only)*
2. TAXABLE SALES *(Whole dollars only)*
3. TAXABLE PURCHASES *(Whole dollars only)*
4. Amount subject to state tax *(Item 2 plus Item 3)*
5. Amount subject to local tax *(Amount for city, transit, county and SPD must be equal.)*

7. **AMOUNT OF TAX DUE FOR THIS OUTLET** *(Dollars and cents)*
(Multiply "Amount subject to tax" by "TAX RATE" for state and local tax due)

TAX RATES

X _____ = 7a. State tax *(include in Item 8a)*

X _____ = 7b. Local tax *(include in Item 8b)*

■ 26180   ■ STATE TAX - Column a   ■ LOCAL TAX - Column b

8. Total tax due *(from all outlets or list supplements)*

01-114 (Rev.2-04/33)

9. Prepayment credit .... −
10. Adjusted tax due *(Item 8 minus Item 9)* .... =
11. TIMELY FILING DISCOUNT .... −
12. Prior payments .... −
13. Net tax due *(Item 10 minus Items 11 & 12)* .... =
14. Penalty and interest *(See instructions)* .... +

15a. Total state amount due   15b. Total local amount due

15. TOTAL STATE AND LOCAL AMOUNT DUE *(Item 13 plus Item 14)* =

Mail to: COMPTROLLER OF PUBLIC ACCOUNTS
111 E. 17th Street
Austin, TX 78774-0100

■ T Code   ■ Taxpayer number   ■ Period   16. **TOTAL AMOUNT PAID** *(Total of Items 15a and 15b)*

26020

Taxpayer name

n.

I declare that the information in this document and any attachments is true and correct to the best of my knowledge.

sign here ▶ Taxpayer or duly authorized agent   Date   Daytime phone *(Area code & number)*

Make check payable to: **STATE COMPTROLLER.**

INSTRUCTIONS FOR COMPLETING TEXAS SALES AND USE TAX RETURN

GENERAL INSTRUCTIONS

WHO MUST FILE THE LONG FORM? If you meet any one of the following criteria, you must file the long form:

- you have more than one outlet;
- you report tax to more than one city, transit authority (MTA/CTD), county or special purpose district (SPD);
- you prepay your state and local taxes;
- you ship outside a transit authority (MTA/CTD);
- you report use tax from out-of-state locations;
- you are a city, county, or special purpose district that has chosen to retain your own local sales and use tax as authorized by the Texas Tax Code;
- you have taken credit for taxes paid in error on purchases; or
- you have custom broker refunds to report.

Returns must be filed for every period even if there is no amount subject to tax or any tax due. Complete and detailed records must be kept of all sales as well as any deductions claimed so that returns can be verified by a state auditor. Failure to file this return and pay applicable tax may result in collection action as prescribed by Title 2 of the Tax Code.

WHEN TO FILE - Returns must be filed or postmarked on or before the 20th day of the month following the end of each reporting period. If the due date falls on a Saturday, Sunday or legal holiday, the next business day will be the due date.

BUSINESS CHANGES - The boxes to the right of the taxpayer name and mailing address should be blackened if your mailing address has changed, if you are no longer in business, if you added a new location, or if one of your locations is out of business or has changed addresses. If you prefer, you may make these changes via voice mail by calling 1-800-224-1844.

INSTRUCTIONS FOR FILING AMENDED TEXAS SALES AND USE TAX RETURNS - To request forms to file an amended return, call 1-800-252-5555 toll free nationwide. The Austin number is 512-463-4600. Forms may be picked up at the Comptroller Field Office nearest you; OR you may photocopy the original, write "AMENDED RETURN" at the top, strike through **Item a**, strike through those figures that have changed, and write the new figures on the return. Sign and date the amended return.

FOR ASSISTANCE - If you have any questions regarding sales tax, you may contact the Texas State Comptroller's field office in your area or call 1-800-252-5555, toll free, nationwide. The Austin number is 512/463-4600. If you are calling from a Telecommunications Device for the Deaf (TDD), our toll free number is 1-800-248-4099, or in Austin, 512/463-4621.

If typing, numbers may be typed consecutively as shown in the example.

```
0123456789
```

If any amounts entered are negative, bracket them as follows: <xxx,xxx.xx>.

SPECIFIC INSTRUCTIONS

Item c. If the return is not preprinted, enter the taxpayer number as shown on your sales tax permit. If you have not received your sales tax permit and you are a sole owner, enter your Social Security number. For other types of organizations, enter the Federal Employer's Identification Number (FEIN) assigned to your organization.

Item d. If the return is not preprinted, enter the filing period of this report (month, quarter or year) and the last day of the period in the space provided. Examples: "Quarter Ending 09-30-03" "Month Ending 10-31-03" "Year Ending 12-31-03."

Item l. If you had zero to report in Items 1, 2, and 3 for all outlets during this filing period, blacken this box, sign and date this return and mail to the Comptroller's office.

Item 1. Enter the total amount (not including tax) of all services and sales, leases and rentals of tangible personal property made during the reporting period for each outlet. Report whole dollars only. Enter "0" if no sales were made during the current reporting period.

Item 2. Enter the total amount of taxable services and taxable sales, leases and rentals of tangible personal property made during the reporting period for each outlet. This amount is the total sales made LESS any deductions. Report whole dollars only. Enter "0" if you have no taxable sales to report.

Item 3. Enter the total amount of taxable purchases that were bought for your own use. This includes purchases from Texas or out-of-state sellers, items taken out of inventory for use, items given away, and items purchased for an exempt use but actually used in a taxable manner. Taxable purchases do not include inventory items being held exclusively for resale. Report whole dollars only. Enter "0" if you have no taxable purchases to report.

Item 4. Add Taxable Sales (Item 2) to Taxable Purchases (Item 3), and enter the result in Item 4. **Do not** include Total Sales (Item 1) in this total. Report whole dollars only.

Item 5. To report local tax by outlet, the amount subject to local tax must be the same for all local taxing authorities (city, transit, county and/or SPD) for that outlet. If any of these local amounts are different for the outlet, you MUST report your local tax on the List Supplement (Form 01-116-A). Report whole dollars only. If "NOT APPLICABLE" is preprinted in Item 5, do not enter an amount.

Item 6. If the return is not preprinted, enter the trade name, actual location and five digit outlet number shown on your sales tax permit for each outlet you are reporting. Use street address or meaningful directions. Do not use P.O. Box or Rural Route Number. Example: "3 miles south of FM 1960 on Jones Road."

- If you do not have a permit, leave outlet number blank.
- If you are reporting use tax from out of state locations, use outlet number "00000."
- If the physical location (outlet) is no longer in business, write "out of business" and date of closing next to any outlet that is no longer in business.
- If the physical location address is different than the preprinted physical location address, make correction next to the incorrect information.
- If a new outlet has been opened, write the outlet trade name, actual location and opening date in a blank space on the return along with a brief description of the business.

Item 7(a,b). Multiply Item 4 by the state tax rate and enter in Item 7a. Multiply Item 5 by the local tax rate and enter in Item 7b. If your return is not preprinted, refer to the booklet, Texas Sales and Use Tax Rates (Pub. 96-132) for a list of the current city, transit, county and SPD rates. If "USE LIST" is preprinted in Item 7b, report the tax on the Texas List Supplement (Form 01-116-A).

Item 8. Combine the state sales tax due from all outlets (Items 7a) and enter the total tax in Column a. Combine local sales tax due from Item 7b from all pages and enter the total tax in Column b.

Item 9. The amount preprinted in Item 9 includes the amount of your prepayment plus the allowable prepayment discount.

- If you prepaid timely and the amount is not printed in Item 9, calculate the credit by dividing the amount you prepaid by .9825 and enter the result in Item 9.
- If the total tax due in either column of Item 8 is greater than the prepayment, enter the difference in Item 10. Multiply the difference by .005 and enter the result in Item 11.
- If the total tax due in either Item 8a or 8b is less than the prepayment credit in Item 9a or 9b enter the difference in Item 10a or 10b. Multiply the difference by .9825 and enter the result in Item 13 to determine the amount of refund. Bracket the amount as follows: <xxx.xx>.
- If you are filing your return and/or paying the tax late, mark out the preprinted amount in Item 9 and enter the actual amount paid with your prepayment report.

NOTE: Discount applies only if all prepayment requirements are met AND your regular sales and use tax return AND any additional payments are postmarked by the due date.

Item 10. Subtract the prepayment credit in Item 9 from the total tax due in Item 8, and enter the result in Adjusted tax due (Item 10).

Item 11. If you are filing your return and paying the tax due on or before the due date, multiply the Total Tax Due in Item 8 by 1/2% (.005) and enter the result in Item 11. (PREPAYERS: See instructions for Item 9.) **NOTE: DO NOT TAKE THE DISCOUNT IF THE RETURN AND/OR PAYMENT IS NOT TIMELY.**

Item 12. If you requested that a prior payment and/or an overpayment be designated to this specific period, the amount is preprinted in Item 12 as of the date this return was printed.

Item 14. Penalty and interest
- 1-30 days late: Enter penalty of 5% (.05) of Item 13.
- 31-60 days late: Enter penalty of 10% (.10) of Item 13.
- Over 60 days late: Enter 10% (.10) penalty of Item 13 plus interest on the amount in Item 7. Calculate interest at the rate published online at <http://www.window.state.tx.us>, or call the Comptroller toll free at 1-877-44RATE4, for the applicable interest rate.

NOTE: An additional $50 penalty may be assessed after more than two returns are received with a postmark date later than the due date.

form 10 • 229

MAIL TO:
CASHIER
TEXAS WORKFORCE COMMISSION
PO BOX 149080
AUSTIN, TEXAS 78714-9080
www.twc.state.tx.us

STATUS REPORT

THIS REPORT IS REQUIRED OF EVERY EMPLOYING UNIT,
AND WILL BE USED TO DETERMINE LIABILITY UNDER THE TEXAS UNEMPLOYMENT COMPENSATION ACT.
(YOU SHOULD RETAIN A COPY FOR YOUR FILES)

IDENTIFICATION SECTION

1. ACCOUNT NUMBER ASSIGNED BY TWC (IF ANY)
2. FEDERAL EMPLOYER ID NUMBER
3. TYPE OF OWNERSHIP (CHECK ONE)
   1. ☐ CORPORATION
   2. ☐ PARTNERSHIP
   3. ☐ INDIVIDUAL (SOLE PROPRIETOR)
   4. ☐ ESTATE
   5. ☐ TRUST
   6. ☐ OTHER (SPECIFY) _____
   ☐ PROFESSIONAL ASSOCIATION
   ☐ LIMITED PARTNERSHIP
   ☐ STATE AGENCY
   ☐ POLITICAL SUBDIVISION

4. NAME
5. MAILING ADDRESS
6. CITY
7. COUNTY
8. STATE
8(a). ZIP CODE
9. PHONE NUMBER ( )

10. BUSINESS ADDRESS WHERE RECORDS OR PAYROLLS ARE KEPT: (IF DIFFERENT FROM ABOVE)
    ADDRESS
    PHONE NUMBER ( )
    CITY
    STATE
    ZIP

11. OWNERS OR OFFICERS [ATTACH ADDITIONAL SHEET IF NECESSARY]
    NAME | SOCIAL SECURITY NUMBER | TITLE | RESIDENCE ADDRESS, CITY, STATE, ZIP

12. BUSINESS LOCATION IN TEXAS [ATTACH ADDITIONAL SHEET IF NECESSARY]
    TRADENAME | STREET ADDRESS, CITY, COUNTY | KIND OF BUSINESS | NUMBER OF EMPLOYEES

13. IF YOUR BUSINESS IS A CORPORATION, ENTER:
    CHARTER NUMBER | STATE INCORPORATED | DATE INCORPORATED | REGISTERED AGENT'S NAME
    ORIGINAL CORPORATE NAME, IF DIFFERENT THAN ABOVE | REGISTERED AGENT'S ADDRESS

EMPLOYMENT SECTION

	MONTH	DAY	YEAR
14. ENTER THE DATE ON WHICH YOUR ORGANIZATION FIRST EMPLOYED SOMEONE IN TEXAS:			
15. ENTER THE DATE ON WHICH YOUR ORGANIZATION FIRST PAID WAGES TO SOMEONE IN TEXAS:			
16. IF YOUR ACCOUNT HAS BEEN INACTIVE: ENTER THE DATE YOUR ORGANIZATION RESUMED EMPLOYING SOMEONE IN TEXAS:			
ENTER THE DATE YOUR ORGANIZATION RESUMED PAYING WAGES IN TEXAS:			
17. ENTER THE ENDING DATE OF THE TWENTIETH WEEK OF EMPLOYMENT IN THE CALENDAR YEAR IN WHICH THIS ORGANIZATION HAD AT LEAST ONE PERSON EMPLOYED IN TEXAS:			
18. IF YOUR ORGANIZATION HAS PAID WAGES OF $1,500 OR MORE IN A CALENDAR QUARTER, ENTER THE ENDING DATE OF THE FIRST QUARTER IN WHICH THIS OCCURRED:			
19. IF YOU HOLD AN EXEMPTION FROM FEDERAL INCOME TAXES UNDER INTERNAL REVENUE CODE SECTION 501(C)(3), ATTACH A COPY OF YOUR EXEMPTION LETTER. ALSO, ENTER THE ENDING DATE OF THE TWENTIETH WEEK OF THE CALENDAR YEAR IN WHICH 4 OR MORE PERSONS WERE EMPLOYED IN TEXAS:			

20. IF THE BUSINESS IN TEXAS WAS ACQUIRED FROM ANOTHER LEGAL ENTITY ENTER:
    PREVIOUS OWNER'S TWC ACCOUNT NUMBER (IF KNOWN) | DATE OF ACQUISITION: →
    NAME OF PREVIOUS OWNER | ADDRESS | CITY | STATE
    WHAT PORTION OF THE BUSINESS WAS ACQUIRED? (CHECK ONE) ☐ ALL ☐ PART (SPECIFY)

21. ENTER THE YEAR(S) YOUR ORGANIZATION WAS LIABLE FOR TAXES UNDER THE FEDERAL UNEMPLOYMENT TAX ACT: (BEGIN WITH MOST RECENT YEAR)
    (YEAR) ___ (YEAR) ___ (YEAR) ___ (YEAR) ___

(CONTINUED ON REVERSE SIDE)

C-1(1199)

EMPLOYMENT SECTION - CONTINUED

22. DOES THIS ORGANIZATION EMPLOY ANY U.S. CITIZENS OUTSIDE OF THE UNITED STATES? ☐ YES ☐ NO

DOMESTIC - HOUSEHOLD EMPLOYMENT SECTION

COMPLETE 23 ONLY IF YOU HAVE DOMESTIC OR HOUSEHOLD EMPLOYEES
(INCLUDES MAIDS, COOKS, CHAUFFEURS, GARDENERS, ETC.)

23. ENTER THE ENDING DATE OF THE FIRST CALENDAR QUARTER IN WHICH YOU PAID GROSS WAGES OF $1,000 OR MORE TO EMPLOYEES PERFORMING DOMESTIC SERVICE: MONTH   DAY   YEAR

NATURE OF ACTIVITY SECTION

24. DESCRIBE FULLY THE NATURE OF ACTIVITY IN TEXAS, AND LIST THE PRINCIPLE PRODUCTS OR SERVICES IN ORDER OF IMPORTANCE:

25. SELECT ONE OF THE SHORT TITLES BELOW WHICH MOST CLOSELY DESCRIBES YOUR BUSINESS OPERATIONS IN TEXAS AND ENTER THE APPROPRIATE CODE IN THE SPACE PROVIDED. →   **INDUSTRY CODE NUMBER**

Code	Description	Code	Description	Code	Description
111	Crop Production	421	Wholesale Trade, Durable Goods	525	Funds, Trusts, and Other Financial Vehicles
112	Animal Production	422	Wholesale Trade, Nondurable Goods	531	Real Estate
113	Forestry and Logging	441	Motor Vehicle and Parts Dealers	532	Rental and Leasing Services
114	Fishing, Hunting, and Trapping	442	Furniture and Home Furnishings Stores	533	Lessors of Nonfinancial Intangible Assets
115	Support Activities for Agriculture and Forestry	443	Electronics and Appliance Stores	541	Professional, Scientific, and Technical Services
211	Oil and Gas Extraction	444	Building Material and Garden Equipment and Supplies Dealers	551	Management of Companies and Enterprises
212	Mining (except Oil and Gas)			561	Administrative and Support Services
213	Support Activities for Mining	445	Food and Beverage Stores	562	Waste Management and Remediation Services
221	Utilities	446	Health and Personal Care Stores	611	Educational Services
233	Building, Developing, and General Contracting	447	Gasoline Stations	621	Ambulatory Health Care Services
234	Heavy Construction	448	Clothing and Clothing Accessories Stores	622	Hospitals
235	Special Trade Contractors	451	Sporting Goods, Hobby, Book, and Music Stores	623	Nursing and Residential Care Facilities
311	Food Manufacturing	452	General Merchandise Stores	624	Social Assistance
312	Beverage and Tobacco Product Manufacturing	453	Miscellaneous Store Retailers	711	Performing Arts, Spectator Sports, and Related Industries
313	Textile Mills	454	Nonstore Retailers		
314	Textile Product Mills	481	Air Transportation	712	Museums, Historical Sites, and Similar Institutions
315	Apparel Manufacturing	482	Rail Transportation	713	Amusement, Gambling, and Recreation Industries
316	Leather and Allied Product Manufacturing	483	Water Transportation	721	Accommodation Services
321	Wood Product Manufacturing	484	Truck Transportation	722	Food Services and Drinking Places
322	Paper Manufacturing	485	Transit and Ground Passenger Transportation	811	Repair and Maintenance Services
323	Printing and Related Support Activities	486	Pipeline Transportation	812	Personal and Laundry Services
324	Petroleum and Coal Products Manufacturing	487	Scenic and Sightseeing Transportation	813	Religious, Grantmaking, Civic, and Professional Organizations
325	Chemical Manufacturing	488	Support Activities for Transportation		
326	Plastics and Rubber Products Manufacturing	491	U.S. Postal Service	814	Private Households (Inc. Domestic Employment)
327	Nonmetallic Mineral Product Manufacturing	492	Couriers and Messengers	921	Executive, Legislative, and Other General Government
331	Primary Metal Manufacturing	493	Warehousing and Storage Facilities	922	Justice, Public Order, and Safety
332	Fabricated Metal Product Manufacturing	511	Publishing Industries	923	Administration of Human Resource Programs
333	Machinery Manufacturing	512	Motion Picture and Sound Recording Industries	924	Administration of Environmental Quality Programs
334	Computer and Electronic Product Manufacturing	513	Broadcasting and Telecommunications	925	Administration of Housing Programs, Urban Planning, and Community Development
335	Electrical Equipment, Appliance, and Component Manufacturing	514	Information and Data Processing Services		
		521	Monetary Authorities - Central Bank	926	Administration of Economic Programs
336	Transportation Equipment Manufacturing	522	Credit Intermediation and Related Activities	927	Space Research and Technology
337	Furniture and Related Product Manufacturing	523	Securities, Commodity Contracts, and Related Activities	928	National Security and International Affairs
339	Miscellaneous Manufacturing	524	Insurance Carriers and Related Activities		

VOLUNTARY ELECTION SECTION

26. IF YOU ARE NOT LIABLE UNDER A COMPULSORY PROVISION OF THE TEXAS UNEMPLOYMENT COMPENSATION ACT, AND YOU WISH TO VOLUNTARILY ELECT COVERAGE FOR YOUR EMPLOYEES, SELECT ONE OF THE FOLLOWING AND ENTER THE YEAR YOU WISH LIABILITY TO BEGIN:

☐ ALL EMPLOYEES
☐ ALL EMPLOYEES, EXCEPT THOSE PERFORMING SERVICE WHICH ARE SPECIFICALLY EXEMPT IN THE TEXAS UNEMPLOYMENT COMPENSATION ACT.

BEGINNING JAN. 1, _____   IT IS UNDERSTOOD AND AGREED THAT AT THE END OF 2 YEARS FROM THIS DATE, OR AT THE END OF ANY
YR   CALENDAR YEAR SUBSEQUENT THERETO, YOU MAY WITHDRAW THIS ELECTION BY FILING A WRITTEN REQUEST. (IF THIS ELECTION IS APPROVED, WE WILL NOTIFY YOU OF YOUR ACCOUNT NUMBER).

FARM OR RANCH EMPLOYMENT

27. DO YOU HAVE ANY EMPLOYMENT IN TEXAS ON A FARM OR RANCH? →
IF "YES", WE WILL SUPPLY YOU WITH A SEPARATE STATUS REPORT TO DETERMINE IF YOU ARE LIABLE FOR YOUR FARM OR RANCH EMPLOYEES.   YES ☐   NO ☐

SIGNATURE SECTION

28. I HEREBY CERTIFY THAT THE PRECEDING INFORMATION IS TRUE AND CORRECT, AND THAT I AM AUTHORIZED TO EXECUTE THIS STATUS REPORT ON BEHALF OF THE EMPLOYING UNIT NAMED HEREIN.
(THIS REPORT MUST BE SIGNED BY THE OWNER, OFFICER, PARTNER OR INDIVIDUAL FOR WHOM A VALID WRITTEN AUTHORIZATION IS ON FILE WITH THE TEXAS WORKFORCE COMMISSION)

DATE OF SIGNATURE: MONTH   DAY   YEAR   SIGN HERE →

DRIVER'S LICENSE NUMBER   TITLE →

Instructions for Status Report (Form C-1)

Purpose of Report: The information in this report will be used to determine if liability has been incurred under the Texas Unemployment Compensation Act.

Who must file: Every individual or employing unit which operates a business or organization in Texas (including domestic and agricultural labor), or which has acquired a business or organization which has operated in Texas.

Employing Unit is defined as any individual or type of organization, including but not limited to any partnership, association, trust, estate, joint-stock company, or corporation, whether domestic or foreign, or the receiver, trustee in bankruptcy, trustee or successor thereof, or the legal representative of a deceased person, which has or, subsequent to January 1, 1936, had in its employ one (1) or more individuals performing services for it within this State.

Detail Instructions:

Item 1: Enter the account number TWC has assigned you. If you have not yet been assigned a number, leave this blank and you will be notified of your number later.

Item 2: Enter the Federal Employer Identification Number the I.R.S. has assigned you.

Item 3: Place an "X" in the appropriate box to indicate your type of business or organization.

Item 4: Enter the names(s) of the legal owner(S). For corporations, enter the corporate name. Do not enter trade names here.

Items 5, 6, 7, 8, and 8(a): Enter the address where you want to receive your mail.

Item 9: Enter the phone number you wish us to use if we need to call you regarding TWC matters.

Item 10: Enter the address and phone number where your payroll records are kept. If it is the same as in items 5, 6, 7, and 8, leave blank.

Item 11: For each owner, officer, or responsible official, enter the name, social security number, title and residence address. If there are more than three, please enter the additional names on a separate sheet and attach it to this report.

Item 12: Enter each trade or business name under which you operate. Also enter the location, kind of business and number of employees at each location. Some examples of kinds of business are: retail store, warehouse, administrative office, factory and auto shop. If additional lines are needed, please continue the information on a separate sheet and attach it to this report.

Item 13: This section should be completed for corporations only. Enter the charter number issued by the state, the issuing state, the date issued, and the original corporate name, if it is different than the name entered in item 4 above. Also enter the name and address of the corporation's registered agent.

Item 14: Enter the first date someone performed services as an employee.

Item 15: Enter the first date someone was paid for their services.

Item 16: If your account with TWC has been suspended, and you are filing this report to reactivate your account, enter the dates someone began performing services and was paid, after you resumed activity in Texas.

Item 17: Enter the ending date (Saturday) of the 20th week of the calendar year in which one or more individuals performed services in Texas. In counting weeks, include any week in which anyone performed services for any portion of a day during that week. This includes part-time and temporary, as well as permanent and full-time employees. If, when counting weeks in the first calendar year of operation, you do not reach 20 weeks, begin counting again with the first week of the second calendar year and count until you reach 20 weeks in that year.

Item 18: Enter the ending date (March 31, June 30, Sept. 30 or Dec. 31) of the first calendar quarter in which wages of $1,500.00 or more were paid.

Item 19: Same as item 17, except that when counting weeks, include only those weeks in which 4 or more individuals performed services. The services do not have to be performed on the same day of the week, and do not have to be performed by the same employee. Also, please be sure to attach a copy of your exemption letter from the Internal Revenue Service.

Item 20: This section should be completed if you acquire all or part of your business or organization in Texas from a previous owner. Enter the TWC account number of the previous owner if you know it. Also enter the name and address of the prior owner, the date the business or part was acquired, and check the appropriate block to indicate "all" or "part" was acquired. If you check "part," describe the part acquired. If additional space is needed, please use a separate sheet and attach it to this report.

Item 21: If you have become liable for taxes to the federal government under the Federal Unemployment Compensation Act, enter your years of liability-beginning with the most recent and working backward.

Item 22: Check the appropriate block to indicate whether you employ U.S. Citizens who perform services outside the U.S.

Item 23: Enter the ending date (March 31, June 30, Sept. 30, or Dec. 31) of the calendar quarter in which $1,000.00 or more was paid to any individual(s) who perform domestic service.

Item 24: Enter a brief description of your business activity in Texas and also list the principle product(s) you produce or the service you provide.

Item 25: Select one of the items which describes your operations in Texas and enter the appropriate code in the block.

Item 26: If your employment experience does not indicate you have become liable under a compulsory provision of the Texas Unemployment Compensation Act, you may voluntarily elect coverage for your employees. To do this, check the appropriate block to indicate whether you wish to cover all employees, or only those who are not specifically exempt by one of the sections of the law which define exempt services. If you have questions concerning exempt services, please contact a TWC Field Tax office. *See your phone book for the office nearest you.*

Item 27: Indicate if you have any employment on a farm or ranch and a separate Status Report will be provided.

Item 28: This report must be signed by an owner, corporate officer, partner, or individual for whom a valid Written Authorization is on file with the Texas Workforce Commission.

Completed forms, inquiries, or corrections to the individual information contained in this form shall be sent to the TWC Tax and Labor Law Department, 101 E 15th St, Room 504, Austin, TX 78778-0001, (512) 463-2699. An individual may receive and review information that TWC collects regarding that individual by sending an e-mail to open.records@twc.state.tx.us or writing to TWC Open Records Unit, 101 East 15th Street, Room 264, Austin, TX 78778-0001.

form 11 ♦ 233

IRS Form 8300 (Rev. December 2001)
OMB No. 1545-0892
Department of the Treasury
Internal Revenue Service

Report of Cash Payments Over $10,000 Received in a Trade or Business
▶ See instructions for definition of cash.
▶ Use this form for transactions occurring after December 31, 2001. Do not use prior versions after this date.
For Privacy Act and Paperwork Reduction Act Notice, see page 4.

FinCEN Form 8300 (December 2001)
OMB No. 1506-0018
Department of the Treasury
Financial Crimes Enforcement Network

1 Check appropriate box(es) if: **a** ☐ Amends prior report; **b** ☐ Suspicious transaction.

Part I — Identity of Individual From Whom the Cash Was Received

2 If more than one individual is involved, check here and see instructions . . . . ▶ ☐
3 Last name | 4 First name | 5 M.I. | 6 Taxpayer identification number
7 Address (number, street, and apt. or suite no.) | 8 Date of birth ▶ M M D D Y Y Y Y (see instructions)
9 City | 10 State | 11 ZIP code | 12 Country (if not U.S.) | 13 Occupation, profession, or business
14 Document used to verify identity: **a** Describe identification ▶ _____
 b Issued by _____ **c** Number _____

Part II — Person on Whose Behalf This Transaction Was Conducted

15 If this transaction was conducted on behalf of more than one person, check here and see instructions . . . . . ▶ ☐
16 Individual's last name or Organization's name | 17 First name | 18 M.I. | 19 Taxpayer identification number
20 Doing business as (DBA) name (see instructions) | Employer identification number
21 Address (number, street, and apt. or suite no.) | 22 Occupation, profession, or business
23 City | 24 State | 25 ZIP code | 26 Country (if not U.S.)
27 Alien identification: **a** Describe identification ▶ _____
 b Issued by _____ **c** Number _____

Part III — Description of Transaction and Method of Payment

28 Date cash received M M D D Y Y Y Y
29 Total cash received $ _____ .00
30 If cash was received in more than one payment, check here . . . ▶ ☐
31 Total price if different from item 29 $ _____ .00

32 Amount of cash received (in U.S. dollar equivalent) (must equal item 29) (see instructions):
 a U.S. currency $ _____ .00 (Amount in $100 bills or higher $ _____ .00)
 b Foreign currency $ _____ .00 (Country ▶ _____)
 c Cashier's check(s) $ _____ .00 ⎫
 d Money order(s) $ _____ .00 ⎬ Issuer's name(s) and serial number(s) of the monetary instrument(s) ▶ _____
 e Bank draft(s) $ _____ .00 ⎪
 f Traveler's check(s) $ _____ .00 ⎭

33 Type of transaction
 a ☐ Personal property purchased
 b ☐ Real property purchased
 c ☐ Personal services provided
 d ☐ Business services provided
 e ☐ Intangible property purchased
 f ☐ Debt obligations paid
 g ☐ Exchange of cash
 h ☐ Escrow or trust funds
 i ☐ Bail received by court clerks
 j ☐ Other (specify) ▶

34 Specific description of property or service shown in 33. (Give serial or registration number, address, docket number, etc.) ▶ _____

Part IV — Business That Received Cash

35 Name of business that received cash | 36 Employer identification number
37 Address (number, street, and apt. or suite no.) | Social security number
38 City | 39 State | 40 ZIP code | 41 Nature of your business

42 Under penalties of perjury, I declare that to the best of my knowledge the information I have furnished above is true, correct, and complete.

Signature ▶ _____ Authorized official   Title ▶ _____

43 Date of signature M M D D Y Y Y Y | 44 Type or print name of contact person | 45 Contact telephone number ( )

IRS Form 8300 (Rev. 12-2001)   Cat. No. 62133S   FinCEN Form 8300 (12-2001)

IRS Form 8300 (Rev. 12-2001)   Page **2**   FinCEN Form 8300 (12-2001)

Multiple Parties
(Complete applicable parts below if box 2 or 15 on page 1 is checked)

Part I — Continued- Complete if box 2 on page 1 is checked

3 Last name	4 First name	5 M.I.	6 Taxpayer identification number
7 Address (number, street, and apt. or suite no.)		8 Date of birth (see instructions)	M M D D Y Y Y Y
9 City	10 State 11 ZIP code	12 Country (if not U.S.)	13 Occupation, profession, or business

14 Document used to verify identity: **a** Describe identification ▶ _____
   b Issued by   **c** Number

3 Last name	4 First name	5 M.I.	6 Taxpayer identification number
7 Address (number, street, and apt. or suite no.)		8 Date of birth (see instructions)	M M D D Y Y Y Y
9 City	10 State 11 ZIP code	12 Country (if not U.S.)	13 Occupation, profession, or business

14 Document used to verify identity: **a** Describe identification ▶ _____
   b Issued by   **c** Number

Part II — Continued- Complete if box 15 on page 1 is checked

16 Individual's last name or Organization's name	17 First name	18 M.I.	19 Taxpayer identification number
20 Doing business as (DBA) name (see instructions)			Employer identification number
21 Address (number, street, and apt. or suite no.)		22 Occupation, profession, or business	
23 City	24 State 25 ZIP code	26 Country (if not U.S.)	

27 Alien identification: **a** Describe identification ▶ _____
   b Issued by   **c** Number

16 Individual's last name or Organization's name	17 First name	18 M.I.	19 Taxpayer identification number
20 Doing business as (DBA) name (see instructions)			Employer identification number
21 Address (number, street, and apt. or suite no.)		22 Occupation, profession, or business	
23 City	24 State 25 ZIP code	26 Country (if not U.S.)	

27 Alien identification: **a** Describe identification ▶ _____
   b Issued by   **c** Number

IRS Form **8300** (Rev. 12-2001)   FinCEN Form **8300** (12-2001)

Section references are to the Internal Revenue Code unless otherwise noted.

Changes To Note

- Section 6050I (26 United States Code (U.S.C.) 6050I) and 31 U.S.C. 5331 require that certain information be reported to the IRS and the Financial Crimes Enforcement Network (FinCEN). This information must be reported on **IRS/FinCEN Form 8300.**
- Item 33 box **i** is to be checked **only** by clerks of the court; box **d** is to be checked by bail bondsmen. See the instructions on page 4.
- For purposes of section 6050I and 31 U.S.C. 5331, the word "cash" and "currency" have the same meaning. See **Cash** under **Definitions** below.

General Instructions

Who must file. Each person engaged in a trade or business who, in the course of that trade or business, receives more than $10,000 in cash in one transaction or in two or more related transactions, must file Form 8300. Any transactions conducted between a payer (or its agent) and the recipient in a 24-hour period are related transactions. Transactions are considered related even if they occur over a period of more than 24 hours if the recipient knows, or has reason to know, that each transaction is one of a series of connected transactions.

Keep a copy of each Form 8300 for 5 years from the date you file it.

Clerks of Federal or State courts must file Form 8300 if more than $10,000 in cash is received as bail for an individual(s) charged with certain criminal offenses. For these purposes, a clerk includes the clerk's office or any other office, department, division, branch, or unit of the court that is authorized to receive bail. If a person receives bail on behalf of a clerk, the clerk is treated as receiving the bail. See the instructions for **Item 33** on page 4.

If multiple payments are made in cash to satisfy bail and the initial payment does not exceed $10,000, the initial payment and subsequent payments must be aggregated and the information return must be filed by the 15th day after receipt of the payment that causes the aggregate amount to exceed $10,000 in cash. In such cases, the reporting requirement can be satisfied either by sending a single written statement with an aggregate amount listed or by furnishing a copy of each Form 8300 relating to that payer. Payments made to satisfy separate bail requirements are not required to be aggregated. See Treasury Regulations section 1.6050I-2.

Casinos must file Form 8300 for nongaming activities (restaurants, shops, etc.).

Voluntary use of Form 8300. Form 8300 may be filed voluntarily for any suspicious transaction (see **Definitions**) for use by FinCEN and the IRS, even if the total amount does not exceed $10,000.

Exceptions. Cash is not required to be reported if it is received:

- By a financial institution required to file **Form 4789,** Currency Transaction Report.
- By a casino required to file (or exempt from filing) **Form 8362,** Currency Transaction Report by Casinos, if the cash is received as part of its gaming business.
- By an agent who receives the cash from a principal, if the agent uses all of the cash within 15 days in a second transaction that is reportable on Form 8300 or on Form 4789, and discloses all the information necessary to complete Part II of Form 8300 or Form 4789 to the recipient of the cash in the second transaction.
- In a transaction occurring entirely outside the United States. See **Pub. 1544,** Reporting Cash Payments Over $10,000 (Received in a Trade or Business), regarding transactions occurring in Puerto Rico, the Virgin Islands, and territories and possessions of the United States.
- In a transaction that is not in the course of a person's trade or business.

When to file. File Form 8300 by the 15th day after the date the cash was received. If that date falls on a Saturday, Sunday, or legal holiday, file the form on the next business day.

Where to file. File the form with the Internal Revenue Service, Detroit Computing Center, P.O. Box 32621, Detroit, MI 48232.

Statement to be provided. You must give a written statement to each person named on a required Form 8300 on or before January 31 of the year following the calendar year in which the cash is received. The statement must show the name, telephone number, and address of the information contact for the business, the aggregate amount of reportable cash received, and that the information was furnished to the IRS. Keep a copy of the statement for your records.

Multiple payments. If you receive more than one cash payment for a single transaction or for related transactions, you must report the multiple payments any time you receive a total amount that exceeds $10,000 within any 12-month period. Submit the report within 15 days of the date you receive the payment that causes the total amount to exceed $10,000. If more than one report is required within 15 days, you may file a combined report. File the combined report no later than the date the earliest report, if filed separately, would have to be filed.

Taxpayer identification number (TIN). You must furnish the correct TIN of the person or persons from whom you receive the cash and, if applicable, the person or persons on whose behalf the transaction is being conducted. **You may be subject to penalties for an incorrect or missing TIN.**

The TIN for an individual (including a sole proprietorship) is the individual's social security number (SSN). For certain resident aliens who are not eligible to get an SSN and nonresident aliens who are required to file tax returns, it is an IRS Individual Taxpayer Identification Number (ITIN). For other persons, including corporations, partnerships, and estates, it is the employer identification number (EIN).

If you have requested but are not able to get a TIN for one or more of the parties to a transaction within 15 days following the transaction, file the report and attach a statement explaining why the TIN is not included.

Exception: *You are not required to provide the TIN of a person who is a nonresident alien individual or a foreign organization **if** that person does not have income effectively connected with the conduct of a U.S. trade or business **and** does not have an office or place of business, or fiscal or paying agent, in the United States. See Pub. 1544 for more information.*

Penalties. You may be subject to penalties if you fail to file a correct and complete Form 8300 on time and you cannot show that the failure was due to reasonable cause. You may also be subject to penalties if you fail to furnish timely a correct and complete statement to each person named in a required report. A minimum penalty of $25,000 may be imposed if the failure is due to an intentional or willful disregard of the cash reporting requirements.

Penalties may also be imposed for causing, or attempting to cause, a trade or business to fail to file a required report; for causing, or attempting to cause, a trade or business to file a required report containing a material omission or misstatement of fact; or for structuring, or attempting to structure, transactions to avoid the reporting requirements. These violations may also be subject to criminal prosecution which, upon conviction, may result in imprisonment of up to 5 years or fines of up to $250,000 for individuals and $500,000 for corporations or both.

Definitions

Cash. The term "cash" means the following:

- U.S. and foreign coin and currency received in any transaction.
- A cashier's check, money order, bank draft, or traveler's check having a face amount of $10,000 or less that is received in a **designated reporting transaction** (defined below), or that is received in any transaction in which the recipient knows that the instrument is being used in an attempt to avoid the reporting of the transaction under either section 6050I or 31 U.S.C. 5331.

Note: Cash does not include a check drawn on the payer's own account, such as a personal check, regardless of the amount.

Designated reporting transaction. A retail sale (or the receipt of funds by a broker or other intermediary in connection with a retail sale) of a consumer durable, a collectible, or a travel or entertainment activity.

Retail sale. Any sale (whether or not the sale is for resale or for any other purpose) made in the course of a trade or business if that trade or business principally consists of making sales to ultimate consumers.

Consumer durable. An item of tangible personal property of a type that, under ordinary usage, can reasonably be expected to remain useful for at least 1 year, and that has a sales price of more than $10,000.

Collectible. Any work of art, rug, antique, metal, gem, stamp, coin, etc.

Travel or entertainment activity. An item of travel or entertainment that pertains to a single trip or event if the combined sales price of the item and all other items relating to the same trip or event that are sold in the same transaction (or related transactions) exceeds $10,000.

Exceptions. A cashier's check, money order, bank draft, or traveler's check is not considered received in a designated reporting transaction if it constitutes the proceeds of a bank loan or if it is received as a payment on certain promissory notes, installment sales contracts, or down payment plans. See Pub. 1544 for more information.

Person. An individual, corporation, partnership, trust, estate, association, or company.

Recipient. The person receiving the cash. Each branch or other unit of a person's trade or business is considered a separate recipient unless the branch receiving the cash (or a central office linking the branches), knows or has reason to know the identity of payers making cash payments to other branches.

Transaction. Includes the purchase of property or services, the payment of debt, the exchange of a negotiable instrument for cash, and the receipt of cash to be held in escrow or trust. A single transaction may not be broken into multiple transactions to avoid reporting.

Suspicious transaction. A transaction in which it appears that a person is attempting to cause Form 8300 not to be filed, or to file a false or incomplete form. The term also includes any transaction in which there is an indication of possible illegal activity.

Specific Instructions

You must complete all parts. However, you may skip Part II if the individual named in Part I is conducting the transaction on his or her behalf only. **For voluntary reporting of suspicious transactions, see Item 1 below.**

Item 1. If you are amending a prior report, check box 1a. Complete the appropriate items with the correct or amended information only. Complete all of Part IV. Staple a copy of the original report to the amended report.

To voluntarily report a suspicious transaction (see **Definitions**), check box 1b. You may also telephone your local IRS Criminal Investigation Division or call 1-800-800-2877.

Part I

Item 2. If two or more individuals conducted the transaction you are reporting, check the box and complete Part I for any one of the individuals. Provide the same information for the other individual(s) on the back of the form. If more than three individuals are involved, provide the same information on additional sheets of paper and attach them to this form.

Item 6. Enter the taxpayer identification number (TIN) of the individual named. See **Taxpayer identification number (TIN)** on page 3 for more information.

Item 8. Enter eight numerals for the date of birth of the individual named. For example, if the individual's birth date is July 6, 1960, enter 07 06 1960.

Item 13. Fully describe the nature of the occupation, profession, or business (for example, "plumber," "attorney," or "automobile dealer"). Do not use general or nondescriptive terms such as "businessman" or "self-employed."

Item 14. You must verify the name and address of the named individual(s). Verification must be made by examination of a document normally accepted as a means of identification when cashing checks (for example, a driver's license, passport, alien registration card, or other official document). In item 14a, enter the type of document examined. In item 14b, identify the issuer of the document. In item 14c, enter the document's number. For example, if the individual has a Utah driver's license, enter "driver's license" in item 14a, "Utah" in item 14b, and the number appearing on the license in item 14c.

Part II

Item 15. If the transaction is being conducted on behalf of more than one person (including husband and wife or parent and child), check the box and complete Part II for any one of the persons. Provide the same information for the other person(s) on the back of the form. If more than three persons are involved, provide the same information on additional sheets of paper and attach them to this form.

Items 16 through 19. If the person on whose behalf the transaction is being conducted is an individual, complete items 16, 17, and 18. Enter his or her TIN in item 19. If the individual is a sole proprietor and has an employer identification number (EIN), you must enter both the SSN and EIN in item 19. If the person is an organization, put its name as shown on required tax filings in item 16 and its EIN in item 19.

Item 20. If a sole proprietor or organization named in items 16 through 18 is doing business under a name other than that entered in item 16 (e.g., a "trade" or "doing business as (DBA)" name), enter it here.

Item 27. If the person is not required to furnish a TIN, complete this item. See **Taxpayer Identification Number (TIN)** on page 3. Enter a description of the type of official document issued to that person in item 27a (for example, "passport"), the country that issued the document in item 27b, and the document's number in item 27c.

Part III

Item 28. Enter the date you received the cash. If you received the cash in more than one payment, enter the date you received the payment that caused the combined amount to exceed $10,000. See **Multiple payments** under General Instructions for more information.

Item 30. Check this box if the amount shown in item 29 was received in more than one payment (for example, as installment payments or payments on related transactions).

Item 31. Enter the total price of the property, services, amount of cash exchanged, etc. (for example, the total cost of a vehicle purchased, cost of catering service, exchange of currency) if different from the amount shown in item 29.

Item 32. Enter the dollar amount of each form of cash received. Show foreign currency amounts in U.S. dollar equivalent at a fair market rate of exchange available to the public. **The sum of the amounts must equal item 29.** For cashier's check, money order, bank draft, or traveler's check, provide the name of the issuer and the serial number of each instrument. Names of all issuers and all serial numbers involved must be provided. If necessary, provide this information on additional sheets of paper and attach to this form.

Item 33. Check the appropriate box(es) that describe the transaction. If the transaction is not specified in boxes a–i, check box j and briefly describe the transaction (for example, "car lease," "boat lease," "house lease," or "aircraft rental"). If the transaction relates to the receipt of bail by a court clerk, check box **i**, "Bail received by court clerks." This box is **only** for use by court clerks. If the transaction relates to cash received by a bail bondsman, check box **d**, "Business services provided."

Part IV

Item 36. If you are a sole proprietorship, you must enter your SSN. If your business also has an EIN, you must provide the EIN as well. All other business entities must enter an EIN.

Item 41. Fully describe the nature of your business, for example, "attorney" or "jewelry dealer." Do not use general or nondescriptive terms such as "business" or "store."

Item 42. This form must be signed by an individual who has been authorized to do so for the business that received the cash.

Privacy Act and Paperwork Reduction Act Notice. Except as otherwise noted, the information solicited on this form is required by the Internal Revenue Service (IRS) and the Financial Crimes Enforcement Network (FinCEN) in order to carry out the laws and regulations of the United States Department of the Treasury. Trades or businesses, except for clerks of criminal courts, are required to provide the information to the IRS and FinCEN under both section 6050I and 31 U.S.C. 5331. Clerks of criminal courts are required to provide the information to the IRS under section 6050I. Section 6109 and 31 U.S.C. 5331 require that you provide your social security number in order to adequately identify you and process your return and other papers. The principal purpose for collecting the information on this form is to maintain reports or records where such reports or records have a high degree of usefulness in criminal, tax, or regulatory investigations or proceedings, or in the conduct of intelligence or counterintelligence activities, by directing the Federal Government's attention to unusual or questionable transactions.

While such information is invaluable with regards to the purpose of this form, you are not required to provide information as to whether the reported transaction is deemed suspicious. No penalties or fines will be assessed for failure to provide such information, even if you determine that the reported transaction is indeed suspicious in nature. Failure to provide all other requested information, or the provision of fraudulent information, may result in criminal prosecution and other penalties under Title 26 and Title 31 of the United States Code.

Generally, tax returns and return information are confidential, as stated in section 6103. However, section 6103 allows or requires the IRS to disclose or give the information requested on this form to others as described in the Code. For example, we may disclose your tax information to the Department of Justice, to enforce the tax laws, both civil and criminal, and to cities, states, the District of Columbia, U.S. commonwealths or possessions, and certain foreign governments to carry out their tax laws. We may disclose your tax information to the Department of Treasury and contractors for tax administration purposes; and to other persons as necessary to obtain information which we cannot get in any other way in order to determine the amount of or to collect the tax you owe. We may disclose your tax information to the Comptroller General of the United States to permit the Comptroller General to review the IRS. We may disclose your tax information to Committees of Congress; Federal, state, and local child support agencies; and to other Federal agencies for the purposes of determining entitlement for benefits or the eligibility for and the repayment of loans. We may also disclose this information to Federal agencies that investigate or respond to acts or threats of terrorism or participate in intelligence or counterintelligence activities concerning terrorism.

FinCEN may provide the information collected through this form to those officers and employees of the Department of the Treasury who have a need for the records in the performance of their duties. FinCEN may also refer the records to any other department or agency of the Federal Government upon the request of the head of such department or agency and may also provide the records to appropriate state, local, and foreign criminal law enforcement and regulatory personnel in the performance of their official duties.

You are not required to provide the information requested on a form that is subject to the Paperwork Reduction Act unless the form displays a valid OMB control number. Books or records relating to a form or its instructions must be retained as long as their contents may become material in the administration of any law under Title 26 or Title 31.

The time needed to complete this form will vary depending on individual circumstances. The estimated average time is 21 minutes. If you have comments concerning the accuracy of this time estimate or suggestions for making this form simpler, you can write to the Tax Forms Committee, Western Area Distribution Center, Rancho Cordova, CA 95743-0001. **Do not** send this form to this office. Instead, see **Where To File** on page 3.

Form **8850**
(Rev. October 2002)
Department of the Treasury
Internal Revenue Service

Pre-Screening Notice and Certification Request for the Work Opportunity and Welfare-to-Work Credits

▶ See separate instructions.

form 12 ♦ 237

OMB No. 1545-1500

Job applicant: Fill in the lines below and check any boxes that apply. Complete only this side.

Your name _____ Social security number ▶ _____

Street address where you live _____

City or town, state, and ZIP code _____

Telephone number (___) ___ - _____

If you are under age 25, enter your date of birth (month, day, year) ___/___/___

Work Opportunity Credit

1 ☐ Check here if you received a conditional certification from the state employment security agency (SESA) or a participating local agency for the work opportunity credit.

2 ☐ Check here if **any** of the following statements apply to you.
  - I am a member of a family that has received assistance from Temporary Assistance for Needy Families (TANF) for any 9 months during the last 18 months.
  - I am a veteran and a member of a family that received food stamps for at least a 3-month period within the last 15 months.
  - I was referred here by a rehabilitation agency approved by the state or the Department of Veterans Affairs.
  - I am at least age 18 but **not** age 25 or older and I am a member of a family that:
    a Received food stamps for the last 6 months **or**
    b Received food stamps for at least 3 of the last 5 months, **but** is no longer eligible to receive them.
  - Within the past year, I was convicted of a felony or released from prison for a felony **and** during the last 6 months I was a member of a low-income family.
  - I received supplemental security income (SSI) benefits for any month ending within the last 60 days.

Welfare-to-Work Credit

3 ☐ Check here if you received a conditional certification from the SESA or a participating local agency for the welfare-to-work credit.

4 ☐ Check here if you are a member of a family that:
  - Received TANF payments for at least the last 18 months, **or**
  - Received TANF payments for any 18 months beginning after August 5, 1997, **and** the earliest 18-month period beginning after August 5, 1997, ended within the last 2 years, **or**
  - Stopped being eligible for TANF payments within the last 2 years because Federal or state law limited the maximum time those payments could be made.

All Applicants

Under penalties of perjury, I declare that I gave the above information to the employer on or before the day I was offered a job, and it is, to the best of my knowledge, true, correct, and complete.

Job applicant's signature ▶   Date ___/___/___

For Privacy Act and Paperwork Reduction Act Notice, see page 2.   Cat. No. 22851L   Form **8850** (Rev. 10-02)

Form 8850 (Rev. 10-02) Page **2**

For Employer's Use Only

Employer's name _____ Telephone no. (___) ___ - ___ EIN ▶ _____

Street address _____

City or town, state, and ZIP code _____

Person to contact, if different from above _____ Telephone no. (___) ___ - ___

Street address _____

City or town, state, and ZIP code _____

If, based on the individual's age and home address, he or she is a member of group 4 or 6 (as described under **Members of Targeted Groups** in the separate instructions), enter that group number (4 or 6) . . . . ▶ ___

| Date applicant: | Gave information __/__/__ | Was offered job __/__/__ | Was hired __/__/__ | Started job __/__/__ |

Under penalties of perjury, I declare that I completed this form on or before the day a job was offered to the applicant and that the information I have furnished is, to the best of my knowledge, true, correct, and complete. Based on the information the job applicant furnished on page 1, I believe the individual is a member of a targeted group or a long-term family assistance recipient. I hereby request a certification that the individual is a member of a targeted group or a long-term family assistance recipient.

Employer's signature ▶ _____ Title _____ Date __/__/__

Privacy Act and Paperwork Reduction Act Notice

Section references are to the Internal Revenue Code.

Section 51(d)(12) permits a prospective employer to request the applicant to complete this form and give it to the prospective employer. The information will be used by the employer to complete the employer's Federal tax return. Completion of this form is voluntary and may assist members of targeted groups and long-term family assistance recipients in securing employment. Routine uses of this form include giving it to the state employment security agency (SESA), which will contact appropriate sources to confirm that the applicant is a member of a targeted group or a long-term family assistance recipient. This form may also be given to the Internal Revenue Service for administration of the Internal Revenue laws, to the Department of Justice for civil and criminal litigation, to the Department of Labor for oversight of the certifications performed by the SESA, and to cities, states, and the District of Columbia for use in administering their tax laws. In addition, we may disclose this information to Federal, state, or local agencies that investigate or respond to acts or threats of terrorism or participate in intelligence or counterintelligence activities concerning terrorism.

You are not required to provide the information requested on a form that is subject to the Paperwork Reduction Act unless the form displays a valid OMB control number. Books or records relating to a form or its instructions must be retained as long as their contents may become material in the administration of any Internal Revenue law. Generally, tax returns and return information are confidential, as required by section 6103.

The time needed to complete and file this form will vary depending on individual circumstances. The estimated average time is:

Recordkeeping . . . . 2 hr., 46 min.
Learning about the law or the form . . . . 36 min.
Preparing and sending this form to the SESA . . . . 36 min.

If you have comments concerning the accuracy of these time estimates or suggestions for making this form simpler, we would be happy to hear from you. You can write to the Tax Forms Committee, Western Area Distribution Center, Rancho Cordova, CA 95743-0001.

Do not send this form to this address. Instead, see **When and Where To File** in the separate instructions.

Form **8850** (Rev. 10-02)

Instructions for Form 8850
(Rev. October 2002)

Pre-Screening Notice and Certification Request for the Work Opportunity and Welfare-to-Work Credits

Department of the Treasury
Internal Revenue Service

Section references are to the Internal Revenue Code unless otherwise noted.

General Instructions

Changes To Note
- The categories of high-risk youth and summer youth employees now include qualified individuals who live in renewal communities and begin work for you after December 31, 2001.
- The work opportunity credit and the welfare-to-work credit are now allowed for qualified individuals who begin work for you before January 1, 2004.

Purpose of Form
Employers use Form 8850 to pre-screen and to make a written request to a state employment security agency (SESA) to certify an individual as:
- A member of a targeted group for purposes of qualifying for the work opportunity credit or
- A long-term family assistance recipient for purposes of qualifying for the welfare-to-work credit.

Submitting Form 8850 to the SESA is but one step in the process of qualifying for the work opportunity credit or the welfare-to-work credit. The SESA must certify the job applicant is a member of a targeted group or is a long-term family assistance recipient. After starting work, the employee must meet the minimum number-of-hours-worked requirement for the work opportunity credit or the minimum number-of-hours, number-of-days requirement for the welfare-to-work credit. The employer may elect to take the applicable credit by filing **Form 5884,** Work Opportunity Credit, or **Form 8861,** Welfare-to-Work Credit.

Note: *Do not use Form 8850 with respect to New York Liberty Zone business employees. Certification is not required for these employees. See* **Form 8884,** *New York Liberty Zone Business Employee Credit, for details.*

Who Should Complete and Sign the Form
The job applicant gives information to the employer on or before the day a job offer is made. This information is entered on Form 8850. Based on the applicant's information, the employer determines whether or not he or she believes the applicant is a member of a targeted group (as defined under **Members of Targeted Groups** on page 2) or a long-term family assistance recipient (as defined under **Welfare-to-Work Job Applicants** on page 2). If the employer believes the applicant is a member of a targeted group or a long-term family assistance recipient, the employer completes the rest of the form no later than the day the job offer is made. Both the job applicant and the employer must sign Form 8850 no later than the date for submitting the form to the SESA.

Instructions for Employer

When and Where To File
Do not file Form 8850 with the Internal Revenue Service. Instead, file it with the work opportunity tax credit (WOTC) coordinator for your SESA no later than the 21st day after the job applicant begins work for you. You may be able to file Form 8850 electronically. See Announcement 2002-44 for details. You can find Announcement 2002-44 on page 809 of Internal Revenue Bulletin 2002-17 at **www.irs.gov/pub/irs-irbs/irb02-17.pdf**.

To get the name, address, phone and fax numbers, and e-mail address of the WOTC coordinator for your SESA, visit the Department of Labor Employment and Training Administration (ETA) web site at **www.ows.doleta.gov/employ/tax.asp**.

Additional Requirements for Certification
In addition to filing Form 8850, you must complete and send to your state's WOTC coordinator **either:**
- **ETA Form 9062,** Conditional Certification Form, if the job applicant received this form from a participating agency (e.g., the Jobs Corps) **or**
- **ETA Form 9061,** Individual Characteristics Form, if the job applicant did not receive a conditional certification.

You can get ETA Form 9061 from your local public employment service office, or you can download it from the ETA web site at **www.ows.doleta.gov**.

Recordkeeping
Keep copies of Forms 8850, along with any transmittal letters that you submit to your SESA, as long as they may be needed for the administration of the Internal Revenue Code provisions relating to the work opportunity credit and the welfare-to-work credit. Records that support these credits usually must be kept for 3 years from the date any income tax return claiming the credits is due or filed, whichever is later.

Cat. No. 24833J

Members of Targeted Groups

A job applicant may be certified as a member of a targeted group if he or she is described in one of the following groups.

1. Qualified IV-A recipient. A member of a family receiving assistance under a state plan approved under part A of title IV of the Social Security Act relating to Temporary Assistance for Needy Families (TANF). The assistance must be received for any 9 months during the 18-month period that ends on the hiring date.

2. Qualified veteran. A veteran who is a member of a family receiving assistance under the Food Stamp program for generally at least a 3-month period during the 15-month period ending on the hiring date. See section 51(d)(3). To be considered a **veteran**, the applicant must:

- Have served on active duty (not including training) in the Armed Forces of the United States for more than 180 days or have been discharged for a service-connected disability and
- Not have a period of active duty (not including training) of more than 90 days that ended during the 60-day period ending on the hiring date.

3. Qualified ex-felon. An ex-felon who:

- Has been convicted of a felony under any Federal or state law,
- Is hired not more than 1 year after the conviction or release from prison for that felony, and
- Is a member of a family that had income on an annual basis of 70% or less of the Bureau of Labor Statistics lower living standard during the 6 months preceding the earlier of the month the income determination occurs or the month in which the hiring date occurs.

4. High-risk youth. An individual who is at least 18 but not yet 25 on the hiring date and lives in an empowerment zone, enterprise community, or renewal community.

5. Vocational rehabilitation referral. An individual who has a physical or mental disability resulting in a substantial handicap to employment and who was referred to the employer upon completion of (or while receiving) rehabilitation services under a state plan of employment or a program approved by the Department of Veterans Affairs.

6. Summer youth employee. An individual who:

- Performs services for the employer between May 1 and September 15,
- Is age 16 but not yet age 18 on the hiring date (or if later, on May 1),
- Has never worked for the employer before, and
- Lives in an empowerment zone, enterprise community, or renewal community.

7. Food stamp recipient. An individual who:

- Is at least age 18 but not yet age 25 and
- Is a member of a family that—

a. Has received food stamps for the 6-month period ending on the hiring date or

b. Is no longer eligible for such assistance under section 6(o) of the Food Stamp Act of 1977, but the family received food stamps for at least 3 months of the 5-month period ending on the hiring date.

8. SSI recipient. An individual who is receiving supplemental security income benefits under title XVI of the Social Security Act (including benefits of the type described in section 1616 of the Social Security Act or section 212 of Public Law 93-66) for any month ending within the 60-day period ending on the hiring date.

Empowerment zones, enterprise communities, and renewal communities. For details about rural empowerment zone and enterprise communities, you can access **www.ezec.gov**, call 1-800-645-4712, or contact your SESA. For details on all empowerment zones, enterprise communities, and renewal communities, you can access **http://hud.esri.com/locateservices/ezec**. You can also call HUD at 1-800-998-9999 for details on renewal communities, urban empowerment zones, and urban enterprise communities.

Note: *Parts of Washington, DC, are treated as an empowerment zone. For details, see section 1400 and Notice 98-57, 1998-2 C.B. 671 (you can find Notice 98-57 on page 9 of Internal Revenue Bulletin 1998-47 at **www.irs.gov/pub/irs-irbs/irb98-47.pdf**). Also, there are no areas designated in Puerto Rico, Guam, or any U.S. possession.*

Welfare-to-Work Job Applicants

An individual may be certified as a long-term family assistance recipient if he or she is a member of a family that:

- Has received TANF payments for at least 18 consecutive months ending on the hiring date, **or**
- Receives TANF payments for any 18 months (whether or not consecutive) beginning after August 5, 1997, **and** the earliest 18-month period beginning after August 5, 1997, ended within the last 2 years, **or**
- Stopped being eligible for TANF payments because Federal or state law limits the maximum period such assistance is payable **and** the individual is hired not more than 2 years after such eligibility ended.

Index

A

accountants, 45, 125, 138, 151
accounting, 3
administrative, 90
advertising, 3, 23, 30, 44, 50, 101, 103, 104, 105, 113, 119
    bait and switch, 102
    deceptive pricing, 102, 103, 104, 113
    endorsements, 102, 103
    federal laws and regulations, 101, 102
    free item, 102
    negative option plans, 103
    state laws, 103, 104
    substantiation of claims, 102, 105
    unfairness, 103
affirmative action, 97
Agricultural Foreign Investment Disclosure Act, 21
AIDS, 86
Alcohol Administration Act, 132
America's Business Funding Directory, 34
American Bar Association, 67
Americans with Disabilities Act (ADA), 37, 40, 79, 86
Amusement Tax, 153
animated gifs, 68
Anti-Cybersquatting Consumer Protection Act, 60
arbitration, 81
assets, 16, 32
Association of Small Business Development Centers (ASBDC), 6, 12
attorney general, 122, 125
attorneys, 15, 20, 21, 45, 49, 53, 66, 67, 77, 97, 104, 107, 110, 111, 113, 120, 125, 143

B

bank accounts, 17, 70
bankruptcy, 32
banks, 32, 117, 143
banner ads, 66
Battery Sales Tax, 153
benefits, 16, 19, 84, 85, 91, 97
blacklisting, 98
Boat and Boat Motor Sales Tax, 153
bookkeeping, 137, 138, 139
breaks, 91
budgets, 3
Bureau of Alcohol, Tobacco, Firearms and Explosives, 47
Bureau of Industry and Security, 48
Business Corporation Act, 16

C

cancellation, 107, 108, 109
    refunds, 109
    right to cancel, 107, 108
capital, 17, 18, 33, 34, 61
Capital Network, 34
cash, 115
Cement Production Tax, 153
checks, 116
child labor laws, 93
Child Protection and Toy Safety Act, 132
Children Online Privacy Protection Act of 1998 (COPPA), 69
Cigarette, Cigar and Tobacco Products Tax, 153
claims, 77, 88, 113

classes of goods, 30
Clean Water Act, 132
Code of Federal Regulations (C.F.R.), 75, 93, 101, 130
Coin Operated Machines Tax, 153
collateral, 32
collections, 120, 122
commercial bribery, 125
commercial discrimination, 124
compliance, 38, 40, 96
Comprehensive Smokeless Tobacco Health Education Act, 132
Consumer Credit Protection Act, 132
Consumer Product Safety Act, 132
Consumer Product Safety Commission (CPSC), 75
Consumer Response Center, 71
contracts, 49, 50, 51, 53, 81, 96, 98, 103, 107–110, 125
    acceptance, 49, 50
    consent, 51
    considerations, 49, 50
    counteroffers, 50
    deaths, 51
    exceptions, 52
    law, 49, 51, 52
    misrepresentation, 51
    mutual mistakes, 51
    offers, 49, 50
    rejections, 50
    rescindment, 51
Controlling the Assault of Non-Solicited Pornography And Marketing Act of 2003 (CANSPAM), 65, 66, 112
copyrights, 62, 68, 126, 127
    infringement, 68
corporations, 15–20, 25–29, 33, 55, 56, 60, 69, 118, 137, 140, 142, 143, 151
    C corporations, 17, 18, 142
    nonprofit, 17
    professional service, 17
    S corporations, 16, 17, 18, 139, 142
county clerk, 19, 26
credit, 118, 120
    worthiness, 30
credit cards, 110, 116, 133
creditors, 39, 122
Crude Oil and Natural Gas Tax, 153
customers, 3, 4, 16, 30, 36, 37, 49, 50, 51, 53, 65, 68, 70, 116, 117, 118, 151

D

damages, 23, 34, 54, 67, 86, 113, 122, 125
Davis-Bacon Act, 97
debts, 17, 19, 52
deceptive practices, 103, 104, 105, 112, 113, 119, 120, 122
Deceptive Trade Practices Act, 113
Department of Labor, 90, 97, 98
disabled, 86, 87, 89
disclaimers, 105

discrimination laws, 85, 86, 87, 95, 98
    equal pay, 85
    sexual harassment, 87, 88, 89
Do Not Call registry, 109, 111
doing business as (d/b/a), 25, 27
Domain Name Rights Coalition, 60
domain names, 29, 59, 60, 61
drug testing, 79
duty to open, 38

E

Earned Income Credit, 144
email, 65, 68, 70
Employee Polygraph Protection Act, 79
Employee Retirement Income Security Act (ERISA), 92
employees, 2, 3, 24, 54, 55, 56, 61, 74–83, 86–92, 94, 97, 98, 125, 143, 144, 145, 152, 156
    foreign, 95
    handbooks, 80
    part-time, 78, 91
    temporary, 83, 84
    theft, 56
employers, 53, 54, 73, 79, 81, 85–90, 95, 97, 98, 152
employment agreements, 80
Energy Policy and Conservation Act, 132
entrepreneur, 1, 29, 33
Environmental Pesticide Control Act, 132
Equal Employment Opportunity Commission, 85, 87, 98
Equal Pay Act, 85
executives, 90
expansion, 24, 25, 29, 38, 39
expenses, 31, 32, 37, 137, 138, 139, 141, 142

F

Fair Credit Billing Act, 118
Fair Credit Reporting Act, 132
Fair Debt Collection Practices Act of 1977, 120
Fair Labor Standards Act (FLSA), 89, 93
Fair Packaging and Labeling Act, 132
Family and Medical Leave Act of 1993 (FMLA), 92
Federal Communications Commission, 47
federal laws, 97, 109, 120, 123, 124, 130, 132
federal regulation, 71
Federal Trade Commission (FTC), 71, 101, 102, 103, 105, 107, 108, 109, 121, 130
fees, 19, 20, 24, 30, 40, 60, 63, 69, 70, 92, 110, 122, 125
FICA, 143, 144
financing, 29, 30, 31, 32, 117, 118, 137
fines, 86, 95, 96, 97, 110, 115, 125, 126, 152
Fireworks Tax, 153
firing laws, 79, 91
    discrimination, 79
    health or safety complaints, 79
    sexual advances, 79
    termination, 80, 83
    unemployment compensation, 77, 78

flaming, 64
Flammable Fabrics Act, 132
Food and Drug Administration (FDA), 48, 74, 103
Food Safety Enforcement Enhancement Act, 132
Food, Drug, and Cosmetic Act, 132
foreclosure, 153
Foreign Investment in Real Property Tax Act (FIRPTA), 21
framing, 68
Free Enterprise and Antitrust Act of 1983, 125
Fuels Tax, 153
Fur Products Labeling Act, 132

G

Gale Research Co., 5, 24
general partnerships, 15–19, 26, 28
gifs, 68
goods, 4, 29, 29, 89, 103, 104, 107, 109, 110, 112, 125, 130, 151
Government Liaison Services, Inc., 24
governmental regulations, 74
growth, 5, 29, 30, 35, 39

H

handicap accommodations, 37
Hazardous Substances Act, 132
hazards, 73, 74
health and safety laws, 73, 78
    federal, 73
        hazardous materials, 74, 75
    state, 76
hiring laws, 77
    at will, 80
    interview questions, 85
    new hire reporting, 79
    off the books, 96
HIV, 86
Hobby Protection Act, 132
holidays, 91
home equity, 30
home solicitation, 105
Hotel Occupancy Tax, 153
hours, 81, 89, 98

I

Illegal Immigration Reform and Immigrant Responsibility Act of 1996 (IIRIRA), 95
immigration laws, 20, 21, 94
    federal, 94, 95
    work visas, 95
income, 29, 30, 31, 91, 115, 137, 138, 139, 141, 143, 151
incorporated, 113
incorporation, 38, 56
independent contractors, 2, 81, 82, 86
injunctions, 125

injuries, 54, 55, 73, 83, 96
Insecticide, Fungicide, and Rodenticide Act, 132
installment sales, 119
insurance, 4, 35, 53, 55, 82, 96, 107, 134
    agents, 53, 56
    auto, 55, 56
    benefits, 53
    bonding, 4, 56
    business interruption, 55
    companies, 53, 54, 56
    coverages, 53, 55, 56
    hazard, 55
    health, 56
    home business, 55
    homeowners, 55, 56
    liability, 54, 56
    premiums, 55
    tenant, 55
    umbrella policy, 55
    worker's compensation, 53, 54, 79, 82, 83, 86
intellectual property, 126, 127
Internal Revenue Service (IRS), 16, 81, 83, 137, 138, 142, 143, 145
    IRS Form 508, 145
    IRS Form 940, 145
    IRS Form 2553, 16
    IRS Form 8832, 142
    IRS Form SS-4, 143, 144
    IRS Form W-4, 143
International Investment Survey Act, 21
Internet, 24, 28, 34, 59, 60, 61, 66–72, 75, 102, 103, 105, 126, 150
    ad trades, 66
    fraud, 72
    privacy, 68
    sales, 105
    search engines, 63, 64, 70
    service providers, 66, 70
    solicitation, 65
Internet Corporation for Assigned Names and Numbers (ICANN), 61
Internet Fraud Complaint Center (IFCC), 72
interstate commerce, 71, 89
inventory, 3, 32
investments, 142
investors, 33, 34
    silent, 33

J

jargon, 61
jewelry, 103, 131
joint ventures, 26
jurisdiction, 66, 67

L

labeling, 130
labor unions, 97, 99
lawsuits, 17, 39, 54, 55, 67, 81, 84, 87, 121
lawyers. *See attorneys*
layoffs, 97
leases, 37, 38, 52, 125
    personal guaranty, 38
legal forms
    form 1, 187
    form 2, 26, 27
    form 3, 30
    form 4, 94
    form 5, 143
    form 6, 82
    form 7, 80, 143
    form 8, 149
    form 9, 227
    form 10, 152
    form 11, 115
    form 12, 87
lenders, 119
liability, 15, 16, 19, 28, 50, 53, 54, 55, 59, 67, 69, 82, 88, 96, 120, 151
    corporate, 17
    personal, 16, 17, 18, 28
    protection, 19
libel, 67
licenses, 19, 20, 44, 47
    county occupational, 44
licensing, 4, 43
    federal, 43
    requirements, 43
    state, 43
liens, 153
limited liability companies (LLC), 15, 18, 19, 20, 26, 27, 69, 137, 151
limited liability partnerships (LLP), 15, 19, 20, 26, 27, 137
limited partnerships, 15, 18, 19, 20, 26, 27, 33
linking, 68
litigation, 53, 153
loans, 12, 31, 32, 119, 120
    credit cards, 32
    personal, 29
locations, 35, 37, 38, 67, 97
    home, 35, 36, 44
    office, 37
    retail stores, 36
losses, 16, 17, 23
lotteries, 104, 134

M

Magnuson-Moss Warranty Act, 132
mail order businesses, 117
    ales, 130
management, 2, 3, 12, 18, 19, 84, 90
manufacturing space, 37
marketing, 65
McNamara-O'Hara Service Contract Act, 97
medical leave, 93
meetings, 20
members. *See partners*
meta tag, 64
Minerals Tax, 153
Miscellaneous Corporation Laws, 16
Mixed Beverage Gross Receipts Tax, 153
money, 3, 18, 29, 30, 31, 33, 34, 49, 70, 77, 120, 157
    inheritance, 31
monopolies, 124, 125
mortgages, 30
Motor Vehicle Sales Tax, 153

N

names, 15, 23, 27, 28
    abbreviations, 27
    assumed, 15
    fictitious, 19, 24, 25, 26, 27, 44
    forms, 26
    incorporated, 25
    legal, 26
    registration, 25, 27
National Labor Relations Act of 1935, 97
National White Collar Crime Center, 72
netiquette, 65
network service providers, 59
Non-Profit Corporation Act, 17
nonprofit organizations, 6, 59
Notice of Cancellation, 105, 107, 108
nuisance suits, 55
Nutritional Labeling Education Act of 1990, 103, 132
NVST, 34

O

Occupational Safety and Health Administration (OSHA), 73, 74
Office of Hazardous Materials Safety, 75
officers, 20, 125
overtime, 2
owners, 4, 5, 17, 19, 55, 60, 92, 123, 153
    foreign, 20, 21

P

partners, 2, 16, 18, 19, 20, 28, 32, 33, 125, 143
partnerships, 137, 141, 142, 143
patents, 126, 127
payments, 32, 108, 115, 118, 153
    cash, 96, 107, 115
    checks, 115, 116
    credit cards, 115, 117, 118
    money orders, 115
    travelers' checks, 115
pension plans, 83, 84, 91
    Individual Retirement Account (IRA), 92
    qualified retirement plans, 92
    SEP/IRA, 92
personal property, 149, 152
    intangible, 149
    tangible, 149
Personal Responsibility and Work Opportunity Reconciliation Act of 1996 (PRWORA), 79
Poison Prevention Packaging Act, 133
poster laws, 97, 152
precious metals, 103
premises, 55
products, 2, 3, 5, 36, 55, 61, 64, 65, 67, 70, 75, 78, 81, 97, 111, 124, 140
professional associations, 28
professionals, 28, 44, 90
professions
    state regulated, 44
profits, 2, 4, 16, 17, 34, 53, 137, 139, 141, 142
property, 39
    buying, 39, 44
    leasing, 44
proprietors, 143
proprietorships, 137
Public Contracts Act, 98
publication, 67, 69, 71, 74
publicity, 3, 23, 59, 65
Pure Food and Drug Act of 1906, 74

Q

Quill Corporation v. North Dakota, 155

R

real property, 21, 110
records, 73, 87, 109
references, 79
refunds, 105, 116
registering, 47, 60, 61, 63, 110, 111, 126, 152
    federal, 47
Regulation Z, 118
renditions, 152
renting, 38, 39
resale, 151
rescission, 105
retirement, 30
retirement plans, 92, 140
right-to-work law, 99
Robinson-Patman Act of 1936, 124

S

safe-harbor guidelines, 156
salaries, 4, 81, 85, 139, 142
Schedule C, 141
Secretary of State, 20, 24, 26, 27, 29, 110
securities, 34, 118
Securities and Exchange Commission, 48
service, 29
Service Contract Act, 98
Service Corps of Retired Executives (SCORE), 5, 12
service marks, 29, 127
services, 2, 3, 4, 29, 36, 55, 61, 65, 81, 82, 97, 103, 104, 107–112, 152
sexual harassment, 87, 88, 89, 112
shareholders, 16, 17, 142
Sherman Antitrust Act of 1890, 124
sick leave, 91
signs, 37, 39, 40, 53
sites. *See websites*
Small Business Administration (SBA), 5, 12, 32, 34
smoking, 76, 77
sole proprietorships, 15–19, 26, 56
solicitation, 101, 107, 125
    door-to-door, 53, 105
    email, 112
    telephone, 109, 110, 111
Solid Waste Disposal Act, 133
spamming, 65, 66
start-up capital, 30
start-up costs, 17
state laws, 98, 110, 111, 121, 125, 133
statutes of frauds, 52
stock, 17, 18, 33, 34, 38
subleases, 38
supplies, 4, 44
Surface Transportation Board, 48

T

taxable services, 149, 151
taxes, 4, 12, 19, 20, 82, 83, 115, 137, 138, 143, 149, 153
    appraisers, 152
    benefits, 86
    business, 156
    Canadian, 157
    credits, 86, 87
    deductible, 92, 96
    deductions, 139, 144
    dividends, 17, 142
    excise, 145
    exemptions, 152
    federal corporate income, 16, 17
    federal laws, 91
    federal withholding deposits, 82
    forms, 17, 139
    franchise, 151
    income, 140, 144
    interest, 119, 153
    Internet, 156
    interstate, 155, 156
    laws, 138

Medicare, 81, 82, 144
personal income, 17
property, 152
rates, 152
returns, 16, 82, 115, 138, 139, 142
sales or use, 40, 140, 149, 151
Social Security, 18, 81, 82, 141, 144
state, 149, 153
taxpayers, 142
Texas franchise, 18, 19
tips, 139
unemployment, 145, 152
unemployment compensation, 77, 82
withholding, 139, 142, 143
technology, 2
telephone lines, 35
telephone solicitation, 109
Texas Deceptive Trade Practices Act, 122
Texas Employment Commission, 94
Texas Labor Code, 93
Texas Minimum Wage Act, 90
Texas Telemarketing Disclosure and Privacy Act, 111
Texas Workers' Compensation Commission, 54
Texas Workforce Commission, 152
Textile Fiber Products Identification Act, 133
top level domains (TLDs), 29, 59, 61
Toxic Substance Control Act, 133
trade associations, 5, 53
Trade Names Directory, 24
trade secrets, 80, 127
trade shows, 156
trade unions, 99
trademarks, 23, 24, 29, 30, 60, 127
    infringement, 64
    registration, 23, 24, 29, 30
    rights, 24
transactions, 49, 105, 107, 108, 110, 115, 117, 118, 124
Truth in Lending Act, 118

U

Uniform Commercial Code (UCC), 123
United States Patent and Trademark Office (USPTO), 24, 29, 30, 126, 127
usury, 119

V

vendors, 49
visas, 20, 21

W

wages, 89, 90, 96, 97, 98, 142, 143, 145, 152
    federal laws, 89, 90
    minimum wage, 89, 90
    overtime, 90
    state laws, 90
Walsh-Healey Public Contracts Act, 97
warehouse space, 37
warranties, 123, 130
Webmaster, 68
websites, 60, 61, 62, 63, 64, 66, 69, 70
    content, 62, 67
    design, 62, 64
    disclaimers, 67
    hosting service, 62
    HTML, 62
    programming, 62
    publicity, 63
    purpose, 61
    structure, 62
    testing, 63
wholesalers, 140
Wool Products Labeling Act, 133
Worker Adjustment and Retraining Notification Act, 97
Worker Protection Standard for Agricultural Pesticides, 74
written agreements, 19, 20, 52, 78, 118, 120

Z

zero tolerance, 89
zoning, 37, 39, 43, 44

Your #1 Source for Real World Legal Information...

SPHINX® PUBLISHING
An Imprint of Sourcebooks, Inc.®

- Written by lawyers
- Simple English explanation of the law
- Forms and instructions included

Quick Cash

Everyone could use more money. This book explores seven fundamental strategies that can be used to raise funds when you experience planned and unplanned financial changes.

256 pages; $14.95;
ISBN 1-57248-385-7

The Landlords' Legal Guide in Texas, 3E

A resource no Texas landlord should be without. Clear, easy to understand explanations of topics including eviction, maintence, liabilities, and much more. Blank forms as well as sample, filled-in forms included.

216 pages; $24.95;
ISBN 1-57248-355-5

The Law (in Plain English) for Small Business

A concise guide that covers every legal topic concerning a small business owner. From hiring procedures to product liability, this book provides answers in simple, everyday language.

320 pages; $19.95;
ISBN 1-57248-337-6

See the following order form for books written specifically for California, the District of Columbia, Florida, Georgia, Illinois, Maryland, Massachusetts, Michigan, Minnesota, New Jersey, New York, North Carolina, Ohio, Pennsylvania, Texas, and Virginia!

What our customers say about our books:

"It couldn't be more clear for the lay person." —R.D.

"I want you to know I really appreciate your book. It has saved me a lot of time and money." —L.T.

"Your real estate contracts book has saved me nearly $12,000.00 in closing costs over the past year." —A.B.

"...many of the legal questions that I have had over the years were answered clearly and concisely through your plain English interpretation of the law." —C.E.H.

"If there weren't people out there like you I'd be lost. You have the best books of this type out there." —S.B.

"...your forms and directions are easy to follow." —C.V.M.

*Sphinx Publishing's Legal Survival Guides
are directly available from Sourcebooks, Inc., or from your local bookstores.
For credit card orders call 1–800–432–7444, write P.O. Box 4410, Naperville, IL 60567-4410,
or fax 630-961-2168*
Find more legal information at: **www.SphinxLegal.com**

Sphinx® Publishing's National Titles
Valid in All 50 States

LEGAL SURVIVAL IN BUSINESS

The Complete Book of Corporate Forms	$24.95
The Complete Partnership Book	$24.95
The Complete Patent Book	$26.95
Employees' Rights	$18.95
Employer's Rights	$24.95
The Entrepreneur's Internet Handbook	$21.95
The Entrepreneur's Legal Guide	$26.95
How to Form a Limited Liability Company (2E)	$24.95
How to Form a Nonprofit Corporation (2E)	$24.95
How to Form Your Own Corporation (4E)	$26.95
How to Register Your Own Copyright (5E)	$24.95
How to Register Your Own Trademark (3E)	$21.95
Incorporate in Delaware from Any State	$26.95
Incorporate in Nevada from Any State	$24.95
The Law (In Plain English)® for Small Business	$19.95
Most Valuable Business Legal Forms You'll Ever Need (3E)	$21.95
Profit from Intellectual Property	$28.95
Protect Your Patent	$24.95
The Small Business Owner's Guide to Bankruptcy	$21.95
Tax Smarts for Small Business	$21.95

LEGAL SURVIVAL IN COURT

Attorney Responsibilities & Client Rights	$19.95
Crime Victim's Guide to Justice (2E)	$21.95
Grandparents' Rights (3E)	$24.95
Help Your Lawyer Win Your Case (2E)	$14.95
Legal Research Made Easy (3E)	$21.95
Winning Your Personal Injury Claim (2E)	$24.95

LEGAL SURVIVAL IN REAL ESTATE

The Complete Kit to Selling Your Own Home	$18.95
Essential Guide to Real Estate Contracts (2E)	$18.95
Essential Guide to Real Estate Leases	$18.95
Homeowner's Rights	$19.95
How to Buy a Condominium or Townhome (2E)	$19.95
How to Buy Your First Home	$18.95
Working with Your Homeowners Association	$19.95

LEGAL SURVIVAL IN SPANISH

Cómo Hacer su Propio Testamento	$16.95
Cómo Restablecer su propio Crédito y Renegociar sus Deudas	$21.95
Cómo Solicitar su Propio Divorcio	$24.95
Guía de Inmigración a Estados Unidos (3E)	$24.95
Guía de Justicia para Víctimas del Crimen	$21.95
Guía Esencial para los Contratos de Arrendamiento de Bienes Raíces	$22.95
Inmigración a los EE. UU. Paso a Paso	$22.95
Inmigración y Ciudadanía en los EE. UU. Preguntas y Respuestas	$16.95
Manual de Beneficios para el Seguro Social	$18.95
El Seguro Social Preguntas y Respuestas	$16.95

LEGAL SURVIVAL IN PERSONAL AFFAIRS

101 Complaint Letters That Get Results	$18.95
The 529 College Savings Plan (2E)	$18.95
The Antique and Art Collector's Legal Guide	$24.95
The Complete Legal Guide to Senior Care	$21.95
Credit Smart	$18.95
Family Limited Partnership	$26.95
Gay & Lesbian Rights	$26.95
How to File Your Own Bankruptcy (5E)	$21.95
How to File Your Own Divorce (5E)	$26.95
How to Make Your Own Simple Will (3E)	$18.95
How to Write Your Own Living Will (4E)	$18.95
How to Write Your Own Premarital Agreement (3E)	$24.95
Law School 101	$16.95
Living Trusts and Other Ways to Avoid Probate (3E)	$24.95
Mastering the MBE	$16.95
Most Valuable Personal Legal Forms You'll Ever Need (2E)	$26.95
The Power of Attorney Handbook (5E)	$22.95
Quick Cash	$14.95
Repair Your Own Credit and Deal with Debt (2E)	$18.95
Sexual Harassment: Your Guide to Legal Action	$18.95
The Social Security Benefits Handbook (3E)	$18.95
Social Security Q&A	$12.95
Teen Rights	$22.95
Traveler's Rights	$21.95
Unmarried Parents' Rights (2E)	$19.95
U.S. Immigration and Citizenship Q&A	$18.95
U.S. Immigration Step by Step (2E)	$24.95
U.S.A. Immigration Guide (5E)	$26.95
The Visitation Handbook	$18.95
The Wills, Estate Planning and Trusts Legal Kit	$26.95
Win Your Unemployment Compensation Claim (2E)	$21.95
Your Right to Child Custody, Visitation and Support (3E)	$24.95

SPHINX® PUBLISHING ORDER FORM

BILL TO:

SHIP TO:

Phone # ____ Terms ____ F.O.B. Chicago, IL Ship Date ____

Charge my: ☐ VISA ☐ MasterCard ☐ American Express

☐ Money Order or Personal Check

Credit Card Number ____ Expiration Date ____

Qty	ISBN	Title	Retail	Ext.
		SPHINX PUBLISHING NATIONAL TITLES		
___	1-57248-363-6	101 Complaint Letters That Get Results	$18.95	___
___	1-57248-361-X	The 529 College Savings Plan (2E)	$18.95	___
___	1-57248-349-0	The Antique and Art Collector's Legal Guide	$24.95	___
___	1-57248-347-4	Attorney Responsibilities & Client Rights	$19.95	___
___	1-57248-148-X	Cómo Hacer su Propio Testamento	$16.95	___
___	1-57248-226-5	Cómo Restablecer su propio Crédito y Renegociar sus Deudas	$21.95	___
___	1-57248-147-1	Cómo Solicitar su Propio Divorcio	$24.95	___
___	1-57248-166-8	The Complete Book of Corporate Forms	$24.95	___
___	1-57248-353-9	The Complete Kit to Selling Your Own Home	$18.95	___
___	1-57248-229-X	The Complete Legal Guide to Senior Care	$21.95	___
___	1-57248-391-1	The Complete Partnership Book	$24.95	___
___	1-57248-201-X	The Complete Patent Book	$26.95	___
___	1-57248-369-5	Credit Smart	$18.95	___
___	1-57248-163-3	Crime Victim's Guide to Justice (2E)	$21.95	___
___	1-57248-367-9	Employees' Rights	$18.95	___
___	1-57248-365-2	Employer's Rights	$24.95	___
___	1-57248-251-6	The Entrepreneur's Internet Handbook	$21.95	___
___	1-57248-235-4	The Entrepreneur's Legal Guide	$26.95	___
___	1-57248-346-6	Essential Guide to Real Estate Contracts (2E)	$18.95	___
___	1-57248-160-9	Essential Guide to Real Estate Leases	$18.95	___
___	1-57248-254-0	Family Limited Partnership	$26.95	___
___	1-57248-331-8	Gay & Lesbian Rights	$26.95	___
___	1-57248-139-0	Grandparents' Rights (3E)	$24.95	___
___	1-57248-188-9	Guía de Inmigración a Estados Unidos (3E)	$24.95	___
___	1-57248-187-0	Guía de Justicia para Víctimas del Crimen	$21.95	___
___	1-57248-253-2	Guía Esencial para los Contratos de Arrendamiento de Bienes Raíces	$22.95	___
___	1-57248-103-X	Help Your Lawyer Win Your Case (2E)	$14.95	___
___	1-57248-334-2	Homeowner's Rights	$19.95	___
___	1-57248-164-1	How to Buy a Condominium or Townhome (2E)	$19.95	___
___	1-57248-328-8	How to Buy Your First Home	$18.95	___
___	1-57248-191-9	How to File Your Own Bankruptcy (5E)	$21.95	___
___	1-57248-343-1	How to File Your Own Divorce (5E)	$26.95	___
___	1-57248-222-2	How to Form a Limited Liability Company (2E)	$24.95	___
___	1-57248-231-1	How to Form a Nonprofit Corporation (2E)	$24.95	___
___	1-57248-345-8	How to Form Your Own Corporation (4E)	$26.95	___
___	1-57248-232-X	How to Make Your Own Simple Will (3E)	$18.95	___
___	1-57248-379-2	How to Register Your Own Copyright (5E)	$24.95	___
___	1-57248-104-8	How to Register Your Own Trademark (3E)	$21.95	___
___	1-57248-394-6	How to Write Your Own Living Will (4E)	$18.95	___
___	1-57248-156-0	How to Write Your Own Premarital Agreement (3E)	$24.95	___
___	1-57248-230-3	Incorporate in Delaware from Any State	$26.95	___
___	1-57248-158-7	Incorporate in Nevada from Any State	$24.95	___
___	1-57248-250-8	Inmigración a los EE.UU. Paso a Paso	$22.95	___
___	1-57248-400-4	Inmigración y Ciudadanía en los EE.UU. Preguntas y Respuestas	$16.95	___
___	1-57248-374-1	Law School 101	$16.95	___
___	1-57248-377-6	The Law (In Plain English)® for Small Business	$19.95	___
___	1-57248-223-0	Legal Research Made Easy (3E)	$21.95	___
___	1-57248-165-X	Living Trusts and Other Ways to Avoid Probate (3E)	$24.95	___
___	1-57248-186-2	Manual de Beneficios para el Seguro Social	$18.95	___
___	1-57248-220-6	Mastering the MBE	$16.95	___
___	1-57248-167-6	Most Val. Business Legal Forms You'll Ever Need (3E)	$21.95	___
___	1-57248-360-1	Most Val. Personal Legal Forms You'll Ever Need (2E)	$26.95	___
___	1-57248-388-1	The Power of Attorney Handbook (5E)	$22.95	___
___	1-57248-332-6	Profit from Intellectual Property	$28.95	___
___	1-57248-329-6	Protect Your Patent	$24.95	___
___	1-57248-385-7	Quick Cash	$14.95	___
___	1-57248-344-X	Repair Your Own Credit and Deal with Debt (2E)	$18.95	___
___	1-57248-350-4	El Seguro Social Preguntas y Respuestas	$16.95	___
___	1-57248-217-6	Sexual Harassment: Your Guide to Legal Action	$18.95	___
___	1-57248-219-2	The Small Business Owner's Guide to Bankruptcy	$21.95	___
___	1-57248-168-4	The Social Security Benefits Handbook (3E)	$18.95	___
___	1-57248-216-8	Social Security Q&A	$12.95	___
___	1-57248-221-4	Teen Rights	$22.95	___
___	1-57248-366-0	Tax Smarts for Small Business	$21.95	___
___	1-57248-335-0	Traveler's Rights	$21.95	___
___	1-57248-236-2	Unmarried Parents' Rights (2E)	$19.95	___
___	1-57248-362-8	U.S. Immigration and Citizenship Q&A	$18.95	___
___	1-57248-387-3	U.S. Immigration Step by Step (2E)	$24.95	___
___	1-57248-392-X	U.S.A. Immigration Guide (5E)	$26.95	___
___	1-57248-192-7	The Visitation Handbook	$18.95	___
___	1-57248-225-7	Win Your Unemployment Compensation Claim (2E)	$21.95	___
___	1-57248-330-X	The Wills, Estate Planning and Trusts Legal Kit	&26.95	___
___	1-57248-138-2	Winning Your Personal Injury Claim (2E)	$24.95	___
___	1-57248-333-4	Working with Your Homeowners Association	$19.95	___
___	1-57248-380-6	Your Right to Child Custody, Visitation and Support (3E)	$24.95	___
		CALIFORNIA TITLES		
___	1-57248-150-1	CA Power of Attorney Handbook (2E)	$18.95	___
___	1-57248-337-7	How to File for Divorce in CA (4E)	$26.95	___
___	1-57248-145-5	How to Probate and Settle an Estate in CA	$26.95	___
___	1-57248-336-9	How to Start a Business in CA (2E)	$21.95	___
___	1-57248-194-3	How to Win in Small Claims Court in CA (2E)	$18.95	___
___	1-57248-246-X	Make Your Own CA Will	$18.95	___
___	1-57248-397-0	The Landlord's Legal Guide in CA (2E)	$24.95	___
___	1-57248-241-9	Tenants' Rights in CA	$21.95	___

Form Continued on Following Page   SubTotal ___

To order, call Sourcebooks at 1-800-432-7444 or FAX (630) 961-2168 (Bookstores, libraries, wholesalers—please call for discount)

Prices are subject to change without notice.

Find more legal information at: **www.SphinxLegal.com**

SPHINX® PUBLISHING ORDER FORM

Qty	ISBN	Title	Retail	Ext.
		FLORIDA TITLES		
	1-57071-363-4	Florida Power of Attorney Handbook (2E)	$16.95	
	1-57248-396-2	How to File for Divorce in FL (8E)	$28.95	
	1-57248-356-3	How to Form a Corporation in FL (6E)	$24.95	
	1-57248-203-6	How to Form a Limited Liability Co. in FL (2E)	$24.95	
	1-57071-401-0	How to Form a Partnership in FL	$22.95	
	1-57248-113-7	How to Make a FL Will (6E)	$16.95	
	1-57248-088-2	How to Modify Your FL Divorce Judgment (4E)	$24.95	
	1-57248-354-7	How to Probate and Settle an Estate in FL (5E)	$26.95	
	1-57248-339-3	How to Start a Business in FL (7E)	$21.95	
	1-57248-204-4	How to Win in Small Claims Court in FL (7E)	$18.95	
	1-57248-381-4	Land Trusts in Florida (7E)	$29.95	
	1-57248-338-5	Landlords' Rights and Duties in FL (9E)	$22.95	
		GEORGIA TITLES		
	1-57248-340-7	How to File for Divorce in GA (5E)	$21.95	
	1-57248-180-3	How to Make a GA Will (4E)	$16.95	
	1-57248-341-5	How to Start a Business in Georgia (3E)	$21.95	
		ILLINOIS TITLES		
	1-57248-244-3	Child Custody, Visitation, and Support in IL	$24.95	
	1-57248-206-0	How to File for Divorce in IL (3E)	$24.95	
	1-57248-170-6	How to Make an IL Will (3E)	$16.95	
	1-57248-247-8	How to Start a Business in IL (3E)	$21.95	
	1-57248-252-4	The Landlord's Legal Guide in IL	$24.95	
		MARYLAND, VIRGINIA AND THE DISTRICT OF COLUMBIA		
	1-57248-240-0	How to File for Divorce in MD, VA and DC	$28.95	
	1-57248-359-8	How to Start a Business in MD, VA or DC	$21.95	
		MASSACHUSETTS TITLES		
	1-57248-128-5	How to File for Divorce in MA (3E)	$24.95	
	1-57248-115-3	How to Form a Corporation in MA	$24.95	
	1-57248-108-0	How to Make a MA Will (2E)	$16.95	
	1-57248-248-6	How to Start a Business in MA (3E)	$21.95	
	1-57248-398-9	The Landlord's Legal Guide in MA (2E)	$24.95	
		MICHIGAN TITLES		
	1-57248-215-X	How to File for Divorce in MI (3E)	$24.95	
	1-57248-182-X	How to Make a MI Will (3E)	$16.95	
	1-57248-183-8	How to Start a Business in MI (3E)	$18.95	
		MINNESOTA TITLES		
	1-57248-142-0	How to File for Divorce in MN	$21.95	
	1-57248-179-X	How to Form a Corporation in MN	$24.95	
	1-57248-178-1	How to Make a MN Will (2E)	$16.95	
		NEW JERSEY TITLES		
	1-57248-239-7	How to File for Divorce in NJ	$24.95	
	1-57248-448-9	How to Start a Business in NJ	$21.95	
		NEW YORK TITLES		
	1-57248-193-5	Child Custody, Visitation and Support in NY	$26.95	
	1-57248-351-2	File for Divorce in NY	$26.95	
	1-57248-249-4	How to Form a Corporation in NY (2E)	$24.95	
	1-57248-401-2	How to Make a NY Will (3E)	$16.95	
	1-57248-199-4	How to Start a Business in NY (2E)	$18.95	
	1-57248-198-6	How to Win in Small Claims Court in NY (2E)	$18.95	
	1-57248-197-8	Landlords' Legal Guide in NY	$24.95	
	1-57071-188-7	New York Power of Attorney Handbook	$19.95	

Qty	ISBN	Title	Retail	Ext.
	1-57248-122-6	Tenants' Rights in NY	$21.95	
		NORTH CAROLINA TITLES		
	1-57248-185-4	How to File for Divorce in NC (3E)	$22.95	
	1-57248-129-3	How to Make a NC Will (3E)	$16.95	
	1-57248-184-6	How to Start a Business in NC (3E)	$18.95	
	1-57248-091-2	Landlords' Rights & Duties in NC	$21.95	
		NORTH CAROLINA AND SOUTH CAROLINA TITLES		
	1-57248-371-7	How to Start a Business in NC or SC	$24.95	
		OHIO TITLES		
	1-57248-190-0	How to File for Divorce in OH (2E)	$24.95	
	1-57248-174-9	How to Form a Corporation in OH	$24.95	
	1-57248-173-0	How to Make an OH Will	$16.95	
		PENNSYLVANIA TITLES		
	1-57248-242-7	Child Custody, Visitation and Support in PA	$26.95	
	1-57248-211-7	How to File for Divorce in PA (3E)	$26.95	
	1-57248-358-X	How to Form a Cooporation in PA	$24.95	
	1-57248-094-7	How to Make a PA Will (2E)	$16.95	
	1-57248-357-1	How to Start a Business in PA (3E)	$21.95	
	1-57248-245-1	The Landlord's Legal Guide in PA	$24.95	
		TEXAS TITLES		
	1-57248-171-4	Child Custody, Visitation, and Support in TX	$22.95	
	1-57248-399-7	How to File for Divorce in TX (4E)	$24.95	
	1-57248-114-5	How to Form a Corporation in TX (2E)	$24.95	
	1-57248-255-9	How to Make a TX Will (3E)	$16.95	
	1-57248-214-1	How to Probate and Settle an Estate in TX (3E)	$26.95	
	1-57248-228-1	How to Start a Business in TX (3E)	$18.95	
	1-57248-111-0	How to Win in Small Claims Court in TX (2E)	$16.95	
	1-57248-355-5	The Landlord's Legal Guide in TX	$24.95	

SubTotal This page _____
SubTotal previous page _____
Shipping— $5.00 for 1st book, $1.00 each additional _____
Illinois residents add 6.75% sales tax _____
Connecticut residents add 6.00% sales tax _____

Total _____

To order, call Sourcebooks at 1-800-432-7444 or FAX (630) 961-2168 (Bookstores, libraries, wholesalers—please call for discount)
Prices are subject to change without notice.
Find more legal information at: www.SphinxLegal.com